BECOME PART OF THE SOLUTION

By

Easton Hamilton

Published by Easton Hamilton

Artwork and cover design by Earl Hamilton

CONTENTS

ACKNOWLEDGEMENTS

In the three previous books, which are part of the Synergy trilogy, I named all the significant individuals who have helped me in some way to assemble the body of work I've put together over the last four decades. I continue to appreciate their contributions, past and present, and they again have been there when I have needed them. I sincerely thank you all... you know who you are.

Become Part of the Solution is particularly dedicated to all those who have trusted me with their hearts, their secrets and innermost fears. I have always considered it an honour and a privilege to walk hand in hand with those who are in despair, who have lost hope and believe only an undesirable future awaits them.

To be able to have helped in some small way makes my heart sing - and for those I have helped find their own song, may we create a chorus together so beautiful that it resonates around the world, inspiring others to find their voices, resurrect their self-belief and fulfil their dreams.

I also want to acknowledge those who have become my partners and allies on this journey, who like me are committed to telling the beautiful and powerful story of synergy. They are busy breaking down barriers and building bridges in their place. They are pioneers breaking new ground and turning barren soil into rich, fertile fields, bursting with abundant harvests that can sustain those who are hungry for positive change.

To each of you who have found the courage and tenacity to walk this path with me, even in the face of opposition, I thank you on behalf of myself and those whose hearts, minds and lives you have helped to change.

To be able to serve in this way is the greatest gift, it needs no acknow-ledgement because it is its own reward.

Finally, I give thanks to my faith and my beliefs which have sustained me on the many dark nights. May you find something that anchors you and supports you at those times when you feel overwhelmed by fear and doubt, because I have found believing in something greater than oneself is a tonic like no other.

If the messages in this book appeal to you then I hope you will share them, particularly with those who are troubled, lost and hurting.

Thank you!

PREFACE

I believe that synergy is beauty... I believe synergy is health... I believe synergy is harmony...

Any time we come across beauty, health and harmony we are experiencing synergy.

It's the lack of synergy that is undermining our world. Whether you are looking at political systems, corporate cultures, social institutions and their various mechanisms, human health, climatic changes, the breakdown of the family and society, the rise in crime, violence and fear, you will always find that there's a lack of synergy at the heart of the problem.

Synergy is the recognition that the whole really is greater than the sum of its parts. No matter how good any aspect of the whole is, a collaborative system where all the elements are valued and positively employed, always leads to a better outcome - whether that be for an individual, the family, an institution, society or the planet.

A collaborative system creates optimum function, greater efficiency and enhanced productivity. Synergy is not some woolly, new-aged concept that should only be taken seriously by a few. It is the essence of what is missing in our modern world and until we take its importance seriously, my proposition to you is that we will struggle to fix what's wrong with ourselves and our world.

We are currently consumed by a culture which is focused on 'me' rather than 'we' and although so much of the work I'm involved in is about strengthening the self by enhancing self-care, this is never at the expense of others. If we strengthen our own position and someone else pays for that, our own position is automatically weakened. And so, our philosophy at Reach is 'we... not just me'. This is synergy in action. In order to save myself I must also invest in saving others. We cannot reach our desired destination unless we hold hands.

The egos and personalities of our modern world have us chasing the idea that happiness, health and well-being are found in becoming celebrities as though only fame and fortune can save us. And yet the research on happiness and longevity tells us time and again that this simply isn't the case. A life of compassion, care, empathy, mutual respect, gratitude and altruism are greater guarantees of sustainable happiness.

We need to move away from the competitive culture which exists in all disciplines. We're so busy trying to prove that our point of view, our knowledge and our philosophy is the one that should be prized above all else, that in the blind pursuit of that, we miss the fact that there is more to be found in inclusion and collaboration.

The current philosophy that dominates modern thinking is one of factions and silos. This can be found in every arena of life and has led to a culture in which one protects one's research, discoveries, knowledge and unique set of insights. This has fostered a competitive environment of self-interest and arrogance. Unfortunately, this attitude and approach has found its way into all aspects of mental health too – as each school of thought professes to have a theory and methodology that is better suited to the problem than the others.

The siloed approach defines human evolution in narrow, separate compartments, as if the best way to classify our knowledge and experience is to keep the different elements of our discoveries separate. This has caused great confusion as we fail to see how things are connected.

The way this has manifested in the field of mental health is that we have developed the strange idea that things are best fixed in parts (part-ology). This means that we habitually pop off to see different people to help us fix our various ailments and concerns, removing the connection and relationship that exists between all the things that make us human. We cease to see how one aspect of our life is impacting on another.

As a result, structures and systems have been created, in which individuals are considered experts in brain health, exercise, bodywork, counselling/ psychotherapy, diet and nutrition, abuse and addiction... and so on. What is almost impossible to find is someone who can pull all these different elements together and not simply revel in the virtues of their own silo and system. I believe that another approach is needed.

We are so busy chasing symptoms, looking for solutions and in the process missing the most important point, which is, that we cannot fix the mind whilst our bodies are ailing... and we cannot fix the body whilst the mind is riddled with fear, anxiety and confusion. Also, we cannot fix the spirit when it has no positive focus, no meaning or purpose. And if we ignore the primacy of the environment, then everything we hold dear is threatened.

The Story of Health was a very big factor in the prequel to this book, but if you haven't read it and have no desire to, please go and take a look at The Story of Health on the Reach website www.thereachapproach.co.uk because it's the centrepiece of our approach and shows synergy in action.

Attempting to address the symptoms will never provide us with lasting solutions because the symptoms are not the problem, they are merely by-products of the real issue(s).

In this final book, I will take you on a journey that shows how broad the synergistic church is. I will be covering topics that on the face of it may seem unrelated, as I look at the body and its primary systems, I will examine the mind's many terrains, expand your understanding of the environment, exposing how truly vast and diverse this topic really is. I will attempt to explain the subtleties of the spirit and its relationship to the world of matter by discussing the role of energy in all things and the metaphysical rhythm at the heart of life.

You could be forgiven for thinking what do the role of the oceans, the lymphatic system, the unconscious mind, alchemy and patternology (the knowledge of patterns), have to do with you becoming part of the solution? My answer is... everything!

The more closely you look, the more I believe you will see the connections between them all and why we need a shift in consciousness. The old, siloed paradigm needs to be demolished and replaced. Everything is connected, from the cell to the cosmos - and my hope is that I will help to open your mind, deepen your understanding and encourage you to actively become a synergist.

For this to happen you will need to surrender what you think you know - your preconceived ideas, prejudices and world view - in order that you can come into contact with the bits of the universe you have not yet seen or experienced.

"We can't solve problems by using the same kind of thinking we used when we created them".

Albert Einstein (1879 - 1955)

INTRODUCTION

I had no intention of writing a fourth book but there was such an overwhelming response and interest in its predecessor Synergy: A Cure for All Ills, that I was compelled to put this final manuscript together. This work is in response to the many thousands of questions over the last seven years, seeking a deeper understanding of synergy in action. What I've attempted to do here is create something that I hope will be memorable and life changing.

The Reach Approach is a model that has organically evolved since 1979 and has been built on research (past and present), client feedback and therapeutic practice. In 1990 Reach was formally launched and its success has led to our work reaching all four corners of the globe.

Over this period, we have produced thousands of written and audio-visual resources; meditations, handouts, worksheets, articles, research documents and an app (Happy Hints), which have generated widespread interest and a substantial following. We are busy helping individuals from a variety of backgrounds, cultures and social experience to improve and realise their potential. Our materials have been translated into numerous languages, making our message more accessible to all, via our websites and the many social media platforms.

I have also developed, with the help of my team, three postgraduate courses for counsellors, psychologists, psychotherapists, holistic practitioners and coaches who are keen to learn a more comprehensive way of responding to emotional and psychological issues.

Our 'principle before profit' philosophy has been valued and respected by many as it has become clear that Reach is an organisation that is putting its message above any material gain. The message is simple... when we put our principles first, we profit in every area of our lives.

It's this philosophy of making our materials available to the widest possible audience that has allowed our message to reach far and wide and it's why we have won the trust and respect of hundreds of thousands of followers and users of our services. It is clear to them that our agenda is to educate and empower. The Reach Approach is a psycho-educational model, designed to help those who are looking for sustainable solutions in a world of quick fixes.

'Become Part of the Solution', is a deeper exploration into all aspects of synergy and is an invitation to become part of the silent revolution for positive change. In this book I explore the subtle politics and dynamics that underpin the human condition. I will also take you further into the metaphysical realm, the arena in which much of what affects human life takes place and yet most of us are unaware of this reality and therefore don't understand its impact on our day-to-day experience. If we were to appreciate the non-physical reality and its impact on the material world and our place within it, then our lives would be much richer.

I think the question-and-answer section (chapter 10) at the end of the book offers good illustrations of the 'person specific' nature of The Reach Approach. In this chapter I demonstrate how seemingly unrelated matters often have common threads that can be identified and offered to a client in such a way that they come to realise that resolution in one area of one's life begins to repair the dysfunction in other areas too.

I do not believe any one thing makes people well. It's the carefully placed strategies and resources that respond to the person's needs that achieve that outcome. It has also repeatedly been my experience that one size does not fit all.

Ten people may be suffering with anxiety and yet the antidote for each is different. One person may be anxious due to chronic dehydration and poor nutrition, both of which impact on the brain's internal workings and processes. Another individual may be suffering with a very similar level of anxiety, which is in fact due to an unresolved trauma, which continues to keep that individual bound to the past.

Both these cases need very different responses if their anxiety is to be arrested and I believe only a model that is holistic and integrative has the versatility to respond to these differences.

I make no apology for saying I'm interested in helping to create synergists – therapists and practitioners who have a well-developed understanding of the factors that impact on human consciousness and have the necessary skills to adapt and mould that understanding around the individual's needs.

Finally, this book is best treated as a reference guide, given the breadth and depth of its content. You can of course read it from cover to cover but should you not be inclined to do so, each chapter can be read as a self-contained piece of work, so feel free to chart your own journey in the way that best suits you.

I hope by the time you get to the end it will have proved as life-changing for you as it has been for me and many thousands of others.

"Complaining is finding faults, wisdom is finding solutions"

Ajahan Brahm (1951 – present)

CHAPTER 1

ENERGY CONTRACTS

"Live as if you were to die tomorrow. Learn as if you were to live forever".

Mahatma Gandhi (1869 – 1948)

What is energy?

Energy is such a difficult thing to describe and define because it has so many manifestations, expressions, shapes and forms, so how could a single definition adequately describe its incredible depth and scope? This nebulous, ethereal, multi-dimensional, metaphysical stuff is to be found everywhere, which makes describing it both easy and complicated – because everywhere we look, it's staring back at us. Defining energy is further complicated because we too are made up of this 'stuff', it is the essence of who we are.

The word energy is derived from ancient Greek (energeia) – it is in Aristotle's work, 400 years BC, that the definition of energy as the operation of 'something' or a description of some 'activity', was arguably first postulated. However, it wasn't until much later in the 17th, 18th and 19th centuries that more precise interpretations and classifications were conceived.

Russian physicist Lev Okun, Professor at the Moscow Institute for Physics and Technology said, "The more basic is a physical notion, the more difficult to define it in words". This is how professor Okun saw energy and although science has now provided us with useful definitions of energy, we need to balance that against the fact that energy has no physical essence, which makes it difficult to quantify.

There is a plethora of famous and lesser-known scientists, researchers and contributors who have each added valuable pieces of understanding to this complex subject. If this is a topic that interests you from a more scientific perspective then you can follow the modern trail starting with Thomas Young, a brilliant physician, philosopher and polymath who is credited as the first person to use the word energy in the modern sense. Young has subsequently been described by many great scientists as; "the last man who knew everything".

He laid a foundation on which others would further develop our understanding of energy. Amongst those others are Gottfried Leibniz in the late 17th century, through to James Prescott Joule and William Rankine in the mid 19th century.

During this period, many different definitions for describing the nature and performance of energy emerged. For example, Rankine coined the term potential energy, and it was Joule who discovered the link between mechanical work and the generation of heat, hence the unit many of us will be familiar with when talking about energy expenditure, joule, was named after him.

The numerous descriptions and ways of quantifying energy did not end there. We now have an extensive list of classifications, which includes thermodynamics, kinetic, mechanical, magnetic, electrical, nuclear, chemical, sound wave and gravitational energy - and subject to which references you consult, there are as many as twelve.

So, it is accurate to say that everything in the known universe is a form of energy and these descriptions are helpful in describing or explaining the many manifestations of energy and how it behaves under certain conditions.

In Synergy: A Cure for All Ills I gave an overview of the four forces, also known as the unified field. The four forces are a summary description of everything in the known universe, classified in one of four categories. These categories are strong nuclear force, weak nuclear force, gravity and electromagnetism.

I don't intend to repeat my explanation of the four forces here, but I do think it's worth saying that all twelve types of energy (some of which I've listed above) are found under the umbrella of the four forces.

The history and science surrounding the subject of energy is a field of study in its own right - it's not my aim to focus on that aspect, as the information has been well documented elsewhere. My aim is to explain how we are inextricably linked to the story of energy, from our DNA through to the stars and the planets – as it is pivotal to you and I and our shared reality.

I want to underline the metaphysical aspects of this topic, which do not tend to be given the same credence and importance, certainly in the world of science. This is unfortunate because apart from a few notable exceptions the lack of acknowledgement of the metaphysical dimension, is in fact in my view impeding science's understanding of this vast subject. I think the inventor and engineer, Tesla, says it beautifully.

"The day science begins to study non-physical phenomena it will make more progress in one decade than in all the previous centuries of its existence".

Nikola Tesla (1846-1943)

Thankfully, there is a handful of committed researchers, pioneers and exponents of energy psychology, energy medicine and metaphysics beating the drum despite the scepticism and opposition - individuals such as Norman Shealy. He founded the American Holistic Medical Association in 1978 and is the CEO of the International Institute of Holistic Medicine. He is a neurosurgeon, considered to be a pioneer in pain medicine and depression management. Shealy has numerous patents in the field of energy medicine and is the inventor of the highly successful TENS (transcutaneous electrical nerve stimulator) machine. He has also written twenty-six books on health and the role of energy in medicine and continues to be a driving force in the field.

Dawson Church Ph.D. is a former student of Norman Shealy, he holds a doctorate in integrative healthcare - and is an author of numerous books, most notably the best seller, Genie in your Genes and most recently Mind to Matter (2018). Church also writes widely for many publications and is the founder of the National Institute for Integrative Healthcare, which is a non-profit institution dedicated to evidence-based research looking at a wide range of healing modalities. His latest book is particularly focused on the relationship between mind and matter and the part energy plays in that.

Bruce Lipton is a developmental biologist most famous for his pioneering work in epigenetics. He has also more latterly become part of the global movement that is quite rightly trying to put consciousness and energy onto the map of science and human understanding. His ground-breaking book, Biology of Belief has proven to be a seminal piece of work highlighting how consciousness moulds biology at every level.

Eckhart Tolle is a renowned spiritual teacher specialising in psychology and metaphysics. He has written several bestsellers, including The Power of Now and A New Earth: Awakening to Your Life's Purpose. His work focuses on inner transformation through consciousness and the act of being 'present in each moment'. He is an advocate for changing one's own energy as the primary vehicle for global transformation, a message that is echoed throughout the centuries.

Dr. Joe Dispenza is a neuroscientist, author, researcher and lecturer with interests in neuroscience, epigenetics, quantum physics and healing. Dr. Dispenza travels the world using science and research to elevate human understanding in order that we might become more passionate about our own healing and ability to facilitate that. Amongst his contributions to the field of neuroscience, epigenetics and energy are films such as: Heal (2017) E-motion (2014) Sacred Journey of the Heart (2012) People Versus the State of Illusion (2011) and there are numerous other written and audio-visual works that could be added to this list.

There are other spiritual teachers, scientists, motivational speakers and researchers who are credited for playing a part in placing consciousness and energy on the radar including: Louise Hay, Wayne Dyer, Caroline Myss, Gregg Braden, Deepak Chopra, Marianne Williamson, Thích Nh?t H?nh, Byron Katie, Michael Beckwith, Rupert Sheldrake and many more. My reference to these individuals is not an endorsement of their work, because although I believe their contributions are very valuable, I also believe as I said in the preface that we need to beware of a 'siloed approach'. My point is that it is important to acknowledge their contributions to the debate and to challenging the current paradigms. It's for you to work out for yourself how much of what they are saying fits with your own philosophy and beliefs.

Energy psychology, although still referred to by many as pseudoscience, is establishing itself as a discipline that needs to be taken seriously, with the rapid expansion of techniques such as Thought Field Therapy (TFT), EFT (Emotional Freedom Technique also known as tapping) and Tapas Acupressure Technique

(TAT), all of which involve working with the mind and body in an energetic way, using affirmations, positive statements, visualisations and specific rituals to bring about the energetic release of negative issues. These techniques have had notable success dealing with anxiety, depression, irrational fears, pain, phobias, negative patterns resistant to change, addiction and a host of other psychological hurts/injuries and physical issues/challenges.

There are now numerous energy focused organisations emerging around the world offering information, research and training, endeavouring to expand the individual's understanding of the topic. There is also the opportunity for therapists and practitioners to become qualified and accredited in the energy disciplines.

Before going any further, I'd like to give credit to the past and many of the Eastern masters, scholars and giants, who first mooted many of the principles that are now being held dear in the spiritual field of energy. I believe they have left us a priceless legacy. These include Buddha, Lao Tzu, Patanjali, Confucius, Mahävïra, Mohammed, Guru Nanak, Bãdarãyana, Wõnhyo, Yi T'oegye, Al-Kindi, Shõtoku Taishi, Rabia al-Adawiyya and many more who are generally not recognised in the West. I offered my tribute to them in Antiquity Comes Full Circle. If you are interested in finding out more about them and their invaluable contributions, then you don't need to buy the book, there are significant extracts on the Reach website (www.thereach approach.co.uk).

By the end of this chapter, I hope you will see that I've chosen to focus on that which I think is most likely to improve your relationship with yourself, your fellow human beings and your destiny. I hope you will be encouraged to pursue a nobler path, one full of grace, conscience and right action.

Now, let's go back to my first question... what is energy? There are so many definitions of energy, here's how I invite you to see it:

It is the incredible fabric that binds all of life together. It is subtle and multi-dimensional. It is complex yet simple, infinitesimal yet vast and expansive. Energy is the very substance of the universe as well as the primary architect within the cosmos – organising the countless functions and activities at the microcosm and macrocosm. It can be defined both by its work and its many and varied manifestations. It is the narrative behind life's diversity and rich expression... and the keeper of the secrets yet to be told.

As we journey together, I will try to unveil further the mystery and magnificence of energy – and in doing so help you to create a positive and special bond, which will liberate you from your destructive patterns and habits.

Energy signatures and energy contracts

The names, descriptions and classifications that we apply to the things around us are merely labels for expressions of energy. Colour, shape and form simply tell us the story of how energy expresses itself in that moment. It's important to understand that all energy is vibrating at its own unique frequency, it has its own signature, its own unique hallmark. No two flowers are precisely the same, no two trees, even from the same species are the same. No two pathogens, whether bacteria, viral or fungal are the same. The latest research around identical twins has overturned the previously held belief that they are identical. We now know that they are in fact virtually the same - and so we can reasonably conclude that energy doesn't ever reproduce itself identically. Everything has its own unique expression.

Energy signatures describe the unique vibration (resonance) of an object, person, system or organism. This is what determines its colour, shape, form and expression. So, when one or more signatories come together an energy contract is formed. And all life depends on these contracts. The more we understand these contractual arrangements, the more we can consciously participate in ways that are beneficial to all.

When one energy enters into a contract with another energy it brings with it its own personality and idiosyncrasies. What this means in practice is that there is an infinite set of possibilities emerging out of every transaction. This is one of the many beautiful things about life – that it is fluid, evolving and endlessly expressive.

Energy signatures are a critical aspect of energy contracts - because they describe what each energy brings to the table and the counter signatories to any contract then influence how that arrangement plays out.

When you understand that everything has an energy signature and every minute of every day, energy contracts are being established, revised, renegotiated and dissolved, you can better see how you fit into your world and your environment. More importantly you can make more conscious contributions to changing the shape of your reality. None of us need be victim to what we are experiencing. If we understand that every transaction is based on a relationship between different kinds of energy, we can ensure that our contribution to that equation is always positive and healthy.

I began using the term energy contracts some thirty years ago, when trying to make sense for myself of the tireless interplay of life, with its countless characters, interactions and transactions. What could be described as chaos, under closer scrutiny is sometimes a thing of great beauty - and hiding beneath its façade at times is in fact a story of collaboration and cooperation.

It became clear through my research, clinical practice and experience of the transpersonal world that we can either be a part of what enhances and enriches our lives, or we can choose to stand apart from these arrangements - at which point our fortune is no more in our control than the roll of a dice. When we choose not to

participate, what we need to understand is that the contractual arrangements continue to take place around us whether we participate or not. In other words, circumstances take over as we surrender our power to choose.

The countless interactions and transactions we all witness every day taking place between people, systems, organisations, countries, continents, the climate, and the cosmos, could appear to be matters of chance, but it's more accurate to describe these dynamics and events as unseen/unknown agreements. There are parts of these agreements that we can see, discuss and even renegotiate should we wish... but there are so many other variables that are not always immediately obvious that are also influencing what is happening. It's at this unseen and often unknown level that the opportunity for positive change exists.

It's dangerous to believe that we are independent forces, able to exist and act without concern for the consequences of our actions. It's this lack of awareness and lack of conscience that keeps us drowning in pollution and yet we keep poisoning the atmosphere, the soil and our water supplies. What's crazy about this attitude is that we are the victims of this neglectful approach and yet seem blind to our stupidity.

If we really understood the interdependency of life then we would respect the other energies and forces around us, fostering healthy relationships with them to ensure mutual survival and continued growth. In other words, forming healthy energy contracts.

We can choose to have healthy relationships with those other systems and forces in our environment, or we can continue to ride roughshod across them, as if our own needs transcend all other needs. But in doing this we are digging our own graves and preparing our eulogies... we are not more important than the other forces with which we share this stage called life. In chapter 2, I will speak more extensively about the interdependency of energy when exploring the four environments.

For now, let me provide you with some examples of energy contracts to further illuminate the importance of this subject and to help you better understand the unseen and unknown elements of the agreements that are taking place in plain sight. Think of the world that we live in where the trees and the foliage, via photosynthesis, draw in the sun's vitality and life force and in return they provide us with oxygen; and with food stuffs that we consume to make ourselves well and whole.

We, as part of that contract, imbibe the oxygen and excrete the carbon dioxide that is needed in the atmosphere - the carbon dioxide that the trees then turn into oxygen. We consume the fruits and the food that are produced, absorbing the sun's energy and light as we do - we are then populated by the photons and nutrients found in those plants and vegetation.

As we are flooded with that energy, we have the capacity choose to use it in a positive way, kindly, compassionately, applying our creative intelligence for the greater good. Then not only do we prosper but the environment prospers too. In this way a healthy energy contract is established where all parties are enriched and empowered.

Unfortunately, this particular healthy energy contract is being undermined through deforestation, where we're felling literally thousands of acres of trees each day, which in turn is altering the atmosphere because the oxygen that the trees promise is no longer delivered in the same quantity, nor does it have the same quality. This is because of the pollutants we're putting into the atmosphere, which amongst other things is creating acid rain. Rain that changes the pH in the soil and with that change, the nature of our food is also substantially changing - because the food is being robbed and stripped of vital nutrients.

Acidity, when it comes to human health, undermines the balance and harmony of the system. Although we do need some acidity to maintain health within the organism – the digestive system and aspects of the immune system are very good examples of this – nonetheless the truth is that a greater degree of alkalinity is essential for human health.

In the example above, not only is the earth being polluted but we in turn are reaping the negative consequences of that pollution. Therefore, this energy contract is no longer working in a way that is optimal – for the planet, humans, animals or natural vegetation.

The extent to which the energy contracts are being reneged on by the choices we are making is quite staggering. The minerals that can be found in the soil are now at a frighteningly low level - we can say that most of what we need for human health can no longer be found entirely within food. We have altered the genetic makeup of the planet and in doing so our food has been altered too.

The earth is always trying to do the best it can with the resources it has, but in truth we are actually polluting it at such a rate that it is struggling to sing its beautiful chorus and the gift of health is increasingly being denied to us all.

Here's another example of energy contracts, clearly described by Dr. Rebecca Jones of the University of Tasmania. In this extract you will see three different energy signatures all forming a part of the energy contract.

"Forests are complex things. They are full of finely balanced illogical relationships often between the most unlikely characters. The close relationship between Tasmania's bettongs, native truffles and eucalyptus is one such story.

In Tasmania, dry sclerophyll forests are dominated by Eucalyptus species. These forests grow on dry gravelly soil, and nutrients are hard for the tree roots to obtain. The trees, however, have a secret accomplice: they have evolved a symbiotic relationship with underground fungi, which grow as a delicate gauze around the trees' finest roots, and extend even finer, highly absorptive threads into the soil to collect water and nutrients. The fungi share these with the tree roots, and in return the tree shares its carbohydrates with fungi. Together, they survive.

Tasmania's forests are full of these harmonious tree-fungi relationships. But there is a problem. The fungi grow their fruit or truffles underground, which means the truffle spores cannot be dispersed by the wind. How then do the fungi spread to new areas to partner with new young trees? Here the forest relationships become more complex again and the third player is introduced.

The Tasmanian bettong, last of its kind (all mainland species have been wiped out mainly by foxes) has become involved in this transaction, presumably to its delight, to dine almost entirely on truffles. Between meals it skips through the forest dispersing the truffle spores, which pass unaffected through its digestive system. The mystery of how the bettong knows where and when to dig for a truffle is uncovered by studying the truffles themselves: they are highly scented when ripe, releasing a perfume that varies according to its location – some smell like lemon, others like pepper – and those volatile chemicals act as signals to guide the bettongs to the feast.

The whole forest is interconnected with relationships like these. Living systems are complex jigsaws of dependent relationships and here we get a small insight into that fascinating story".

The more we examine the dynamics and intricacies of the earth and environment, the more we discover that energy contracts are everywhere. I will explore more of these environmental examples in chapter 2, but for now, I 'd like to look at a couple of different examples to illustrate how far-reaching energy contracts are.

In Synergy: A Cure for All Ills, I discussed the intimate relationship between the mouth and the mind. I also introduced the notion of quantum dissonance (disease) and quantum coherence (health) as these are pivotal concepts illuminating the incredible and powerful dialogue between mind and body. These are also excellent examples of energy contracts as they highlight the fact that there's always a conversation taking place and subject to the terms and conditions, those conversations either produce health or disease, happiness or chaos.

The body promises to deliver optimal health and maximum functioning, so long as it is provided with the necessary hydration, nutrients, sleep, relaxation, joy and happiness that it needs. If we meet those minimum requirements, then the body's immune and detoxification systems will be capable of managing the many insults to health. This in turn will enable our creative intelligence to fully blossom.

However, if we are not meeting the minimum requirements for self-care the body cannot deliver on its promises and instead of health being our prominent experience, we'll find ourselves being victims of dis-ease and as a consequence disease will follow - whether that be physical or mental ill health, or in some cases both.

At every stage, the body is saying 'provide me with the right energy and I will deliver the promise of health and well-being'. But unfortunately, many of us are no longer meeting those minimal requirements and as a result the body cannot deliver. It will always do its best... it will always try to work with what we've given it. However, without the right nutrients and correct configuration of those compounds, then the body will fail in that task and as a result we will find that we fail in our primary task of being the best we can be.

Let's look at one more example to illustrate the point further. Relationships provide us with countless opportunities to examine energy contracts.

Each one of us is vibrating in our own unique way. When we come into contact with others, we can experience their vibration and they indeed can experience ours – whether either party is conscious of this or not, a transaction of some kind takes place.

When there is harmony of intention, desire, values and beliefs then these exchanges are experienced by both parties to be positive, inspiring, uplifting. However, when these exchanges are taking place where the intentions, beliefs, aspirations, values and philosophies are different, it is more likely that a tension will be experienced. And in that tension, there's nearly always one who will feel less than and it's possible that the other will feel more than. That said, differences in resonance don't automatically mean conflict will ensue. It is possible that the difference in 'spin rate' (the way that energy moves/expresses itself) can lead to a transaction that is mutually beneficial. This depends on how wedded each one is to their own point of view.

Equally possible is that both parties feel hurt, damaged, even poisoned by the interaction and neither party wants to have that experience again. Whenever you feel you're in the company of those that make you feel more than you would by yourself, you're likely to be attracted to being in their company; you're more inclined to pursue that relationship. Whereas in an interaction where you feel there's something that doesn't sit right (even though you might not be able to explain it) then those encounters and relationships are ones you're less likely to pursue.

All of us can think of examples like this. There are those individuals that we want to be around and treasure their company and those we would rather have little or nothing to do with.

Hopefully by now you're beginning to see that energy contracts are not something we can really opt out of, although we may make that decision. But as explained earlier, if one forfeits one's right to choose, then circumstances will choose for you. This is just another energy contract, but not one that is in your best interests.

In a world that's interdependent, where synergy is at the heart of everything, then energy contracts are the lifeblood of that system. However, we can choose how we sign up to those contracts. We can, through our philosophy and beliefs, our intentions and actions, enter into these contracts in a very different and conscious way. Rather than being victims of what's taking place and unfolding, we can decide to be conscious contributors to the transactions, making sure that our part in the energy contract is positive and unambiguous.

By removing ambiguity and better still negativity, our energy contracts, or rather our contribution to them, can lead to a much better experience for ourselves and those around us which means that our contribution to the world can be more constructive.

Electromagnetic fields – how energy gets the job done

At the outset of this chapter, I stated that I didn't want to get too bogged down in the science because there's plenty of research documented elsewhere. I also felt there was a danger of the metaphysical importance of this subject getting lost. That said, I believe energy signatures and contracts are better understood if we have some understanding of electromagnetic fields, as they are the primary context in which these transactions take place.

Electromagnetism as a field, combining electricity and magnetism, is widely accepted to have begun with Hans Christian Ørsted in 1820 who fortuitously noticed how the electric current from a battery influenced the movement of a compass needle. He wasn't initially able to explain what he'd witnessed but it began a period of intense research where he was subsequently able to prove that an electric current did indeed produce a magnetic field. The unit of magnetic induction named ørsted is an acknowledgement of his contribution to electromagnetism. It was Ørsted's research that began the revolution that followed in this field - and it is widely accepted that it is his work that helped create the foundation for a unified concept of energy.

French physicist, André-Marie Ampère, took Ørsted's work further by developing a physical and mathematical theory which explained the relationship between electricity and magnetism, and he produced a single mathematical formula to explain the magnetic forces between current carrying conductors; as a result, Ampère's law was established – and the ampere (amp), the unit of measurement of an electric current, was named after him.

What followed was a synergy of seismic contributions from, James Clerk Maxwell, Michael Faraday, Heinrich Hertz and Oliver Heaviside - as a result of their ingenuity, research and discoveries a rapid period of growth took place during the 19th century, leading also to a growth spurt in mathematical physics, which provided a language and a set of equations that underpinned electromagnetic theory and a unified concept of energy emerged.

This subsequently led to a greater understanding of the nature of light (photons), overturning the previous paradigm in the process with a proposition that connected the whole field of energy. Put simply, different frequencies of oscillation create different forms of electromagnetic radiation (energy) from radio waves through to gamma waves (see: the electromagnetic spectrum, to see the vast range of this continuum). This highlighted the fact that there is a common thread that runs through all energy manifestations... namely light - and the electromagnetic field is the matrix that 'holds', facilitates and maintains the shape and form of these transactions.

This is a topic I briefly covered in Synergy under the heading 'the story of light'. There is also a summary of this topic under that name on the Reach website, should you wish to explore it further.

The electromagnetic field is now known to be one of the four primary forces, which collectively underpin the world as we know it. The other three you may remember are: weak nuclear force, strong nuclear force and gravity. These are all forms of energy and part of the incredible story of light.

To conclude this brief summary on electromagnetism I would like to include the work of Dr Harold Saxton Burr, as his research developed the picture further. He was a professor of neuroanatomy and bio-electrodynamics at Yale University, School of Medicine for over forty years - from 1914 until the late 1950s.

Here's an overarching summary he offered about electromagnetic fields:

"The universe in which we find ourselves and from which we cannot be separated is a place of law and order. It is not an accident, nor chaos. It is organised and maintained by an electro-dynamic field capable of determining the position and movement of all charged particles. For nearly half a century, the logical consequences of this theory have been subjected to rigorously controlled conditions and met with no contradictions."

This quote and the forty years of research that underpins it is why I believe Dr Burr's contribution is worthy of special mention in the explanation of 'what is energy?' He discovered what he called electro-dynamic fields (which are also known as fields of life or L-fields for short). Dr Burr was able to demonstrate through his research, using voltmeters that all living organisms emit volts and are moulded and controlled by these electro-dynamic fields. He was convinced, that these electromagnetic fields were the blueprint for all life on this planet. They offered a clear explanation and a testable formula, which illustrated how the body, trees, animals and other organisms kept their shape under the relentless metabolic/structural changes that all living organisms go through. Burr's work solved this mystery because the electro-dynamic fields he discovered provided a template that maintained the shape of an organism/system, as it undergoes the unfathomable number of changes that sustain life.

The magnet and iron filings experiment most of us would be familiar with as children performed in the science lab is often used to illustrate the electromagnetic fields phenomenon. If you scatter iron filings on a card or piece of paper with a magnet underneath, you'll notice they arrange themselves in lines that match the force field that the magnet creates. If the filings are discarded and fresh filings are placed on that same paper/card, then they will replicate the pattern of the previous iron filings.

This is an excellent analogy for what is happening in the human body (and nature generally) because regardless of the billions of activities taking place each second of every day the cells and molecules within our bodies are managed and kept in position by these electrodynamic fields. So, as cells and molecules are broken down and discarded, new cells and molecules are created out of the food that we eat - and the electrodynamic field serves as a mould/matrix allowing new molecules and cells to arrange themselves in accordance with the same pattern.

Another very helpful analogy for understanding this phenomenon is a jelly mould. When we make jelly and pour it into the mould, we know exactly what shape the jelly will take on. The electrodynamic fields provide us with a similar level of accuracy and prediction about outcomes. Although the L-fields are invisible and intangible, they are nonetheless able to be measured - and based on the voltages of an organism, it is possible to predict the patterns of behaviour and activity of that organism.

Dr. Burr decided to examine the electrical properties of cancer-susceptible mice. He wanted to see if the voltage would change during the initiation and growth of cancer tissue and what he discovered was quite startling - that in less than 30 hours after the implementation of cancer cells there were measurable changes in the voltage and according to the level of the voltage, he could predict progression rates and potential recovery rates.

What Burr was trying to establish is whether the L-fields could become a valuable diagnostic and therapeutic tool. He wondered if establishing an electro-metric scale for different organisms would make it possible to identify when the disease state is emerging before there are visible symptoms. In other words, if the mould has in some way become damaged then that could be detected and measured, so like the jelly mould when you pour the jelly into it, the jelly reflects those imperfections.

Burr concluded:
"We had reason to believe that the electro-dynamic field could serve as a signpost for a variety of conditions because our experiments had confirmed our basic assumption. This was that the organism possesses a field as a whole, which embraces subsidiary or local fields, representing the organism's component parts. We assumed, then, that variations in the subsidiary fields would be reflected in variations in the flow of energy in the whole system - we decided, therefore, to look for further practical consequences of the theory".

Dr Burr's research went much further than mice, he used his electro-metric technique in neurological and psychiatric cases. He and Dr. Leonard J. Ravitz Jr., also a teacher and researcher at Yale University, in the psychiatric department, found they could establish a baseline voltage which demonstrated normal mental functioning and when patients were not at that point on the scale some mental dysfunction would be visible. They also noted that readings could come back into the normal range when a patient received therapeutic intervention or had a positive change in circumstances.

Burr's extensive body of work is well documented in over 90 scientific papers and his experiments covered diverse areas of interest - each time confirming the L-fields were indeed the guiding hand pointing to the expression of health or disease, balance or chaos, and so if we could listen in on those conversations it would be possible to notice dysfunction in the field, which would later manifest as a problem in the organism.

Understanding the incredible matrix that the electromagnetic fields create, helps us to appreciate how the unimaginable web of action and reaction taking place within the universe is possible. It also helps us to understand how the cause-and-effect dynamic brings about an equal and opposite reaction. The electromagnetic fields are like information highways, allowing data to travel backwards and forwards between two or more objects. Their sophistication is such that if we could see the field with the human eye, what we would see would resemble the most incredible web of light. We would see that every thought, word and action carries its own resonance (vibration) along these pathways, communicating its messages as it goes – which ultimately impacts on both the transmitter and receiver.

This offers us incredible insight as we take this journey towards becoming part of the solution - and extricate ourselves from the problem.

Once our relationship to electromagnetic fields is understood, we realise that most of the harm and damage being done in life is beyond the field of the visible. In fact, the damage and harm that we see is largely the consequence of what we don't see. There are unimaginable numbers of transactions taking place each day impacting on our souls and the quality of our lives.

We misguidedly believe that we're in control of our fortunes, but where the real control lies, is not always immediately obvious to us. The invisible and intangible world is the real architect in the universe. If we align ourselves to this world then we can be co-creators. If not, we simply become casualties of fate. If we want to influence our own destiny, we need to understand the relationship between free will and the world of energy, both metaphysical and physical. Only then can we plug the holes in the soul and stop our energy seeping away.

Energy stealers

This is a vitally important aspect within the huge subject of energy and is something we need to understand in order that we can manage this phenomenon and avoid losing our energy, otherwise our best efforts will continue to be undermined.

The list of energy stealers is quite extensive and so I won't cover them all, but I would like to draw your attention to some of the primary ones.

The list below is in no particular order because some will apply to some people and not others and also the extent to which they apply will be different from one person to the next. See if you can pick out your energy stealers.

Making mistakes and not learning from them:
This is a major energy stealer. Mistakes are arguably our best tutors but when we deny and justify our actions, we are denied the lessons and the growth they offer and are destined to make even more mistakes of the same nature.

Trying to unnecessarily control situations and people:
To take control can be a virtue in the right circumstances, but so many of us are actually trying to control things out of fear; fear that we won't get what we want, fear that s/he will get it wrong, the belief that only I can do what's required, which simply disempowers all parties. This kind of control is toxic because it harms the one doing the controlling and those being controlled.

Making excuses:
This is one of the most common ways of covering up what we haven't done. It's often our attempt to make us look better and to cover our shame. All it really does is stunt our growth.

Defending oneself and one's perspective at all costs:
A dogmatic approach to life is responsible for nearly every conflict and war that's ever been fought. When we hold onto our prejudices, points of view and beliefs, unwilling to see another perspective or negotiate, we make ourselves blind.

Harsh negative thoughts against oneself:
Negative thoughts are arguably the worst energy stealers. They can send us spiralling down at a great rate of knots. Compassion towards oneself is the swiftest way to achieve positive change. The kind mind erases all negative objections, enabling us to find a smoother path.

Negative, critical judgement towards others:
Hardening our hearts towards others denies us access to our better natures and we are weakened in the process. We cannot avoid making judgements because it's the nature of the mind to try and make sense of what it's seeing and experiencing. However, we can ensure that our judgements are kind.

Not facing one's own demons:
There is much talk about 'living in the now' but can we truly live in the now whilst we have a litany of issues that remain unattended to? Without resolving the past to the best of our ability we remain chained to it and the gift of the present is never fully unwrapped.

Impatience:
Impatience is responsible for so many disasters. It believes that the best route is always the shortest or the quickest and yet impatience almost always doubles the length of the journey. Impatience mistakes force for strength and doesn't realise that the reason the fruit has not ripened is because it has sucked the life out of it.

Not accepting the way things have played out:
Non-acceptance has us constantly revisiting the past, seeking a different outcome. This is futile because we can't change the past, but we can change how we relate to it. Acceptance is a great virtue and requires much strength. When we fight against the way circumstances have unfolded, we can waste so much energy and time, which would be better spent learning what we need to learn and planning a better strategy.

Disrespecting time:

Those who disrespect time will find their best laid plans in tatters at their feet, often looking for someone to blame. It's impossible to claim back time that has been wasted, because it is gone. What we can do however, is to take our lessons with us and make a pledge to value and respect time going forward. Those who do this will find she has a very forgiving nature.

Maintaining unhealthy relationships:

Company colours. The people you spend time with and share your mind and heart with are the people most likely to influence you. This is why it's so important that they are hand-picked. Those who do not add value to your life should not be condemned but are best avoided.

Inadequate investment in self-care:

Self-care is the key to positive change. You cannot be the best version of yourself whilst you neglect your own core needs. Identify what those are and prioritise them. Then you will turn from a stone into a diamond.

Poor nutrition:

Human beings are made up of food, water, air and light. To achieve the best in well-being we need all four, in sufficient quantities. Nutrition is essential to physical and mental health. Where there is inadequate nutrition both body and mind struggle to fulfil their meaning and purpose and we are plagued by stress.

A lack of order in one's life:

Order creates peace, chaos creates confusion - look honestly at your life and the people around you and the proof of this will be blindingly obvious. So many of us waste time and energy wading through our mess and in the process our contentment is replaced with frustration and fatigue.

Poor sleep hygiene:

Most of the body's housekeeping and maintenance duties are carried out whilst we are asleep. Sleep is one of the cornerstones of good mental and physical health. So, ensure that you take all the necessary steps to make your sleep beneficial. Focus on creating an environment that naturally induces sleep. In the hour before going to sleep it is best to avoid overly stimulating activity.

Dehydration:
We are vertical rivers. Our bodies cannot perform any of their functions without water. Of the things we put into our bodies, water is by far the most important. Without it we cannot even think straight and focus properly as dehydration undermines all cognitive functions. This energy stealer accounts for so many problems in relation to human health.

Not being sufficiently vigilant with one's own health:
If you listen in, you will notice that your body is communicating with you all the time. It prods and pokes you in little ways, inviting you to meet its needs. So, don't neglect these nudges (symptoms/feelings). They are often the best indicators of something needing your attention. Listen to that voice within.

Lack of personal responsibility:
The blame game may be very comforting as it provides the illusion that the only thing right with the world is you! To those who find comfort in this position, all learning and growth is denied. It's only when we take responsibility for those 'things' we get right and wrong, that we can find our way through the maze of life.

Not chewing food thoroughly:
It has long been said you are what you eat. However, it is more accurate to say that you are what you absorb from what you eat. Digestion begins in the mouth. Bowel disorders are on the rise and a lack of chewing is arguably the number one reason for this, because undigested foods cause a plethora of problems – altering the brain and body chemistry in the process.

Saying one thing and doing another:
Words are powerful vehicles of energy. They can uplift and inspire. They can undermine and destroy. We need to employ them mindfully. We also need to realise that when we say one thing but do something else the incongruence of this resonates within us in such a way that we are unable to find peace or clarity.

As I said at the outset, this is not a definitive list, but it is a good place to start and clearly shows that there are many ways that energy can seep away from us and if we are to prevent that from occurring then we need to be aware of these drainage points and plug them with the appropriate response.

If you're not sure if something is an energy stealer, the simple test for checking is to ask yourself the following questions:

> Does it lower your mood?
> Does it steal your focus?
> Do you keep going around in circles, experiencing the same disappointing outcomes?
> Do you find that no matter what you do, you can't progress?

Test anything you're not sure about against these criteria. If you feel weakened by a course of action you are taking, then something is wrong.

Energy enablers

These are the best ways to make positive investments in your life. They also provide you with some of the antidotes to the energy stealers.

Make a list of non-negotiables:
There is no doubt that the best way to break the negative cycles that send our minds spinning in the wrong direction, is to create a set of non-negotiables – promises and pledges to oneself that we aim never to break. What this means in practice is carrying out these non-negotiables at least 80% of the time. You will then find you accrue the power to meet all life's challenges with grace and strength.

Forgiveness unblocks our energy fields:
Forgiveness is often mistaken for letting the other person off the hook, having not secured justice. As a result, many shun forgiveness, not realising that a lack of forgiveness weakens them. For those who can walk this challenging path there is healing and transformation. Their anger, revenge and pain are converted into a more useful force for change.

Gratitude strengthens our resolve:
One of the positive statements I use a lot in my work is 'a mind full of gratitude has no room for complaint'. This attitude to life really works. The more we count our blessings the more blessings we end up having to count as the magnet of appreciation creates good fortune and positive outcomes. Practise saying thank you, which will create feelings of gratitude and heartfelt appreciation will follow.

Humility always wins the day:
For some humility is the greatest virtue of them all and experience has taught me that this is indeed true. It has been postulated that if you put humility on one side of the scales and all the other virtues on the other side, humility would still be greater in value. Humility should not be mistaken for weakness. One who stands in this position is not interested in being right but pursuing what is right. Humility is not false modesty. It knows its own value and celebrates that, whilst never seeking to diminish another. It does not seek or need title, recognition or reward.

Listening – the jewel in the crown:
The best way to see is with your ears! The eyes miss so much and are easily flattered and deceived. The ears on the other hand are the portholes to insight, clarity and the 'real' conversations of life. To one who is really listening, every moment is packed with benefits. The listener is a perpetual student, researcher and expert and as such is always growing. A true expert is one who is experienced in the topic(s) they are presenting. Theirs is not merely a theoretical appreciation of the subject. They have immersed themselves in that subject over time to such an extent that they embody it.

Patience is the mother of wisdom:
Those who understand that change is a process, not an event, are happy to wait because they know life guarantees to match their intentions. They do not fret and stress because the outcome they seek has not yet turned up. They are anchored to faith... they know that by doing the right things the best outcomes do eventually emerge in their lives. This attitude and approach conserves so much energy.

Feed the mind and body well:
It is important to make introspection a central feature of each day in order that the mind is adequately fed. I've covered introspective practices comprehensively in my work and those familiar with The Reach Approach will know there is no shortage of options. The mindfulness and meditation revolution that's taking place is also helping to underline the importance of cultivating our inner world. The body needs daily attention too. This has been well documented in my work entitled Persuading the Body (to find out more, see the Reach website). So, make sure you fulfil the needs of both, and you will flourish.

Make time for joy:
We live in the world of our attention. Where our attention goes our energy flows. No matter how busy you are you must make time to soak up the wonders of life. There is so much joy to be found in both the great and the small things, but we really need to be paying attention so that we do not miss those treasures.

Find and fulfil your meaning and purpose:
A lack of meaning and purpose is one of the key reasons that mental ill health is on the rise. We need to find value and meaning in our lives - to exist is not enough. Many find themselves slipping into anxiety and depression, when they can see no light on the horizon. You must first find and cultivate the light in you and your path will be illuminated.

Pursue kindness in all things:
Kindness tops up your pot of good energy. It keeps the virtuous cycle spinning. If you treat others the way you wish to be treated, you'll find that life lifts you up onto its shoulders, helping you to wade through troubled waters more easily.

Empathy changes our experience of reality:
The more we practise seeing reality from the other person's position, the more our own awareness grows. Empathy makes us more than we would otherwise be. Seeing the world through someone else's eyes enhances our connection with the world, it also offers greater insight and as a result our spirit soars.

Sincerity ensures our success:
Sincerity unlocks every door. The sincere heart can access the unseen parts of itself. It can also find solutions where there appear to be none. The whole universe conspires to help sincerity to achieve its objectives. The more sincere you become, the richer your heart and soul.

Aspire for authenticity in all things:
Keep trying to be the best you can be. Authenticity is not about pretending to be something you're not. It's about accepting the truth about yourself and kindly nourishing that. Those who aspire for authenticity are helped by all that is good in the world and will eventually meet their very best selves.

Courage teaches you to fly:
When we take a step in the right direction, even when it's the last thing we really want to do, we are elevated by our ancestors and all those courageous souls who've gone before us. Every time you find the courage to face your fears, fear loses its grip over you and your spirit learns to fly. Be brave!

Embrace your ambivalence:
Integrity does not mean we are without flaw and contradiction. The one who lives a life of integrity is the one who accepts their ambivalence and finds ways to be true, whilst they are changing. They do not condemn themselves because they know transformation will not be possible without acceptance. Integrity is to be transparent, to be truthful about where you are. There is great power to be had in this position.

Become part of the solution:
It's so easy to keep finding fault with everything and everyone. This really takes no effort. The real challenge is to find goodness where there is little, to find hope where there is none, to find a way forward when the path is blocked. Those who are looking for solutions to the problems are the ones most likely to find them. And surprisingly they seem to have extra fuel in their tank. Life loves those who are trying to find the best way forward and goes out of her way to support them.

There are many more ways to invest energy in order to sustain yourself and maintain your growth. However, this list is a good starting point. These energy enablers feed off one another. The more you immerse yourself in them and incorporate them in your life, the more resilient and resourceful you'll become. You will feel yourself growing in stature and real power will emerge. As a result, you will find the confidence to continue pursuing the best path for you.

Those who conserve their energy and invest in the right things, find they care very little about how others see them. Their focus is on how they feel about themselves, because they know this is where they will find peace of mind and bliss.

Creating your own energy contract

Hopefully by now, the depth and breadth of this subject has become clear. Everything is energy of one kind or another. It's the essence of you and me and everything we can see, touch and even that which is beyond our sensory perception is made of energy. I've referred to it in previous works as the story of light, because energy is light; and light is energy. It's important with this understanding in place that we become part of the conversations taking place around us and so creating an energy contract for ourselves is the starting point for this incredible voyage.

Once you've created your energy contract, see it as a document that you may need to revise over time, as you deal with life's ebbs and flows and learn to master your ambivalences and contradictions. It's not a static agreement, it's fluid and adapts to your circumstances and situations, as they change and as you grow.

The obvious place to start is by limiting your energy stealers. Eliminating them will take time, so don't expect to do this overnight. There may be some that are easier to overturn than others but it's more important to do this well than do it quickly.

Sit quietly and consult your heart... take a good look at both these lists and be honest with yourself about what it is you need to do. Don't worry about doing this 'correctly' - there is no right or wrong way, it's simply a case of working out what is the best fit for you.

Once you've done your honest audit, you will be left with a list of things that need to be removed and a list of things that need to be added. This will provide the foundation of your energy contract. Set yourself small, manageable targets. Be careful about how many things you try to address simultaneously. It's better when looking at the energy stealers to identify the key ones, because they are the ones that will feed the other stealers – as there is a relationship between all of them. When you dismantle those primary stealers, you'll find the fabric of the others begins to fray and disintegrate.

For example, if we take non-acceptance to illustrate this point, you will often find that when you can accept the things you cannot change, the negative commentary that relentlessly undermines your best efforts, begins to wane. It loses one of its primary lifelines and with that its power. This new-found acceptance makes it easier to embrace your mistakes in a positive way, extracting the lessons and the learning and using them as building blocks for positive change. As a result, your negative judgements and criticism of others become an unwanted habit, which is no longer palatable. Your respect for yourself and time changes. All of this achieved by dealing with one energy stealer.

When looking at the enablers, there will also be primary ones and if you choose them at the outset, you will find that you generate more traction and momentum, and positive change is more readily available to you. This is because they too have an intimate relationship with one another. Therefore, it makes sense to look at those energy enablers that may uplift three or four areas in addition to the one you're focusing on.

For example, when you identify what gives your life greater meaning and purpose you will find the courage that had eluded you, begins to emerge. This is because in finding meaning and purpose feelings of self-belief and confidence are generated. You may also find as a result of this pairing that you begin to listen differently, both to yourself and others. You now hear things you had previously missed. And with that comes a greater degree of empathy and kindness. Again, we see that by focusing on one enabler the power of the primary enabler brings the others to the fore. As a result, a better outcome is produced.

When you've written your energy contract, make numerous copies – have it as a screen saver on your phone or your computer, put it on a message board in the kitchen or your office. Have a copy inside your diary. The more you can keep bumping into the contract and remind yourself of what you've promised to do, the more likely you are to do it.

As well as having this in a written form, create a vision board, something that beautifully illustrates your hopes, dreams and intentions. Let your creative intelligence conjure up something that illuminates the life you wish for yourself. I have found that those who create vision boards that clearly itemise their ambitions and goals, the nature of their relationships with others, how they plan to manage their health, the kind of environment they need to flourish, are much more likely to succeed in achieving their objectives.

It's extremely important when seeking to fulfil your energy contract, to act 'as if'. Those who are familiar with energy medicine and positive psychology will not be surprised by this, as the idea 'fake it 'til you make it' has now become part of mainstream psychology. But what does this really mean? For many it is about doing the thing you most fear, finding the courage to act when everything else would have you run away. This is certainly one interpretation, but I feel that it doesn't go far enough. I have seen many who have not achieved their objectives by solely employing this approach.

What's required is that you become what I refer to as a metaphysical magician, one who consciously and positively manipulates energy. Metaphysics, as I stated earlier, describes the intangible forces, which we can neither see nor touch. Being a metaphysical magician is working with those invisible forces because s/he understands the subtle relationship between the visible and invisible. As a result, the magician becomes a divine intermediary in those transactions and special things begin to happen.

Once you've written your contract and your aims and objectives are clear, you now need to visualise what that contract would look like in practice. If you've described taking better care of your body and your health, you would need to see yourself drinking water, eating the rainbow diet, doing the stretching and exercise that that requires. If amongst your promises it's about having more fun and adventure, you'd be seeing yourself learning to dance, being amongst nature more often, spending more time with those who uplift your spirit.

But it's not enough to visualise. You need to visualise regularly and most importantly with sincerity of heart. It's sincerity that enables you to become the magician. It's sincerity that allows you to mould and manipulate the energy and exploit the energy fields in a positive way. To visualise is to imagine the possibilities, but sincerity calls those possibilities into being. It breathes life into them.

When you've made your vision board, if possible, include at least one image of yourself, looking happy and healthy. If you don't feel you have an appropriate image, then choose an image that reflects those qualities for you. When you spend time looking at the vision board, what you should see looking back at you are images that depict nourishing and wonderful relationships, pursuits that bring you peace, joy and contentment and images that promote feelings of hope and inspiration. It's important not only to see this in your mind's eye, but to feel it, touch it and taste it too. The more tangible you can make your experience, the more the energies conspire to create what you're seeing.

You need to climb inside your vision to such an extent that you're not watching the movie as a member of the audience, you're one of the leading characters in the film. But don't be content with just being a leading character, become the director of the film too. Decide exactly what part you're going to play and how all the elements are going to come together to make your dream a tangible reality.

Acting 'as if' is not merely putting yourself in the uncomfortable position of trying to do something you struggle with, because that is not enough and can lead to you falling flat on your face. Acting as if is also about seeing that scenario in your mind's eye again and again. It's only with this practice that the acting as if formula beds itself into your consciousness. These frequent mental rehearsals provide you with a better chance of success when you do put yourself in a position you find difficult. This is because every time the brain goes around a positive loop that you have created in your mind, the more it creates the neurochemicals that support your beliefs and mental health. You also create, by changing the neural pathways, better templates, which will influence how you will act and react in those scenarios you've imagined. In other words, the brain will have greater confidence that you can succeed, and the mind can take centre stage, less fearful of failure. This process has been described by neuroscientists as synaptogenesis, which has been summarised as 'neurons that fire together, wire together' and 'neurons not in sync do not link'.

Building an energy contract in this way means that you become a 'signatory of influence' in all the contracts you form. You become a real co-creator. Your life is not dictated to you by circumstances and chance because you have exercised positive choice and the fruits of that are immense. Please take this route and you'll be surprised at the outcomes.

Another very good option is to record your energy contract on your phone or other device and listen to it often. When you listen to your own voice recounting what it is you intend to do it has the incredible ability to influence you more than hearing the same message in any other voice. It should be said for balance that it's also where you may meet the greatest resistance as your unconscious mind will cross-reference what it's hearing against your experiences up to that point and if it cannot find sufficient evidence for your plan/intentions there is the possibility of it dismissing what it's hearing.

However, if you continue listening to your contract regularly, you'll find that that resistance will subside, and it will be replaced by the warm embrace of hope and that which seemed beyond you will come and greet you. This is a very powerful way to rewire the brain and refocus and channel the energies of the mind.

For the first three months it would help to read/listen to your contract every day or as often as you can, to help you remember and keep your promises to yourself. You need to hold yourself to account. You may find it helpful to do this with someone else as this often increases your commitment to yourself and the likelihood of success. However, this person needs to be one who has 'kind eyes'. This means that they are kind in their comments and judgements, which empowers you and enhances your vision. Criticism delivered with love and kindness is a gift that can liberate, so do not be afraid of it. Equally, criticism delivered with harshness and ill intent will rob you of your dreams.

Remember, an energy contract puts you on the positive side of negotiating with your life and reality. It enables you to tap into the electromagnetic fields and influence the perpetual conversations that we are all a part of.

Also remember, if your intention is not in the right place the outcomes that you seek will move further away from your grasp. Instead of becoming a magnet for what you need and want, you will in fact, unknowingly, repel the very things that would enrich your life.

Be sure to make your intentions as noble as they can be because the outward appearance of your action has little bearing on the metaphysical conversation that you are trying to influence. This is not something you can bluff your way through. It requires clarity, focus and sincerity. It's important to decide where you want to position your heart and then obsess your way to that place.

As you go further on this voyage, the all-pervading nature of energy signatures and their contracts will be seen everywhere. This I hope will positively influence the contracts you establish for yourself.

"When you show deep empathy towards others, their defensive energy goes down, and positive energy replaces it. That's when you can get more creative in solving problems".

Stephen Covey (1932 – 2012)

Points to remember

- Everything is energy of one form or another. Energy can be classified in many ways: kinetic, magnetic, nuclear, gravitational, solar, each name tag describing the multiple personalities and expressions of energy.

- There are so many definitions of energy, here's how I invite you to see it:

- It is the incredible fabric that binds all of life together. It is subtle and multi-dimensional. It is complex yet simple, infinitesimal yet vast and expansive. Energy is the very substance of the universe as well as the primary architect within the cosmos – organising the countless functions and activities at the microcosm and macrocosm. It can be defined both by its work and its many and varied manifestations. It is the narrative behind life's diversity and rich expression... and the keeper of the secrets yet to be told.

- Everything we give a name to has an energy signature, which is its own unique resonance. The energy signature describes the personality, characteristics and the potential of that thing or that force. We all have an energy signature of our own and we're all capable of feeling and detecting the infinite number of energy signatures around us.

- Energy signatures are the basis of all contracts. A contract is always made up of at least two energy signatures. Energy contracts underpin all activity in the universe at the micro and macro levels.

- Energy has a physical and a metaphysical dimension. The mind via the thoughts generated (which are metaphysical) orchestrates the countless activities taking place in the brain and body. This contract is arguably the most intimate in the universe, certainly as far as human life is concerned. Life is packed with many metaphysical and physical contracts. The relationship between food and mood is another powerful example of this. This is when biology interfaces with psychology. Look closely and you will see these contracts are everywhere.

- Energy contracts are not something we can opt out of. All energy is in some way connected. What we can do is choose what kind of contracts we bind ourselves to. By making a conscious choice we can ensure we are no longer victims to the 'randomness' of life. Choose to use your energy wisely and make agreements within your environment that are mutually uplifting. That which benefits others and/or the space that you are in automatically benefits you.

- Electromagnetic fields are the environmental context in which energy contracts take place. These fields provide a template for the countless transactions happening every minute of every day. Without them the mechanism to facilitate the innumerable energy contracts on which life depends, wouldn't exist. Remember that the electromagnetic fields provide a mould which allows energy to keep its shape, form, and regenerate, maintaining its identity and primary characteristics in the process.

- Energy stealers are those things which deny us access to our most virtuous selves. They include, impatience, making excuses, blaming others, being defensive, a lack of self-compassion, not facing one's own demons. Energy stealers should be avoided at all costs.

- Energy enablers are where we form healthy contracts, committing our intention, time and resources to the greater good. These include, kindness, altruism, active listening, gratitude, patience, humility, forgiveness of the self and others, creating and honouring a list of non-negotiables. These energy producers are lifesavers.

- Sit quietly and reflect on the contents of this chapter and see if you are using your energy signature to create the best contracts for yourself. Identify where you are losing or wasting energy and are therefore working against the very things that you ache for. Be clear about what you want, what is missing, and identify the antidotes required to address your deficiencies - and then obsess your way to positive change.

- Remember to act 'as if' your vision, hopes and dreams have already happened. When you stand in the certainty of their manifestation you increase your magnetism, your energetic ability to draw that thing towards you and make it part of your life. Energy is always waiting for your instructions. Remember, it doesn't respond well to mixed messages, so make your instructions clear.

Please note:

What follows is a meditation script that I invite you to read and where the dots appear in the script, please pause before reading on as it's not meant to be read as one continuous piece. The pauses allow for reflection on what you're saying.

You can simply read these meditations in the way I've suggested, or better still, you can record them and listen to them at regular intervals, to extract even greater benefit. When we hear something positive recorded in our own voice, it has the capacity to go even deeper into the unconscious mind, bringing about positive change.

There is a meditation that reflects the theme at the end of each chapter. I hope you find these useful.

A meditation to remind you of the primary themes of this chapter...

I live in a universe of energy... a universe of light... all the forces we are surrounded by and have classified are all manifestations of light... these forces underpin and make up this wonderful, choreographed performance called life... even that which has been described as random, and by chance is part of the sea of light... and has the principles of order flowing through its veins...

As I look around me, I can see there are countless actions, interactions and transactions taking place... each one striving to fulfil its reason for being.... its meaning and purpose... there is no luck or coincidence in a cause and effect universe... there is only the law of action and reaction... one energy pushing or pulling in order to fulfil its part of the contract... even though it isn't always immediately obvious, it's a system with justice beating at its heart...

There are countless energy contracts at play... and I can simply stand by and be mesmerised by the vastness of this web... or I can marvel in its wonder and find my place in the dance... I choose to find my place...

Having understood I have an energy signature of my own... and that I am unique in my ability to contribute to what is taking place in the world... I choose now to call on my divinity, my greatness... so that I can form positive energy contracts wherever I go...

I forge healthy connections with my family, friends and colleagues... I find positive ways to contribute to my community and the wider social context... I realise that my 'vote' matters and so I must use my energy wisely... I really do make a difference, but I need to find ways to positively engage my energy...

As I connect to the truth about myself... that I am a being of light, living in a sea of light... I realise that I can illuminate the path for myself... and can help to do that for others... to achieve this, I must regularly spend time in silence... silence is more than the absence of sound... in fact, silence has a sound of its own... and it invites me into its sanctuary in order that it can share its secrets with me... enabling me to find my true meaning and purpose... and gather the courage and tenacity that I need to be my very best me...

I can now see myself standing at the top of the mountain of life... a magnificent being of light, exuding light... and my light is rippling out into the world... touching the hearts and minds of those that I know... but also those that I don't know... my light lends its support to Mother Earth, as I can hear her cries... and I add my light and love, in order that I can be part of the solution...

I can now feel that I am making a positive contribution with every breath that I take...

CHAPTER 2

THE FOUR ENVIRONMENTS

"We begin to see the importance of selecting our environment with the greatest of care because environment is the mental feeding ground out of which the food that goes into our minds is extracted".

Napoleon Hill (1883 – 1970)

In order for us to better understand and meet the needs of the environment we need to appreciate its four distinct aspects – the environment of the self, the environment of the body, the external environment (social and community) and the wider environment of the planet.

Once we understand these different environments, we can begin to see that meeting the needs in each area requires different things. It's important to say that although these four environments do require different focus and resources, there is an intimate relationship between them as each one underpins and supports the others. The overlap and connections between these four environments are countless, and in this chapter, I aim to give you some sense of their relationships - and what it is that we can do to enhance our relationship with them.

The environment of the self

What do I mean by the environment of the self? This is your inner landscape. It includes your thoughts, emotions, feelings, all your experiences and their impact on your identity and how you feel about yourself.

This is a very delicate ecosystem. If left unattended it can be like the most barren sun- drenched desert, or the coldest, harshest Siberian blizzard. It can feel like such a dark and inhospitable place, an environment we perpetually seek to escape. Many of you will have had moments where your inner world has felt like this. Some will have experienced days, weeks, months even years in this inauspicious place.

Don't be fooled into thinking that this environment runs itself. It is an environment that is run on the beliefs you have about yourself... and those beliefs are constructed out of your thoughts, feelings, experiences and relationships. If you want to change those beliefs and alter the terrain then you need to change the thoughts that you have about yourself, which in turn will change the feelings, which will shape your experiences and the nature of your relationships.

Then the inhospitable will become a warm, welcoming space; a sun-drenched beach, a welcoming sea with kind, gentle winds, inviting you to drink from nature's nectar.

Once you understand you can make your inner world hell or heaven and that your reality is not something that is 'happening to you', then rather than being driven by circumstances and events, you can drive your reality through the power of choice, developing new experiences that will uplift your heart and mind.

Here are some examples of how this can be done:

Creating a habit of introspection is crucial to our internal mindscape

Positive silence alters the way the brain communicates with itself. With the advances in technology this communication can be interpreted and understood through our brain waves and other biological measurements – so we now know that positive silence brings harmony to mind and body.

The excellent work of Dr. Shanida Nataraja illustrates how meditation, prayer and other reflective practices change the conversation that the brain is having with itself and in that process replaces confusion with clarity. For those of you who are interested, see her work, The Blissful Brain.

The introspective habit covers thoughts, feelings and beliefs and how they shape our biochemistry. Dr. Nataraja's work is a helpful introduction into neuroplasticity (our ability to change the architecture of the brain). The brain is malleable and its ability to adapt itself to its environment is arguably its greatest asset.

The environment that most influences the brain's structure is the internal one (beliefs, thoughts and feelings). If we do nothing to change these where they are causing harm, then the amazing opportunities for positive change remain beyond our reach.

Neuroplasticity has indisputably shown that what we think and feel but most of all what we believe, shapes our perspective. The placebo and nocebo effect are wonderful illustrations of this. I gave an overview of this topic in Synergy: A Cure for All Ills, outlining John Haygarth's valuable contribution to this subject in the eighteenth century, followed by the important work of Émile Coué.

The neuroplastic revolution is building on the work of Haygarth and Coué offering up a plethora of research with valuable illustrations of how belief creates biochemical reactions which have far-reaching effects, not simply on the mind but also the body. For those of you interested in finding out more about neuroplasticity, a good place to start is with the work of Dr. Andrew Newberg (neuroscientist) and Dr. Norman Doidge (psychiatrist) – both are playing key roles in asking and answering the difficult questions about the brain's capabilities and how we might make best use of its resources.

An example of neuroplasticity in action found that some breast cancer survivors who regularly practised stress reduction techniques, including mindful meditation and yoga, physically changed their cells, despite no longer receiving treatment. This is one of many studies illustrating that what we do with our minds really matters.

Dr. Linda Carlson of the Tom Baker Cancer Centre in Alberta, Canada was the lead researcher and author of that study, which was published in the journal, Cancer (2014) where she stated: "We already know that psychosocial interventions like mindfulness meditation will help you feel better mentally, but now for the first time, we have evidence that they can also influence key aspects of your biology".

In summary, the research found that positive activities protected our telomeres.

Telomeres are protective lengths of protein that exist at the ends of chromosomes. These get shorter after replication and determine how quickly the cell ages. When the telomeres are gone, the chromosome begins to degrade, which is bad for the health of the cell. After the study period had ended, the two groups that had practised mindfulness and went to weekly meetings had preserved their telomere length, while the control group that did not learn mindfulness had shorter telomeres. From the current scientific data, we can conclude that telomere longevity and length have a bearing on our chromosomes and therefore on our health and well-being.

Fabrizio Benedetti, a neuroscience professor at the University of Turin's School of Medicine, is considered to be one of the world's authorities on the placebo effect. He's also a member of the Placebo Study Group of the mind/brain/behaviour initiative at Harvard University. He said: "The placebo effect has evolved from being thought of as a nuisance in clinical pharmacological research to a biological phenomenon worthy of scientific investigation in its own right".

The part that belief plays in both the healing and disease process is generating a lot of exciting research. Let's take a look at a few more examples. Symptoms of Parkinson's disease arise from impaired production of a neurotransmitter called dopamine, which affects movement. Canadian researchers (2010) have clearly shown that Parkinson's patients who were given a placebo but were told it was an anti-Parkinson's drug, found that their movement improved to varying degrees. This research went further - brain scans of the patients showed that the brain was activated in the area that controls movement and that dopamine was actually being produced! So, the improvement was not just psychological, it was accompanied by an actual physical release of dopamine and yet an anti-Parkinson's drug was not being taken. The patients simply 'believed' they were taking one. This has led to an interesting discussion as to whether placebos should be an integral part of treating Parkinson's.

This production of chemicals generated by belief was first proven in 1978 when scientists at the University of California showed that placebo analgesia (when a person gets pain relief from a placebo) actually occurs because the brain produces its own natural analgesics (painkillers). What was discovered then is that the body produces its own opiates like morphine, but these are the body's own natural versions and therefore not synthetically constructed. However, these endogenous opiates, as they came to be known, did the job certainly as well and arguably better than conventional medication. So, the brain produces its own natural painkillers.

Similar studies that have looked at depression illustrate that the brain produces its own natural antidepressants, such is the power of belief, the power of the mind. When the individual believes that something can and will make a difference, they kick start their own unlimited pharmaceutical factory that produces the necessary compounds to address the presenting problem. This is mind over matter at the molecular level. Science is just beginning to understand a subject that the spiritual masters have been explaining through the vehicle of their experience and philosophies over the last two and a half thousand years. You can find wonderful examples of transcending pain in the yogic philosophies and also the Taoist tradition. In both instances there is the recognition that the mind has the ability to produce the antidote for the challenge or trauma that one is beset by.

Laughter is a wonderful tonic

There is now a mountain of research highlighting all the wonderfully protective and healing neurochemicals that are produced as a result of laughter, well-being and happiness. Amongst those that have been studied and found to be life-enhancing are endorphins, oxytocin, prolactin, BDNF (Brain-Derived Neurotrophic Factor) and dopamine. In fact, there is a plethora of substances that are produced in the brain and then flood our bodies with their magic.

Prolactin is a hormone, which enables women to produce milk and therefore is normally associated with this function. However, prolactin has a far wider range of influence, as it is essential in the function and regulation of the immune system and it also plays a critical role in metabolism and in the development of the pancreas.

Research has shown that those with lower levels of prolactin are more likely to be depressed. As prolactin increases there is greater neural connectivity, which enhances cognition and influences how we perceive reality. In other words, even though circumstances may not have changed in a way that is favourable to us, our perception gives us another pair of spectacles through which we can see other permutations and possibilities - therefore, finding positivity at times when we're surrounded by challenge and threats to our well-being.

Whilst examining the role of prolactin, it is helpful to understand the impact of stress on this picture.

In Synergy I spoke at some length about the HPA axis (hypothalamus, pituitary, adrenal) and for those of you not familiar with this term it is worth taking a brief look at this subject because it is helpful to our understanding of the fight, flight and freeze responses, which we are subject to at times of trauma and fear. The HPA triangulation is at the heart of so much that is taking place between the limbic system (the emotional centre of the brain) and the neocortex (the higher executive function of the brain). Below is a brief summary of the transactions that take place between these three key agents.

The hypothalamic-pituitary-adrenal axis is our central stress response system. When a threat is perceived, the hypothalamus (the mood centre) releases corticotropin-releasing factor (CRF). When CRF binds to CRF receptors on the pituitary gland, adrenocorticotropic hormone (ACTH) is released. ACTH binds to receptors on the adrenal cortex and the release of cortisol results. In response to stress, cortisol will be released for several hours after encountering the stressor.

When a certain blood concentration of cortisol is reached, when the system is working efficiently, the process is reversed... which causes a decrease in the secretion of CRF from the hypothalamus, a decrease in the pituitary release of ACTH and subsequently decreased levels of cortisol released by the adrenals. At this point, systemic homeostasis returns, that is, a state of balance.

However, with on-going or repeated exposure to one or many stressors, (real or perceived) there follows repeated and sustained HPA axis activation. If this mechanism remains 'switched on' for too long, it sustains the uncomfortable and unhelpful symptoms of anxiety. The mechanism is now operating without an 'off switch' and the neurological, biochemical and psychological consequences cause untold damage to the human body.

The role of prolactin here is an interesting one as it is produced in numerous places within the body such as the prostate, uterus, breast, lymphocytes and it is also produced in the pituitary. The hypothalamus is like a conductor in this scenario, because subject to how the individual is feeling, we can see from the summary above that it instructs the pituitary to produce ACTH, but if the mood is one of joy and laughter then greater amounts of prolactin are produced, which is an excellent anti-depressant, due to its mood elevating properties.

This is a very good example of how we can change the biochemical conversation by virtue of how we are feeling, which of course is determined by our inner narrative.

BDNF is a protein released by the brain when it is under stress. It is therefore protective. Amongst its numerous functions is its ability to repair our memory neurons, which is of course valuable because stress has a way of 'stealing' our memory – more accurately disengaging us from our ability to access memory.

BDNF also has the ability to 'reset' our brains, so after a stressful episode we can find clarity and insight reinstated which can be very useful in making sense of our experiences.

A final example of the good guys – the happy hormones – is the endorphins. Endorphins are also neurotransmitters (including neuropeptides) which means they can pass their messages from one neuron to another. This is a very large family of neurochemicals and so at different times, different endorphins and neuropeptides are created and dispatched. In some quarters of the cognitive neuroscientific community, as well as the epigenetic fraternity endorphins have come to be known as molecules of emotion, a phrase coined by Candace Pert in the late1980s.

What we now know is these happy hormones are generated at times of relaxation, fun, exercise, positive social interactions and when we are pursuing those things that we're passionate about.

Therefore, it's important to consciously make time to listen to or watch things that are positively stimulating and/or make us laugh. It's also extremely valuable to spend time with those who enhance our moods and lighten our spirits, then both our physical and mental health will be enhanced.

Everybody wins in a charitable world

This is another Reachism which we seek to promote in all aspects of our work.

Kindness benefits everyone - the giver, the receiver and the observer are all elevated by acts of kindness, big and small.

- There is an extensive body of research that has developed around kindness and compassion and so for those who still need persuading of the merits of kindness and need a scientific basis to underpin their belief, then you'll have no problem finding many examples – see the work of Professor Paul Gilbert, Dr. David Hamilton, Dr. Robert Emmons, Professor Sonja Lyubomirsky and Matthieu Ricard to name a few. These are just some of the ambassadors promoting the health benefits of kindness, happiness and gratitude.

- The subject of altruism, which is the highest form of kindness, is fraught with debate and some disagreement. It seems that the majority of commentators do not believe that human beings are capable of altruism because in the final analysis, even if it's only biological benefits, there is some reward and true altruism is an act of kindness where no reward is attained by the giver.

- I believe this is a misunderstanding of altruism. Altruism, like kindness comes down to intention. We need to be aware that the outward appearance of an action does not tell us the full story. Something may appear kind but if carried out with an ulterior motive, then the action is tainted by that intention. Altruism is not about whether one is rewarded for one's actions. Altruism is about the true nature and intention of one's actions. Someone who genuinely gives without concern or need for acknowledgement, who really gives without counting, has performed an altruistic act.

- I'm not suggesting giving in this way is easy, although it can be with practice. What I am saying though is that we should not believe that we are not capable of the highest form of kindness because we are - and furthermore we should actively pursue it.

Psychologists have identified a euphoria related to charitable activity. This in some areas has come to be described as the 'helper's high'. James Baraz and Shoshana Alexander (2010) postulated that those who engage in charitable activities, responding to pain with compassion, care and generosity, experience a more joyful life as a result of the endorphins produced.

Research at the National Institute of Health and at Emory University demonstrated that kindness (giving to charity and more generally helping others) activates the same part of the brain that experiences pleasure.

Focused meditation has been found to have the same effect as illustrated by Richard Davidson (Wisconsin University) in his extensive research on the effects of loving-kindness and compassion meditation.

In his research (2008), two groups of subjects included inexperienced meditators (students) and very experienced meditators (Buddhist monks). He used MRI brain scans to monitor both groups. This research has been replicated numerous times in the last decade.

The results revealed that all the subjects, both competent meditators and novices, showed increased activity in the regions of the brain responsible for managing one's emotions, planning and positive emotions such as happiness.

Interestingly, regions that keep track of what is 'self 'and what is 'other' seem to morph into one another. In other words, a sense of our own identity fades and the distinction made between 'me' and 'you' evaporates and is replaced by a feeling of 'we'.

There's a powerful quote from Sharon Begley's book (Train Your Mind Change Your Brain) where she takes her students on the same journey as Davidson took his subjects in the research above.

One of her students, beautifully illustrates the benefits of loving kindness and compassion meditation at all levels to the self:

"When you tune in to another's suffering and send out compassionate thoughts to them, rather than draining you, it actually fills you up with more energy. You seem to clear out the confusion of your small mind and replace it with something much more vast and vibrant. Under all the chatter in your mind, there's a basic goodness you touch that's deeper and more profound. When you let down the fear, you get filled up with that basic goodness and sweetness of your caring heart".

In a cause-and-effect universe one cannot perform an action without some return but it's the desire or lack of desire for return that determines whether something is altruistic or not. Although the meditator is reaping the benefit of their kind action it's perfectly possible to be engaged in this kind of activity with the sole intention of giving without desire for reward. There are many who practise LKM quite simply because they want to give with no desire for return.

Remember it's the intention or motivation that dictates whether an action is negative, ordinary, good or exceptional. When thinking about this subject in relation to yourself check the compass of your intentions – and be honest with yourself about its position.

Find ways to be altruistic and your spirit will soar.

Let us now explore the second of the four environments...

The environment of the body

The body has often been described as our temple and I believe that it is worthy of our reverence and respect. One of the seminal pillars in The Reach Approach is entitled Persuading the Body. It's how we at Reach strive to help those we work with to set up a loving contract with their bodies - one in which they meet the body's needs and in doing so the body in turn supports them in all their endeavours.

I have written at some length, in Synergy, about forging a contract of love with our bodies, so I'm not going to explore it at the same depth here, but what I do want to underline is that the body never knowingly works against itself. It is always trying to make the best of the situation it finds itself in.

In the next chapter Protection and Growth, I will say much more about the survival instinct and its role in every arena of human life. I believe this instinct is so pivotal that until we work with it, it can appear to be working against us, when in reality nothing could be further from the truth. The body is a wonderful example of this. There are approximately sixty trillion cells that are conspiring to keep us alive, even in the face of our neglect, abuse and disrespect.

If we are to take this crucial aspect of The Story of Health (the environment) seriously, then, in addition to improving the conditions of our inner world, (the psychological, emotional and spiritual) we also need to extend the attitude of self-care to the physical one too. Only then can we realise our potential.

Here are some examples of what is required to achieve this:

Nutrition is the lifeblood of the body

If we are not meeting the nutritional needs of the body then we actually alter our brain chemistry, which in turn impacts on our perception and how we feel about ourselves.

Did you know that the human gut holds over a hundred trillion bacteria? There are in fact more bacteria in the human body than there are human cells. These hundred trillion bacteria are responsible for 70% of the body's immune system, so any imbalance or deficiencies here are bound to have some impact on one's overall health.

Bacteria are typically made up of just a single cell. Unlike the cells that make up the human body they do not have a membrane-bound nucleus. Neither do they have membrane-bound organelles, such as the mitochondria, which are effectively the batteries found in all cells.

Although bacteria are often perceived as the enemy, the fact is that the vast majority of the bacteria found in the gut are critical to human health. Gut microorganisms benefit the host by collecting the energy from the fermentation of undigested carbohydrates and the subsequent absorption of short-chain fatty acids. This incredible relationship begins from the moment we are born, because most of the microflora found in the gut, which includes bacteria, comes from the mother's birth canal and is transferred to the child during the birth process.

By the time we are fully developed as adults the bacteria that live in the gut weighs about the same as the human brain. There's an interesting parallel here because the latest research looking at the connection between the gut and the brain, is helping us to understand that there is a busy dual carriageway between the two. This is why in some quarters the gut has come to be known as the 'second brain' – whatever is happening in one organ is pretty accurately mirrored in the other, such is the strength of connection between the two.

It is now being suggested that the microbiota found in the gut almost certainly is involved in a host of conditions such as: anxiety, obesity, Parkinson's disease and a range of mood-related conditions.

What does the research indicate?

This relationship between gut flora and various physiological conditions is a complex one and the research continues to mount. Dr. Jane Foster (McMaster University in Canada) has done a lot of ground-breaking work, which highlights that there is a relationship between the microbiota and behaviour. However, the results are not yet conclusive – what is clear, is that the flora in the gut does influence mood and anxiety and this is particularly noticeable when the levels of good bacteria are insufficient.

The growing evidence that bacteria in our guts influences our mood and with that our behaviour, is something that we now need to take very seriously indeed. Our obsession with and overuse of antibiotics, to rid the gut and the body of bad bacteria, has led to a situation where healthy bacteria is eliminated in the process. What we are discovering now is that this doesn't simply lay us open to re-infection from a variety of pathogens it also leads to dysfunction in the brain and the mind.

The work of Professor Emeran Mayer (a gastroenterologist at the University of California, Los Angeles) has exposed the connection between the age of our bodies and the activity, or reduced activity, of the microbiota. His work has exposed that the lack of maturation in children of the healthy flora in the gut is one of the reasons they remain vulnerable to their environments, especially in their first three years – interestingly the picture is similar as we get older.

As we get older, the bacterial quota in the gut starts to decline both in terms of diversity and abundance, and what is then observed could be described as a reverting back to a childhood state of immunity and vulnerability. Professor Mayer has concluded that it is very likely that the deterioration of brain functions we see in the elderly is strongly connected to the reduction of healthy bacteria in the gut, which could at least in part explain the rise in the incidence of dementia and Alzheimer's.

The mechanisms and processes at work here have not yet been fully understood but what we know is that the gut bacteria and the molecules they produce, interact with the vagus nerve in the gut (the vagus nerve is the primary dual carriageway carrying vital data between the brain and the gut). This interaction in turn affects hormonal signalling and the immune system via the neurons within the gut lining and the vagus nerve. This sophisticated communication between the gut and the brain is influenced moment by moment by what is happening in terms of the good and bad bacteria – subject to their respective levels our physical and mental health is either reduced or enhanced.

Professor John Cryan (from the University of Cork) found that the impact of the probiotic Lactobacillus rhamnosus on mice, dampened down their anxiety - they actually 'chilled out', and their brain chemistry was altered, further indicating the relationship between good bacteria and mental health.

Psychobiotics and mental health

In one trial (2015) healthy people given a blend of the probiotics, bifidobacteria and lactobacillus for thirty days were found to fare better according to their answers in questionnaires, which sought to assess anxiety, depression and stress levels. This was better than those who were given a placebo. This and other similar research have led to the development of what is being described as 'psychobiotics' – which is the system where probiotics and prebiotics are prescribed to help treat people who are suffering with various mental health conditions.

The medicine of tomorrow almost certainly will include taking the microflora of the gut more seriously and prescribing probiotics and prebiotics alongside other treatment regimes. There is, however, a word of caution coming out of this research, which is that given the huge numbers and types of bacteria it is difficult to know exactly which particular strains are impacting on our mental health in a detrimental way.

Prebiotics are fibrous substances we cannot digest that promote the growth of beneficial bacteria in the colon. They occur naturally in some foods and include carbohydrates such as inulin, galacto-oligosaccharides and FOS. Probiotics on the other hand are live microbes. They are often administered in liquid drinks, supplements and yoghurt. The health benefits of probiotics are quite wide and varied, as each strain has different capabilities and potential.

In my practice I have seen the enormous benefits of prebiotics and probiotics being used for both issues of the gut and more widely for mental health issues such as anxiety, panic attacks and depression. They are not a panacea but should be considered when evaluating a treatment plan, as they are so easily overlooked.

Research involving Dr. Kirsten Tillisch and Professor Emeran Mayer (2015) found that probiotics within as short a period as four weeks actually influenced the connectivity between various brain regions.

In this research, a group of women split into three categories, those having a probiotic yoghurt, those having a probiotic-free dairy product and the third group having nothing at all, were compared over this four-week period.

Their brains were scanned at the beginning using functional magnetic resonance imaging (fMRI) and after four weeks the brains were scanned again. There was a clear difference between the way their brains connected in the resting state. What was of particular note is when the women were shown images of angry or frightened faces the probiotic group showed a marked decrease in the activity of the brain regions involved with emotion and sensation. Dr. Tillisch and Professor Mayer concluded that the gut-brain relationship is clearly an intimate one, where the bacterial ecosystem has a bearing on the brain and human emotions.

I believe, given the mounting evidence across numerous disciplines, that a new paradigm is needed, one where we appreciate that physical and mental health are intimately entwined, and our health strategies increasingly need to bear this in mind.

I would not recommend on the basis of the ever-growing research that an individual mindlessly takes pre or probiotics, without looking at their health in a holistic way.

What I would recommend is examining diet, hydration, sleep, exercise and nutrition in the widest sense. We also need to factor our thoughts (self-talk) into this equation. Without proper attention to all these areas, looking exclusively at the connection between the gut and the brain is likely to be insufficient when dealing with the complexities of mood, personality and behaviour.

Assuming that you are addressing all the other relevant aspects of health, choosing a probiotic to supplement your diet is generally a very good option. When doing so it is much better to choose a probiotic which has in excess of twenty billion viable organisms and also has a multi-strain profile. This ensures much better protection and is more likely to help you achieve the results you're looking for, for both brains. That said, always consult a qualified practitioner who can best advise you on your personal needs.

Avoid dehydration alert

Water is essential for human life. It accounts for 50% - 70% of our body weight and is crucial for most bodily functions. Any deficit in normal body water – through dehydration, sickness, exercise or heat stress – can cause a medley of symptoms.

Amongst the symptoms we are likely to feel is a change in mood/temperament as our brains are unable to work optimally. We can feel fatigued, suffer headaches, experience constipation and become part of the 'sickly well' – which means we function relatively normally, but there's always some niggly complaint not very far away.

This is because insufficient water in the body creates panic within the cells. This has been described as dehydration alert. The body is unsure whether there'll be adequate water to carry out all its tasks and under these conditions it moves into a protective mode. This means that whatever water is contained within the system, is held onto by the body for fear that it will not have a sufficient supply to carry out the necessary functions. The intracellular fluid (found within the cells) containing waste products is not being sufficiently released and the extracellular fluid, trying to find its way into the cell with vital nutrients for health and healing is unable to gain full access.

Movement is essential for health whereas stagnation provides the environment for disease. This stagnation is the foundation for all ill health because we need to release the waste products that have accrued – and without absorbing the necessary nutrients, how can we possibly be the best versions of ourselves?

Therefore, to address this position, we have to provide the body with more water to create the necessary movement. We have to persuade the body to open up the cell membrane, thus allowing waste products to leave the cell, and provide the necessary environment and safe passage for the nutrients to enter the cell - leading to well-being.

Dehydration causes stress throughout the whole body, taxing every organ and system. The more you examine dehydration, the more you can see it's at the root of so many diseases, mental and physical.

We need to understand that stress is not purely a mental phenomenon, brought on by external events such as: relationships, work issues and other emotional and psychological challenges. Hunger, poor nutrition, a lack of sleep and dehydration are all stressful events and have the same impact on the body – in some cases it is worse.

Some examples of dehydration

We continually lose water (on average two and a half litres per day) as we breathe, sweat, pass urine and excrete faeces. By the time you feel thirsty your body is already dehydrated; our thirst mechanism lags behind our actual level of hydration. There are other signs that come before that point. These will vary from person to person but can include feeling foggy, unable to concentrate, headaches, constipation and moodiness.

Research shows that as little as 2% dehydration negatively affects your mood, attention, memory and motor coordination. Although some of the data is contradictory, it nonetheless appears that brain tissue fluid decreases with dehydration, thus reducing brain volume and temporarily affecting cell function.

As we 'lose' body water without replacing it, our blood becomes more concentrated. This triggers our kidneys to retain water. The result: we urinate less.

The thicker and more concentrated our blood becomes, the harder it is for our cardiovascular system to work optimally. It increases heart rate in an attempt to maintain blood pressure. This can cause us to faint, for instance, when we stand up too quickly.

Less water also hampers the body's attempts at regulating temperature, which can cause hyperthermia (a body temperature greatly above normal). At a cellular level, 'shrinkage' occurs as water is effectively borrowed to maintain other stores, such as the blood. The brain senses this and triggers an increased sensation of thirst.

Research has shown that dehydration has a number of negative neurological and psychological effects.

Dehydration affects your mood: a number of studies have identified a link between dehydration and mood disturbances. Most notably, in a 2012 study, Armstrong et al, at the University of Connecticut, induced dehydration in healthy young women, through exercise and through exercise plus the use of a diuretic, and assessed the effects on their mood. The dehydration that was brought on, resulted in a measurable increase in 'total mood disturbance'. Other cognitive deficiencies were also noted.

Dehydration reduces your cognitive and motor skills: according to the findings of a 2015 study conducted at Loughborough University, we should avoid driving whilst dehydrated. Volunteers committed a significantly greater number of errors such as lane drifting and late braking in a two-hour driving simulation when they were dehydrated. Drivers' performances were found to be similar to those who were driving under the influence of alcohol having reached the legal limit - and so it was concluded that dehydration reduces concentration and reaction times.

Dehydration makes you more sensitive to pain: in a 2014 study by Japanese researchers, dehydration was found to increase pain sensitivity. Volunteers were asked to immerse one arm in cold water to test their pain sensitivity while having their brains scanned. They reported a lower pain threshold, which was measured according to how quickly they felt pain, whilst dehydrated. These subjective reports were confirmed using brain scans, which highlighted increased activity in brain areas involved in the experience of pain.

Dehydration affects your memory: in 2010, researchers at Ohio University measured the hydration status in a group of twenty-one older women and also had them complete tests to measure declarative memory (also known as explicit memory) and working memory (short-term memory). A strong link between their hydration status and memory skills was found, with the most dehydrated subjects performing most poorly on the tests.

Over the last decade or so there have been numerous studies underlining the importance of water and the primary conclusions cannot be ignored. The examples above are just a snapshot of why we should be taking water much more seriously in relation to both physical and mental health.

Recent imaging data suggests that the brains of the elderly and children are more vulnerable to deficiencies in water. This is almost certainly because children's brains are not fully developed and so dehydration will impact on all aspects of brain health. Older adults are more likely to be affected by dehydration because their brains need greater care and nutritional support due to the ageing process.

This doesn't mean that the rest of the populace should underestimate the value of hydration because we are all vertical rivers and any deficiency in the volume of water in the body is impacting on one of three things: perception, personality and performance.

When there is insufficient water in our systems, perception is arguably the first thing to be distorted. We are unable to see things clearly because the way the brain communicates with itself is significantly altered. Under these conditions we no longer see the world as it is... we begin to see things as 'we are'.

Swift on the heels of perceptual changes come changes in our personality (temperament and mood). Deficiency in water can make us more irritable, impatient and reactive. We are not quite so 'cuddly' as our nature becomes more prickly - the change in perception means we're seeing things with a more negative slant, so how we feel about ourselves and others is impacted upon.

Last but not least in this trilogy is performance. Literally anything we do in a dehydrated state will be impaired. The concentration, memory and focus required to complete a task to our full potential simply isn't there. We might perform adequately, even very well, but it would not be optimal, because without water lining the hallways of consciousness, our creative intelligence runs dry.

How much should we drink?

Normal water needs range significantly due to a number of factors, such as: age, body composition, metabolism, diet, climate, other environmental factors and lifestyle.

According to the Institute of Medicine (2004), the adequate water intake for adult men and women is 3.7 and 2.7 litres per day, respectively. This figure is based on water losses throughout the day, which I gave an overview of earlier.

There is some contradictory data about where this water should come from. On one side of the divide there are those who would say that any fluid constitutes water – which includes tea, coffee, soft drinks etc. On the other side of the debate are those who state that water should come from the least contaminated sources possible and should not include diuretics, such as caffeine and alcohol (which also have a number of other biological disadvantages).

I believe that the more you understand the anatomy and physiology of the body the clearer it becomes that acquiring water from the least polluted sources is unquestionably the best route to take and here are some of the reasons why.

1. If you remember the primary premise of chapter 1, energy contracts, then it's easy to understand that every transaction taking place in the universe requires energy. When we eat and drink energy is expended in order to acquire the energy we need. So bottom line, we need to expend less energy in the consumption of food and drink to ensure the energy we acquire from it is beneficial to us.

   In other words, if we are spending more energy on something that we're imbibing than we're getting from it, we put ourselves in negative equity. Negative equity is a precursor to dysfunction and disease.

   When we take in water from other sources the body has to work hard to clean up that fluid in order to extract the water. This puts a demand on the kidneys and lymphatic system. Water that comes into the body filtered does not require the same clean-up operation and therefore can get on straight away with the tasks at hand.

   This does not put us into negative equity and in terms of health, we are benefiting from this contract.

2. When our fluid intake comes via diuretics water is actually being taken out of the system, which means the billions of activities that water is responsible for initiating and supporting are in some way undermined. What is then set up in our bodies is a competitive state where the body is having to make moment to moment calculations about the best distribution of the fluid. This is very well illustrated with the intracellular

and extracellular fluids (which I spoke about earlier) leading to waste products not leaving the body efficiently and nutrients not reaching the cells and therefore not generating sufficient energy for all other bodily functions.

3. The overall pH of the body is 7.4, so we are slightly alkaline. There are areas of the body where acidity needs to dominate in order for good health to prevail. The gut is the best example of this – the pH here needs to be between 1 and 2.5 in order to keep our bacterial balance in the right place.

   When we are not conscious about our fluid intake, we impact on the body's need to be alkaline. This is because juices, carbonated drinks, caffeine and alcohol all impact on the body's pH in a way that nudges us towards acidity - and so acidosis (an acidic state) should be avoided because it's a precursor for so many states of ill health. It should also be said for balance that alkalosis (being too alkaline) also carries with it a range of health problems.

This summary of dehydration alert I hope will inspire you to create a healthy relationship with water where you give it the respect it deserves - because I promise you if you do it will serve and respect you.

Consciously support your immune system

In a world that is increasingly polluted, the body is under perpetual challenge. Therefore, it's not always possible to avoid the environmental assaults but what is possible is boosting our primary line of defence against these pollutants and pathogens.

I believe that The Story of Health is the 'missing link' – the piece of the jigsaw puzzle we keep overlooking. Without it our best endeavours to achieve health are foiled. With it, the story of disease also becomes clear and so what's required to transform our fortunes becomes visible.

If we are to achieve the best immunity, we must meet the needs of the mind, body and spirit and make the adjustments to our environment that will support all three. That said beginning with your physical immune system is a good place to start.

Unfortunately, we're losing the battle because we give our power away, through poor food choices, insufficient sleep, continual exposure to stressful situations, inadequate hydration and overtrading – all of which make us vulnerable to our environments.

When it comes to maintaining good health, the immune system is absolutely critical in this regard. It offers us protection against both common infections and the deadliest diseases. Yet despite modern scientific advances in medical treatments infection is still the commonest cause of illness and death worldwide. Cancer in all its forms (breast, stomach, bowel, lung, prostate and cervix) is rapidly closing the gap, as the incidence of cancer continues to rise.

So, what is going wrong? We are now, despite all the research and colossal investment in cancer, repeatedly told that by the 2020s we can expect one in two of us to be suffering with cancer. Clearly the current strategy is not working.

In our attempts to destroy the many pathogens, toxins, microorganisms and cancer cells that exist in our bodies, we've lost sight of the need to strengthen our immune systems. It's clear that our attempts to annihilate those things that attack our bodies has proven to be an unsuccessful strategy, as we have created a generation of superbugs, which are a direct response to our attempts to deal with those pathogens. Health has to be about prevention as well as cure. Far too often we busy ourselves only responding once the problem has turned up. What about trying to do something before the problem actually emerges?

The evidence is clear that since the 1950s, despite our powerful technologies, vaccinations, antibiotic treatment programs, radiotherapy and chemotherapy, disease in all its forms continues to rise and despite our best efforts our immune systems are struggling to cope.

As human beings we have a tendency, when things are not working, to keep doing them, but only harder! We think if we push harder, we will get a different result, when in fact most of the time what we really need to do is to rethink our strategy.

It's time for us to work with nature and the natural healing powers of our own bodies. Our 'warlike' model and adversarial approach has failed us. Life is not a battle between us and the microorganisms or cancer cells – it is this approach that has left us reeling.

There are two immune systems – the acquired immune system and the innate immune system. The immune system as a whole is not well understood by the medical profession, most of whom are far more familiar with adaptive (or acquired) immunity. It is still not recognised, for example, that it is the innate rather than the acquired immune system that is more important in keeping us free from infection.

They may know that the innate immune system is damaged by excessive hygiene (the 'hygiene hypothesis'), which has removed important immune-priming compounds from the food chain. However, there is relatively little awareness that innate immune function can be enhanced by the use of immuno-primers; among which the lead candidate is undoubtedly yeast-derived 1-3 and 1-6 beta glucans. Thankfully awareness around this is developing.

These beta glucans are now the subject of intense research programmes; a simple search of the medical and scientific databases reveals a rapid proliferation of publications citing the 1-3 and 1-6 beta glucans in a wide variety of applications. They are being seen as valuable therapeutic tools of intervention. For those of you who want to explore the topic further, see the work of Dr. Paul Clayton.

The FDA is currently supporting their development as pharmaceutical agents in cancer therapy and as agents to reduce the incidence of post-surgical infection. The Technical University of Berlin is using them to replace antibiotics in animal feed, as has already occurred in aquafarming across the world. The University of Oslo is working on their ability to reduce the severity of allergic disease, in parallel with medical institutions in Brazil and Japan.

The American Armed Forces Radiobiology Research Institute has demonstrated the ability of beta glucans to protect against bone marrow suppression and the Canadian Department of Defence has also established that beta glucans offer comprehensive protection against even weaponised anthrax.

Any strategy for strengthening our immune system should be considering the potency of these superheroes as they can help provide a wonderful fortress of protection.

The pioneers of microbiology, Louis Pasteur, Antoine Béchamp and Claude Bernard encouraged us to think of the microorganisms and pathogens as 'agents' of disease and not the causes of disease. This is where we have lost our way because if we think of the diseases we are afflicted by as the problem then the causes of those diseases will continue to elude us.

This is where the founding fathers of medicine, those from the Ayurvedic tradition and Hippocrates and Plato laid a beautiful foundation, which we have continued to ignore. Their message was simple – we can't heal the mind without healing the body and we can't heal the body without addressing the needs of the mind.

Plato went even further in underlining this approach to health because he said that "where we ignore the relationship between mind and body, such an approach could not even be called medicine, as it was a crime against the obvious".

And here we are, over two thousand years later, with all our advances in medicine, still committing this crime against the self and common sense. How can we 'dismember' the body, brain and mind and believe we can get the best results when we treat them as separate 'bits' that do not relate to one another?

Prevention is better than cure

The sad truth is, although we are busy denying it, many of the diseases that we are afflicted by exist as a result of our toxic environments, poor diets (even where there is an abundance of food), poor hygiene and a lack of strategy and policy to address poverty and malnutrition.

Furthermore, we continue to rape our soils, not replenishing them with the essential minerals they need to maintain the vitality of our food. The list of crimes against our planet and ourselves is growing all the time and our responses to these crimes are simply inadequate. If we want better health, then we need to start thinking in terms of prevention rather than cure. We can't keep waiting until there is a problem before we act. We are rapidly running out of options. So, what can we do?

I started by looking at the immune system over thirty years ago because it has so much to teach us; but we need to put down our weapons and listen to its very simple message. Prevention is the answer.

As indicated earlier, some of the giants of microbiology, Pasteur, Béchamp, Lister, Ehrlich and Koch recognised that the microorganisms that they sought to find an antidote for were in fact the agents of disease and the impact they had on the body was determined by the biological terrain they encountered. In other words, subject to our immune health we would either be contaminated by the pathogen or it would be neutralised by our system. This means the pathogen alone is not the problem.

What does prevention look like? Well, we need to change our diets to ensure that they are diverse and colourful. What we eat must be as close to nature's original composition as possible. The more we interfere with the molecular structure of food, the more we interfere with the molecular structure of our bodies. This in turn undermines our natural defences – especially the immune system.

If we are to get the best from the foods that we eat we must chew thoroughly. Digestion begins in the mouth. There are so many health problems that begin with poor digestion, which leaves food rotting in the gut due to inadequate mastication. The digestive system then has to work far too hard to extract the necessary nutrients from the food and then dump the toxic compounds. This habit of poor chewing and inadequate digestion leads to the reabsorption of waste, turning our bodies into cesspits in the process.

This position is worsened by inadequate hydration. When we don't drink sufficient water, nutrients are not adequately distributed and waste products are not fully flushed out of the system and as you can imagine, that does not create an effective ecosystem able to meet the challenges of disease, in all its forms.

This is one of the ways that we have contributed to creating autoimmune diseases – where the immune system 'appears' to work against itself. When the immune system is weakened it cannot defend us and even worse than that, as a result of the chemical confusion that has been caused, it can seemingly work against itself. In truth it is trying to survive in the best way it knows how but the result is conditions such as: rheumatoid arthritis, lupus, AIDS, ME, type 1 diabetes and many more conditions caused by the immune system attacking its own body cells, as if they are foreign organisms.

In order to strengthen our immune systems, in many cases we need to detoxify the body first. This can include following specialist diets, lymphatic drainage, massage, acupuncture, intensive juicing and raw food regimes, colonic irrigation and enemas.

There is no one route to be championed above another – most people need to pursue more than one anyway, subject to their particular problem. You will almost always need some advice from a good, reputable health practitioner and consulting your general practitioner is also advisable.

In your endeavour to strengthen the immune systems (acquired and innate) the body will probably need the support of targeted supplementation, herbs, homoeopathic remedies and other natural potions to give it the best chance of recovery and maintaining good health.

Remember what the founding fathers of medicine said about the mind and the body – they are inextricably linked and so any strategy for recovery or prevention must include the mind, which means changing your thoughts. Until you change and improve the way that you think, the ability of negative thoughts and feelings to pollute the body must not be underestimated. In fact, the pollution of the body, as a consequence of our own thinking, ought to be as great a concern to us as external contaminants.

It's time we recognised that the mounting evidence, from cognitive neuroscience, epigenetics, psychoneuroimmunology and the noetic sciences is clearly showing us that consciousness is not only a significant player in the story of health and disease, but in fact it is the most critical of all the factors – and so we ignore its importance at our peril. Below are some more of the things you can do to improve your immunity:

Avoid stress: chronic stress causes the adrenal glands to secrete higher levels of corticosteroids, which depress the immune system. High adrenaline levels, also caused by an increase in stress lead to a decrease in T-helper-cell activity and an increase in T-suppressor-cell activity, which leads to a degeneration of lymphoid tissues, increasing the overall vulnerability of the body. Chronic stress is a major risk factor in the development of all illness but particularly cancer and heart disease. Try practices such as: deep breathing, positive affirmations, meditation, self-hypnosis, regular exercise and yoga as antidotes to stress.

Avoid pollution: this is increasingly difficult in a world that is becoming ever more polluted. However, where you can reduce your exposure to microwaves, computer screens, television, mobile phones, radio transmitters etc. it is important to do so, because they are all able to scramble the electrical signals in the body. Also avoid pesticides, herbicides and insecticides where possible. Endeavour to improve the hygiene in your home to reduce your exposure to house dust, dust mites and moulds. One way of doing this is to open all the windows in your home every day for at least 5 to 10 minutes. It may surprise you to know that there is more pollution inside our homes than outside.

Control your weight: obesity in the developed world has reached epidemic proportions and is clearly related to the high incidence of coronary heart disease, type II diabetes, the risk of cancer and premature death. Managing one's weight through diet and exercise is critical. Our sedentary lifestyles and our over consumption of processed foods and sugars have made this a much greater challenge. Make a plan to eat more sensibly and exercise more. If you can embark on this challenge with others, it's easier to maintain your motivation and the success rates tend to be higher.

Take regular exercise: the latest research has confirmed what common sense has long known, that regular exercise is not only good for you it actually prevents disease. In fact, it has been proven to enhance immune function, therefore protecting you against conditions such as: cancer, heart disease and osteoporosis. Evidence also shows that three or more thirty-minute exercise sessions a week, such as brisk walking, jogging, cycling or swimming, all enhance immunity. A word of caution though – over exertion suppresses the T-cell function and other immune responses and therefore that should be avoided. Also, excessive exercise produces too much lactic acid, which disturbs the body's pH, increasing acidity. So, the message is clear, we need balance here too.

Avoid/reduce alcohol, cigarettes and drugs: although in the developed world alcohol has become a cultural norm and some believe is essential to their lives, the truth remains that it depresses immune response and is clearly associated with heart disease, hypertension, pancreatitis, peptic ulcers, serious liver damage, strokes, gastritis and a deterioration in mental function (Wernicke-Korsakoff syndrome). Some of the other recreational drugs also add to this damaging list of health conditions as they undermine nutrients (many are anti-nutrients), which in turn compromise immune competence. Tobacco contains high concentrations of dangerous chemicals such as benzene, carbon monoxide and cadmium, which is a powerful immunosuppressant (also found in fungicides, fertilisers and rubber tyres).

Work with nature: it is infinitely better to use nature's pharmacy wherever you can, rather than suppressing the symptoms with drugs. With many minor illnesses, it is far better where possible to let the immune system do what it is designed to do. Our job should be to support it with the right nutrients. It is our interference that often causes the most problems. According to the WHO, Iatrogenesis is the fifth leading cause of death in the world. Iatrogenesis is composed of two Greek words, iatros, which means physicians and genesis, which means origin. Therefore, iatrogenic illness is where the physician, (which includes diagnosis, prescribed drugs and the medical institution) is seen as the agent responsible for the illness. In other words, there are millions of deaths a year actually caused by medical intervention. This doesn't mean we should not be seeking medical care when needed, because that would be folly. What it means is that we should also consider what naturopathic remedies may also assist us with our ailments.

In my work, I use the term 'persuading' a lot. This is because I believe in cooperation, rather than competition. Conflict is far too common in our world and keeps us in the fight, flight or freeze mode, where nothing works optimally.

'Persuading the Body' as I said earlier is one of the central tenets of The Reach Approach, which explores the relationship between mind and matter. This is where mind does not seek to impose its will on matter but rather it enters into a loving and mutual arrangement, an energy contract. It is my experience and belief that this is the best way to achieve sustainable health and so the things I've listed above are starting points for this journey. I hope you will consider them seriously.

The external environment

We would probably largely agree on what is meant by the term external environment, but to avoid any confusion, let me tell you what I mean. The external environment includes: our physical space, our families, relationships, communities and society.

Our physical space is primarily the place we inhabit. This needs to feel like a sanctuary, a sacred space that embraces us, leaving us feeling rejuvenated and refreshed. Our physical space also includes where we work. We may not be able to entirely control every aspect of this but bringing some order to your personal and working environments will bring peace and clarity to your mind.

When it comes to families, they can either be the best of institutions or the worst. We may not always be able to control the dynamics within our families but what we can do is manage our temperaments and responses and move towards that which is good and healthy and move away from that which is not. This can be said about all of our relationships. It's important that we are not bound to things or people that are not good for our souls.

To address this will take great courage for many, because our need to fit in and belong often leads to self-betrayal. Hopefully, as you take this journey you will find the courage to do what's right for you in each aspect of your life.

The individual who has addressed his or her physical space and relationships makes the best contributions to his or her community and becomes a valuable member of society. It's not the role or the position from which that contribution is made that is important, it's the nature of the contribution that matters. Authenticity and sincerity are the primary currencies required for the best outcomes.

Here are some examples of how you might cultivate this third environment:

Where possible, create a physical sanctuary

This should be a special space for reflection and self-nurture. Having a space that's dedicated to positive mental activity helps in developing the discipline of self-care. This is because routine is good for establishing new patterns and habits.

The impact of the environment on our mental health cannot be overstated. For those who want to change outdated and unwanted patterns, attending to your environment must become a priority. There are many things that need to be taken seriously with regards to this subject; first and foremost is decluttering.

In chapter one I provided an overview of energy signatures and the contracts formed around them. There are very few places where energy signatures and contracts matter more than in our homes.

Holding onto those things we no longer need keeps us trapped in the past, tied to old ideas, unhelpful memories and stale, stagnant experiences, which in turn pollute our minds and deceive our hearts. That which is no longer useful and is surplus to requirements, vibrationally adds nothing to the space it occupies. At best it will be neutral in its impact but in most cases it will in fact diminish and subtract energy from the space.

When we sit in a space that is saturated by the past and by things and objects that now carry little energetic value, our minds can become cluttered and confused - then doubt and fear easily emerge out of those unhelpful vibrations. A space can either be inspirational, neutral or negative subject to the value of the objects in that space and the way things are ordered and arranged.

Chaos creates an uneasiness and uncertainty. It keeps us locked into self-limiting habits and tendencies. This is why it is vital that you look around and ask the question, what in my immediate environment is adding value and what is not? Then make the time to do something about it. Don't continue to live in a cluttered space, as it's a form of self-harm.

I spoke earlier on about quantum coherence (a state of bodily harmony and health) and quantum dissonance (a state of bodily dysfunction and disease). When quantum coherence is present, there is a beautiful conversation taking place between food, water, air and light - our bodies, brains, minds and souls. The better aspects of our nature become visible and are sustained by our positive choices.

Quantum dissonance on the other hand is where the conversation has broken down, usually because of our poor decision-making and choices vis-a-vis our health. At this point our system is working to survive rather than thrive. The cooperation of the coherent state has been replaced by the disorder of dissonance.

This dynamic is relevant to our relationship with physical spaces. One of the ways that quantum dissonance is perpetuated and sustained is by sitting in spaces where the energy is negative and does not lend itself to the upliftment of the spirit. Decluttering is one of those activities, which impacts equally on mind, body and spirit.

Marie Kondo is a professional consultant in the joy of attaining minimalism. Her first book, The Life-Changing Magic of Tidying Up: The Japanese Art of Decluttering and Organising, is an international bestseller.

Kondo's simple and interesting approach is one where she sees tidying as a 'cheerful conversation' in which anything that doesn't spark joy is to be thanked and ceremonially sent on its way towards a better life elsewhere, where it can discover a more appreciative owner. This wonderful approach to decluttering and recycling is definitely what the world needs right now.

Part of what makes her method effective is that instead of decluttering room by room, she tackles belongings by subject, starting with what is easiest to part with. So, for example, she may begin with all the clothes, then all the books, the difficult to classify, then documents and last and most difficult for many, photos and mementos.

Instead of deciding what to get rid of, she says the focus should be on what to keep: those things that uplift your heart and/or are truly necessary. This way one is left only with items that make the heart sing and which do not keep transporting the mind back to moments and things that are best left behind.

Once you have found a better home or use for the things you don't really need, Kondo suggests that the next step is to organise what is left. The key, she says, is storing things mostly in drawers, arranged so everything can be seen at a glance and nothing is stacked.

Her philosophy is simple, "The inside of a house or apartment after decluttering has much in common with a Shinto shrine... a place where there are no unnecessary things, and our thoughts become clear... it is the place where we appreciate all the things that support us. It is where we can review and rethink about ourselves."

Although many may not want to go as far as Kondo is suggesting, there is no doubt that there is a lot of merit in following these core principles.

I have had the great fortune of working with people from so many walks of life, suffering with every ailment imaginable and wrestling with demons that have seemed invincible to them. I've lost count of the number of times that I have seen changes in the environment bring about changes in one's hopes, perspective, motivation and energy and this has convinced me beyond doubt that a physical sanctuary, a space that is clean, ordered and free of clutter, can be a catalyst for unimaginable change.

Here are some other facts and figures worth bearing in mind.

Researchers at the Princeton University Neuroscience Institute published the results of a study they conducted in *The Journal of Neuroscience* (January 2011) that relates directly to uncluttered and organised living. The report was entitled Interactions of Top-Down and Bottom-Up Mechanisms in Human Visual Cortex. Below is the primary conclusion of their research.

"Multiple stimuli present in the visual field at the same time compete for neural representation by mutually suppressing their evoked activity throughout visual cortex, providing a neural correlate for the limited processing capacity of the visual system".

To paraphrase, when your environment is cluttered, the chaos reduces your ability to focus. The brain's ability to process information is also diminished. This is because clutter distracts the brain and leads to 'data overload' - so we are unable to process information as effectively as we would in an ordered and uncluttered environment.

The researchers gathered the data by using functional magnetic resonance imaging (fMRI) and other physiological measurement tools to map the brain's responses to organised and disorganised stimuli. They then monitored the subjects' performance within those different contexts.

The conclusions were indisputable - if you want to focus to the best of your ability and process information as effectively as possible, you need to clear the clutter from your home and work environment.

This research clearly shows that we would all be distracted less often, able to process information more efficiently and be more productive and less irritable with an uncluttered and organised home and office.

Dr. Christine Carter, a sociologist with a particular interest in health, goes on to support the findings that came out of Princeton University. Her research indicates that an environment that is cluttered reduces our ability to manage other things in our lives well. As a result, emotional challenges and issues may be avoided because we don't feel we have the energy to meet them head on. Those unresolved issues can then create a mental backlog, further denying us inner peace, which feeds into other aspects of our lives, affecting our moods, quality of sleep and our relationships.

Here we see a pattern emerging which common sense confirms, that is, if we have energy dispersing in many directions at the same time, we undermine our ability to be truly focused. It's difficult to formulate priorities when we're distracted, we may even feel disheartened because of the number of tasks in front of us - and so avoidance may feel like an attractive option when in fact we're simply stockpiling those things that need our attention. This disempowers us, compounding our feelings of inadequacy, and unhappiness. This left unchecked can become a mental health issue.

Professor Sharon Macdonald and Dr. Jennie Morgan are anthropologists from York University who were engaged in a four-year study (2015-2019) looking at all aspects of decluttering. In their study they examined both the domestic context as well as a variety of organisations and institutions to assess what the impact is of the mass production, consumption and explosion of consumer goods on our mental health.

During a series of workshops conducted under their 'Profusion' study, they particularly focused on household and domestic excesses. The purpose of these workshops was to get the participants to look at their attachments to the various items and objects they were reluctant or struggled to let go of.

Predictably most candidates had not looked at their relationships to the things they held onto - and the habit of not letting go featured quite prominently. In other words, we often make decisions based on our attachment to things rather than on their usefulness, illustrating that many of our choices are unconscious ones.

At the end of the workshops Professor Macdonald and Dr. Morgan invited attendees to treat decluttering as if they were going on holiday - only taking that which was really essential and necessary and getting rid of everything else -

something that many taking part in the study understood intellectually but emotionally found challenging.

In summary, moving in this direction may at first be difficult but taking baby steps to change your physical space will prove really good for the soul. The goal is minimalism. The definition that most resonates with me is 'minimalism is a tool to rid oneself of life's excess, in favour of focusing on what's important'. This is a growing movement and is essentially a response to the extremes of the world. Some parts of the world have too much whilst other parts have too little.

The minimalism movement is not against the acquisition of things, especially where those things add value, it's a response to greed, the acquisition of things for their own sake and a selfishness that doesn't see the needs of others as vital to a world that works for us all.

Those of you who would like to find out more about this topic may be interested in the work of Joshua Fields Millburn and Ryan Nicodemus who have compiled via a number of media, some persuasive arguments for us living more mindfully and relating to our environments in less harmful ways.

Developing a social conscience is vital

As part of your manifesto for positive change it's important to develop a social conscience. What this means in practice is to remember that 'everybody wins in a charitable world'.

It's important to take a good look at your contribution (what you energetically and practically put into your relationships), to assess what your net contribution is. Look at your relationships with your family, friends, colleagues and wider community; this is where a social conscience begins.

You will remember, earlier in this chapter I spoke about the 'helpers high' which explains not only the nature of the virtues inherent in helping others but the incredible advantages that one gets from giving without desire for reward.

Imagine a world where instead of waiting to see what we will receive for our efforts and contribution, we're so focused on giving, that we simply enjoy the enrichment provided by kindness. Now that would be heaven.

There are numerous initiatives, projects and activities that are encouraging a greater social conscience in a variety of forms. A good example of this is what is being described as the 'gift economy'. Nipun Mehta, the founder of Service Space has been promoting the concept of 'giftivism' since 2001.

His primary message is summarised in this mission statement – "moving from consumption to contribution, from transaction to trust, from isolation to community and from scarcity to abundance".

The Service Space movement is now said to have over half a million followers. These are volunteers using their talents and technology to create greater participation in the name of benevolence - encouraging each person to find a way that they can contribute by using their skills, time and energy to help others.

The organisation has developed many projects and resources since its inception to encourage philanthropy, altruism and kindness. Amongst its offerings is: Karma Kitchen, which is a volunteer run restaurant with branches in California, Chicago, London, Washington DC... and there are others joining this wonderful experiment around the globe.

All the food is cooked by volunteers, served with love and described as a gift given to those who come to the restaurant. Guests make a contribution in the spirit of 'pay it forward'. Those who dine out there do not have to pay for their meals, the bill is always zero. Those guests who have benefited from the gift are then invited, should they wish, to pay it forward with their contribution. This approach encourages an attitude of selflessness and generosity.

The whole point of Karma Kitchen is to demonstrate that we can design a world with kindness at its heart. However, in order to do that, we must move away from the 'I' consciousness that is currently dominating our world, to a 'we' consciousness.

Another valuable project offered by Service Space and funded by the volunteers' acts of kindness and generosity, is Daily Good, a website that focuses exclusively on positive news around the world.

What's so wonderful about the Daily Good website, is that it recognises our obsession with negative news, which is piped into our homes and brains 24 hours a day, is not good for our souls. This diet of negativity is rewiring our brains, encouraging us to focus on what is bad rather than what is good.

If you're interested in becoming part of the gift economy, you could become part of something that's already organised and well established or alternatively seek to do things in your immediate environment. Start in small and realistic ways. Help your neighbour and those that are disadvantaged in some way. Donate your time, energy and resources to causes that will benefit others. Engage in selfless activities with no desire for reward and simply rejoice in the wonder and upliftment of giving. As Gandhi so eloquently put it: "The fragrance always remains on the hand that gives the rose". Giving is always mutually beneficial, which is why I passionately believe everybody wins in a charitable world.

The evidence of a social conscience is also beginning to make an impact in the world of business. The term corporate social responsibility (CSR), also referred to by some as corporate social and environmental responsibility (CSER), is part of the new language underlining a commitment to an ethical way of working. Broadly speaking CSR is a description of the company's commitment to manage their business affairs in a way that takes account of social, economic and environmental impact. It also is a commitment to human rights and equality.

The underpinning philosophy for most embarking on this way of conducting their business is to consider all the stakeholders. This means looking at suppliers, employees, consumers and communities. When making decisions those acting with corporate social responsibility would be checking whether all the relevant parties have good practices both in terms of their workforce, health and safety and the environmental consequences of their business. With regards to employees those adopting a CSR approach would be ensuring their staff are in receipt of the best pastoral care and are working in an environment that is positive, encouraging and rewards performance and contribution.

Consumers are considered critical to the success of any business and so offering products and services that meet a high ethical standard and offer the best product to the client is also integral to the CSR approach.

Last but not least, those operating under the principles of social responsibility would be seeking to embrace their community. This can take on many forms such as: taking part in charitable initiatives, offering internships, supporting volunteer programmes and sponsoring local events.

Evidence is mounting with regards to the benefits of businesses and corporations of all sizes working to service the needs of their stakeholders, which in turn positively impacts on profits. Amongst the benefits, operational costs are reduced, better brand recognition, increased customer sales and greater loyalty to the brand.

What's also becoming clear is that those who value and incorporate social responsibility in their business activities retain their staff and attract those with greater ability and talent, as more individuals want to be associated with organisations with these codes of conduct.

The evidence also illustrates that such businesses improve their reputation, which in turn gives them a better profile in their respective markets. The excellent report overseen by Professor David Grayson, Director of the Doughty Centre for Corporate Responsibility (Cranfield School of Management) and Stephen Howard, Chief Executive for Business in the Community (BITC), lays out clearly and eloquently a rationale for businesses embracing social responsibility at the core of their philosophy. Not just because it improves the bottom line, but more significantly because it provides sustainability.

Their research indicates that taking a short-term view based primarily on the financial health of an organisation almost certainly promises a future of decline. This is because the true health of the organisation is determined by how one looks after one's employees.

Their report itemises seven benefits that come from undertaking more responsible business practices. First and foremost is meeting the needs of the primary stakeholders and the workforce. This has been identified as arguably the key business strategy that should be pursued because it improves the social and mental health of the workforce as well as operational effectiveness.

Project ROI (return on investment), which is a voice for the corporate responsibility movement, has produced extensive research and reports on the essentiality of a business that has at the heart of its governance an environmental and social strategy. They argue that corporate responsibility does not automatically bring improvement unless it is done well. Therefore, it should not simply be an 'add on' to an existing business model, the model needs to be built around CSR.

In the United States, according to Project ROI, 76% of those described as millennials (those reaching young adulthood in the early 21st century) would be reluctant to take a job with a company that had a bad reputation. 45% state they would be happy to take a cut in pay for a company that has an ethical approach to the environment and society.

The research data that is amassing is overwhelmingly clear that organisations and businesses that look after their staff are more effective, they produce better goods and offer better services. As a result, their customers are happier. Such organisations make positive contributions to their communities. Another wonderful by-product of their success is that they are more likely to have and maintain ethical arrangements with their suppliers, which leads to greater profits for all parties.

So why adopt any other strategy when it's clear that a social conscience creates a win-win situation?

The role of attachment

Attachment theory has helped us to better understand the nature of relationships; that is the relationship we form with our environment (in the first instance our caregivers) and as a result of those relationships the relationship we form with ourselves.

If you are interested in exploring this topic more thoroughly then beginning with the work of John Bowlby (1958), who was the first behavioural psychologist to establish a working theory around attachment, is a very good place to start.

What Bowlby was able to demonstrate through his research is that attachment is an emotional bond with another person - and the emotional bonds that are formed with one's caregivers have a tremendous impact throughout one's life. One of the primary messages of attachment theory is that the relationship with your primary caregiver will determine the bond you create with yourself and the world.

Initial theories around attachment suggested that it was food that led to the forming of attachment behaviour, but Bowlby was able to illustrate that the nurturing provided by those who are responsible for the child's needs allowed the child to develop a sense of safety and security, which is described as a secure attachment.

In the prequel to this book, I discussed at some length the three As. These are: attention, affection and affirmation. These three primary needs/drivers are critical to the formation of secure attachments; when they are absent insecure attachments are formed.

Secure attachments are categorised as a state where the child experiences their caregivers to be emotionally available and responsive to their needs. It is an environment of certainty, which allows the child to develop a clear sense of self; an environment that allows for adventure and creative expression. Such an environment fosters trust in the child because of the consistent reassurance and comfort provided by the parent. Those who have enjoyed the benefits of secure attachment confidently express their individuality. They form healthy, trusting and positive relationships. As a result, they are much more likely to be successful in whatever they do and where misfortune does befall them, they have a greater resoluteness and self-belief that enables them to find positive solutions.

There are subtle differences in interpretation with regards to attachment theory, which is inevitable given the different contributors as the theory has developed over the last sixty years or so. However, one of the primary elements where the consensus is fairly unanimous is the description of insecure attachments. There are essentially three types of insecure attachment, and they are: anxious ambivalent, anxious avoidant and anxious disorganised.

The common theme with these three insecure attachments is mixed messages (something we focus on a lot at Reach because so many clients are the victims of this phenomenon, without knowing it). In each case, the child is unable to fully trust its environment. The caregivers to varying degrees are inconsistent with their warmth, attention to the child's needs, love and affection. As a result, the child is unsure of who s/he is and how to behave.

What follows is a summary of the three insecure attachment styles. The anxious ambivalent (also referred to as ambivalent attachment) is an emotional state created when the child feels anxiety when separated from the primary caregiver. However, when the primary caregiver returns the child does not feel reassured. This is because the parent/caregiver even at times of nurturing is often preoccupied, not truly present and therefore not attuned to the needs of the child, so the child doesn't feel soothed by their presence.

At other times the caregiver is insensitive, emotionally unavailable and at other times can be intrusive in ways that obstruct the child's development. As a result, the child becomes confused and insecure not knowing what kind of response or treatment they will receive - and so they become untrusting and ambivalent. Those who fall into this category continue to carry that ambivalence with them through their life - and nothing seems able to quell that underlying anxiety and the doubt and suspicion they feel.

Those who suffer with anxious avoidant attachment issues (also referred to as avoidant attachment) are those who have come from environments where the primary caregiver is largely emotionally unavailable and did not respond to their core needs. This leaves the child feeling rejected and abandoned - as a result these infants oscillate between being demanding and clingy - and at other times they randomly express anger, which to the observer, seems disproportionate to the situation.

Eventually, such children shut down, avoiding the pain of the rejection and lack of intimacy. As adults this avoidant and withdrawing pattern is carried into the world and underpins their relationships and interactions. These individuals prematurely learn to become independent but in fact their independence is a defence mechanism, a way of protecting themselves from pain.

Anxious disorganised attachment (also referred to as disorganised attachment) stems from the child being fairly consistently exposed to an unpredictable and disruptive environment. The child feels no sense of safety or security because the primary caregiver fluctuates far too much to provide the child with a helpful reference point, an anchor around which to build a sense of self. Those exposed to this kind of unpredictability and culture of uncertainty are likely to develop adult personas that are emotionally unbalanced - their own identity is obscured - and chaos is more likely to be a refuge for them. As adults these individuals struggle to feel at home in relationships. This is generally because those who have been exposed to this kind of environment are much more likely to be entangled in their subpersonalities and have a false sense of self.

Since the time of Bowlby and his protégée Mary Ainsworth (1970s) there have been numerous studies, which have further underlined the validity of these four categories of attachment, and a host of statistics have also emerged from the plethora of research from the late 1950s up to the present time.

If we are to believe the data, then 50% of the population enjoys a secure attachment. Approximately 20% are anxious avoidant, there is a similar percentage that are anxious disorganised (although this figure is considered by many to be more, especially in cases of neglect and abuse), which leaves approximately 10% who would be described as anxious ambivalent. It should be said for accuracy these figures do vary slightly according to the source of the data.

I do not believe that 50% of the population is enjoying the fruits of secure attachment - as if this were the case we would be living in a much better world. Based on my professional and personal experience as well as the research I have undertaken, I think at least two thirds of the population is suffering with one form of insecure attachment or another - and in some cases are evidencing that they are victims of a more complex web of insecurity that doesn't fall neatly into only one of these categories.

Although some classification around emotional and psychological conditions is useful, I have seen how those very labels can become a problem both for the one wearing the label and those trying to help. It's easy when seeing a client or patient as a named condition, to stop seeing their humanity, as the clinician and those who are close to the individual focus on what the label says. The client or patient can be further disempowered when they see themselves as that condition. This can lead them to believe there is little they can do to transform their reality because their issues become the lens through which they see themselves – and they are disabled in the process.

When I'm working with those who are suffering with whatever emotional, psychological or physical distress, I only ever use the label they come with as a point of entry into the process, but I do not get caught up in the story that comes with the label. I have found this often deceives and has led me down paths that are not useful or relevant. We have to be aware of the story but not defined by it. This applies to both the practitioner and it also applies to the one suffering. Otherwise, the categorisation can limit the opportunity for growth.

That said I wanted to provide this overview because if we are to understand how we build healthy relationships, then having some idea of how our formative years shape that process will also provide us with some clues about what we need to do to disentangle ourselves from any unwanted patterns and habits.

If you want to immerse yourself more in this subject, then in addition to looking at Bowlby's work, you may want to take a look at the work of; Mary Ainsworth (Strange Situation study), Harry Harlow (Maternal Deprivation study), Rudolf Schaffer, Peggy Emerson (the Stages of Attachment) and Sue Gerhardt (Why Love Matters).

All of these individuals have contributed in some way to the subject and our understanding of how being present, offering love, consistency, attention, affirmation and affection contribute to creating a sense of safety and security, which in turn enables the child and eventually the adult to move forward confidently in their life.

Building healthy relationships

There are so many points of view on this topic, it could leave one's head spinning. However, I believe there are some common threads that are required to build and maintain healthy relationships.

The primary ones are communication, trust, empathy, conscious intimacy, compromise, compassion, humour, forgiveness, adventure and the pursuit of common interests. There are other key factors that could be added to this list such as: sensitivity, awareness, tolerance and light-heartedness. This is not meant to be the ultimate declaration on healthy relationships but those who pursue these values will find that whatever issues do prevail can be surmounted when these ingredients are present. Let me provide you with a few examples of the primary components:

Communication: this is about open and honest dialogue and is arguably the greatest evidence of love. Through open and honest communication, the bridges of understanding, trust and respect can be built. Unless we dare to step into another person's reality, we are left standing on the platform of assumption. Sometimes our assumptions will be accurate, but often they will merely reflect our own projections. Healthy communication is built on respect and kindness. It avoids conflict in the name of resolution. What this looks like in practice is finding the earliest point in time to express your concerns but ensuring you do not do that from a place of anger.

Reactive communication is rarely productive. It serves to hurt the heart of the other person and whatever message is being conveyed is generally lost. Those who invest regularly in communicating sensitively and from the heart, remembering that the other person's point of view is as valid and valuable as their own, are able to see the bigger picture. As a result, both parties feel heard and valued, which is important because so many arguments and disagreements are about not feeling heard and valued by the other.

Make time regularly to share your innermost thoughts and feelings with those you are closest to. One needs to feel safe when taking this kind of risk, so it's important to ensure that the other person also shares these values.

Empathy: this is a wonderful companion of communication. If we want to truly connect with another person, we have to make a conscious effort to step away from our own point of view. Empathy demands that we look at the issue from the other person's perspective. It asks us to put to one side our view of reality and dare to examine the world with another pair of eyes. This kind of empathy is not easily attained. It requires practice. However, when we do look at the world through the other person's eyes our own view of reality is significantly enhanced.

Empathy makes both parties better. If I have the humility to consider I may well be wrong and cannot see the whole picture, then empathy will fill in some if not all of the gaps.

When you're next communicating with someone you love, or someone you're trying to build a relationship with, consider their argument from their point of view. That way when you offer your own perspective there's more likely to be understanding which makes compromises much easier to achieve.

Conscious intimacy: intimacy can take on so many forms – kind words and deeds, stroking, embracing, expressing interest and exhibiting warmth. Intimacy is not exclusively about romance and sexual relationships. What I mean by conscious intimacy is making time regularly to show interest in the other person, making time to enquire about their inner world, their day, their challenges, hopes and dreams. It costs us very little to make another person feel valuable. Use touch mindfully. Connect with another person in ways that say, 'I'm here', 'I'm interested' and 'I'm listening' and this will enrich the quality and the nature of the connection and dialogue.

Our attitude whilst communicating with others, including the way we use our voices, influence the bonds of trust we are able to develop. When we feel that others care about us, not only do we in turn care more about them, we risk sharing our vulnerabilities with them. As indicated in my summary around attachment, it all depends on creating an environment that is safe and secure. Conscious intimacy enables a relationship to find safe and common ground.

Humour: it has been repeatedly and wisely stated that laughter is the shortest distance between two people. It's amazing how humour can connect people and enable the most difficult of discussions to take place in a more amicable way.

The ability to laugh at oneself is so empowering because it offers us a third person perspective. Some useful research conducted in 2016 with Waterloo and Yale universities demonstrated that adopting a third person perspective when looking at romantic relationships was a valuable way to look at difficult issues. The emotional distance and perspective offered can help the person to better see themselves, the other person's perspective and examine differences and conflicts. This more detached view of a problem or issue enabled couples to have a better handle on fixing what was wrong.

Humour has a way of moving us out of our own self-absorption into a more empathic position. This research encouraging adopting a third person perspective by Alex Huynh and Daniel Yang was not focused on humour but on the value of distancing ourselves from challenges in relationships. They found that if we could project ourselves into the future and view the problem from there, we could often find better solutions. This is the value that comes from changing one's perspective and I've found that humour offers us this advantage.

Common interests: for a relationship of any kind to flourish there needs to be a shared experience. It is difficult to build dialogue and intimacy without sharing our time, energy, thoughts and feelings - and so it's vital to build a language that both parties understand.

Very few things do this better than developing a shared interest. It doesn't matter what this is. It could be walking, playing chess, salsa dancing, abseiling, cooking, being part of a book club... whatever brings both hearts joy will work.

When building a relationship, you may need to engage in something that initially you're not interested in. Building a common language often requires experimentation, a willingness to compromise and putting to one side preconceived ideas and prejudices. Bear this in mind when thinking of compromise, it is the willingness to suspend your promise (to yourself or to your beliefs) in order that the other person can find and fulfil their promise (their potential).

When we dare to engage in something that helps us to build a bond with another person not only are they enhanced by the experience we can also discover uncharted territories and find new loves that we didn't know existed.

So, when exploring common interests be prepared to go on an adventure if that is what is required, because building and consolidating relationships is life's ultimate thrill. In the end it's the nature and the quality of the relationships we have built that gives us the greatest sense of safety, security and joy.

The environment of the planet

Although I am choosing to discuss this environment last it needs to be understood that it is in no way least. There are many who would say it should come first because without it the lives that we cling to, treasure and want to improve, would simply not exist. We are so dependent on Mother Earth. However, we are unlikely to be passionate and committed about saving the planet if we have not first looked at ourselves, developed a respect for our bodies and developed a relationship with our physical space and those we share it with.

It's often when these three are properly understood and valued that the individual feels compelled to find ways to make a difference, however small. There is the overwhelming realisation that one might not be able to change the world, but one can influence the part of the world one comes into contact with. If we can take on this mantra and make this part of our life's mission, then we have a chance of creating something that's better for all of us and those who will come after us.

There are those who champion one environment over another because they are convinced that's where their attention should go, but we are all made weaker when we don't see the synergy of these four environments and the wondrous web that they weave. They are forever entwined.

The environment of the planet is such an enormous subject and is very topical at this time due to the substantive climatic changes that are taking place. However, my aim is not to drown you in facts and figures that can actually leave one feeling even more disempowered, my aim is to highlight what you can do. So, here are three examples of why the fourth environment is critical to our survival and may they inspire you to make a contribution.

Soil erosion

This is considered one of the most serious environmental and public health problems facing human society. The loss of soil from land surfaces is widespread globally and is adversely affecting the productivity of all the natural ecosystems. As a result, it is suggested that the biodiversity of plants, animals and microbes in the soil is being damaged, which in turn affects the nutrient profile – this has been much researched and exposed since the 1990s.

Added to the diminishing quality of the soil, which in turn is reflected in the inconsistency of minerals and vitamins found in our fruits and vegetables, there is also the contentious debate around acid rain, which, it is claimed, is altering the pH in the soil. Some researchers and health professionals suggest that this has dire consequences for health given that the pH of the body is considered the regulatory authority that controls most cellular processes. The pH balance of the human bloodstream is recognised by medical physiology texts as one of the most important biochemical balances in all of human body chemistry (Simoncini, 2007 and Sircus, 2010).

There are many factors linked to soil erosion, such as: loss of soil structure, poor drainage, soil acidity, soil degradation, soil compaction and low organic matter. In addition, water, wind and ice are key contributors to the loss of soil potency. If environmental factors are the main reasons for soil erosion, what can we do about that?

Well, we need to understand that human activity is a key factor in soil erosion and so we can start by looking at our contribution to the loss of soil structure, the increase in soil acidity and degradation. Also, how can we improve the organic matter found in the soil, ensuring it can be nutrient rich? These are all things that with human imagination, ingenuity and the desire, we can have an impact on.

So, what can we do?

Well, land tillage (the agricultural preparation of soil) is certainly an area worthy of our attention. As farming methods have become more advanced, more aggressive methods of agitating/turning the soil have been employed. Before the huge mechanical plant machinery that is now being used the turning and agitation of the soil (tilling) would have been undertaken by human power such as digging and turning the soil manually, using shovels, pickaxes and hoes (in some cases horses and ploughs would be used). This form of tilling was less destructive to the soil, leaving many more microbes and nutrients intact as a result.

Modern methods on the other hand have caused more disruption and destruction to the soil and where the soil has low organic matter, which is not being replenished, such aggravation naturally leads to soil erosion and reduces the crop yield. Something modern farming has also reduced given the demands of consumerism, is allowing the field to lie fallow. Giving the land a chance to recover after harvest is certainly one of the things that would significantly help with soil erosion. If after the field was harvested it were simply left and not ploughed or mechanically agitated in any way this would allow for some renewal. In addition, leaving the previous year's crop residue in situ helps with soil enrichment. Adding organic matter at this point would further help with the soil structure and pH levels.

Overgrazing is another reason that the soil quality is becoming poorer. We need to understand that the animals living off the land are extracting nutrients for their own growth and survival, which is all part of the natural cycle of life. But as we farm the land as custodians of the planet, it's important that we ensure that we're doing everything we can to put those nutrients back in otherwise the food crops we extract from the soil will be insufficient to support our own biological needs.

There are many things that we can do to reduce the impact of soil erosion. Afforestation (planting trees) is one of the key things that can help with erosion as the roots of the tree bind the soil, improving its structure and integrity, making it much more difficult for water, wind and ice to cause the soil to be washed away. Adding mulch and fertiliser to the topsoil is extremely valuable too, as it helps reduce the water run-off, which displaces and diminishes the soil and can help with nutrient enhancement and retention.

In addition to planting trees, planting herbs and wildflowers are also excellent ways of helping retain soil in a particular location as they have an intricate root system which binds the soil, making it more robust and resistant to environmental ravages. In fact, planting any kind of natural vegetation will help with soil erosion. It's probably the easiest thing we can do to stem the tide.

Slopes present us with another challenge when it comes to soil erosion because the incline makes it easier for the wind and the rain to wash away the topsoil, which is a real problem given the immense value of topsoil. This is why contour ploughing (ploughing that follows the natural shape of a slope), terrace farming (creating flat areas on a previously sloping piece of land and providing catchment areas for water) and strip cropping (where different crops are planted in strips alongside one another to minimise soil erosion) are all excellent ways of helping to mitigate against topsoil loss.

One of the biggest crimes we are committing is deforestation. As I said, afforestation helps with the soil structure, integrity and resilience, so it's hardly surprising that deforestation does the complete opposite. In addition to dismantling the soil, deforestation leads to a huge reduction in biodiversity. Over 80% of land animals and plants live in our forests, so millions of species increasingly lose their habitats which has a bearing on the wider ecosystem.

One of the worst examples of deforestation is taking place in the rainforests of Indonesia, which is the second largest rainforest in the world after Brazil. Huge areas are being flattened and burnt at a terrible rate by large multi-nationals, particularly for the production of palm oil. This is because of the cheapness of the product and its multiple uses. But this terrible devastation taking place in the name of profit, is destroying over six million acres a year and is having a massive impact on the climate in the form of greenhouse gases.

This is why the frightening rate of deforestation has to be quelled because we may think of it happening in another part of the world and therefore, we do not need to concern ourselves, but the rate of tree loss and other natural vegetation is also reducing the quality of oxygen available to all of us and when this is aligned to the amount of pollution we're generating, it does not make for a positive or hopeful picture.

As we consider the global issues, we could be forgiven for thinking what's the point, as there is so little any of us can do to alter the current decline. But this is not the case. We can join conservation groups, look at ways to enhance our local community, protest peacefully against land grabbing and further encroachments on areas of outstanding beauty, look to reduce our own carbon footprints, reduce waste and recycle where we can and join the non-plastic revolution.

If you are lucky enough to have a garden or some land, then engage in those activities that will help with soil erosion. There are simple things like building retaining walls to hold soil in place, creating rockeries is another way to minimise soil erosion, don't allow the soil to become compacted because it needs to breathe to maintain its potency. Equally don't over-till the soil, try and strike a balance. Either produce your own compost or buy good quality compost to ensure soil enrichment. Plant small trees, wildflowers and herbs where you can.

If we have a mind to, we can all become part of the solution in some way, rather than considering it someone else's role or responsibility.

The carbon cycle

We are now, through the popular media, becoming increasingly aware of the role and importance of carbon and given that all life is in some way bound up with the carbon cycle, it is imperative for our own salvation and that of the planet to understand our relationship with this critical element.

You may remember in chapter 1 I introduced the topic of energy contracts. The carbon cycle is one of the most important energy contracts. At each stage of the cycle there is a transaction that supports some aspect of life. If it were not for the carbon cycle, life as we know it simply wouldn't exist.

The system that we live in is described as a closed system, which in essence means there is a finite amount of energy within the system – hence the first law of thermodynamics states that energy cannot be created or destroyed. It's always being recycled, changing its form and structure but ultimately returning to its original state.

In our closed system the sun is the source of all energy but it's only plants, algae and a few types of bacteria that can actually use sunlight as a direct source of energy. This means that no other organisms including humans can convert the sun's energy into the nutrients needed to maintain life.

Therefore, we are totally dependent upon the nutrients from plant sources for our survival. Those plants need the carbon dioxide that is found in the atmosphere along with the light energy from the sun, to manufacture those nutrients. This is truly an interdependent system. Without the sun and carbon dioxide, plants would not create the nutrients that we need – and without that plant vegetation providing essential nutrients and emitting oxygen we would not survive.

Our part in the carbon cycle is also significant because the carbon dioxide that we and animals produce at the point of exhalation goes into the atmosphere, helping to maintain the carbon balance which ensures the survival of trees, shrubs and all vegetation.

All the proteins, amino acids, carbohydrates and DNA in our bodies contain substantial amounts of carbon. Carbon is also found in abundance in the earth in the form of fossil fuels (coal and oil) and in the atmosphere in the form of carbon dioxide.

There are four primary steps in the carbon cycle that describe the journey of carbon atoms and the consequences along the way. These are: photosynthesis, respiration, combustion and decomposition.

Photosynthesis describes the process where plants and other organisms use light energy to convert water and carbon dioxide into oxygen and carbohydrates. Respiration is the process in which a living organism or cell takes in oxygen from the air or water and distributes carbon dioxide back into the biosphere. In other words, photosynthesis takes carbon out of the atmosphere and respiration puts it back. It is this transaction that needs to be kept in balance.

Combustion occurs when any organic material is burned in the presence of oxygen giving off carbon dioxide, water and energy in the process. This is where we can see the human impact on the carbon cycle when organic materials and fossil fuels such as: coal, oil and methane (natural gas) are burned. There are other organic materials that include some carbon, hydrogen and oxygen such as: paper, wood, plastics and cloth and when they are burned in the presence of oxygen, carbon dioxide and other compounds are released into the atmosphere.

When looking at the role of combustion it's important to consider metabolism in animals and humans as a similar process takes place. Once plant material and/or animal products are consumed a series of complex actions and reactions occur at the cellular level in the presence of oxygen, which converts those products into glucose sugar, carbon dioxide, water and energy, which the body then uses to support all the other activities of the organs and systems.

Decomposition is a critical phase in the carbon cycle as it facilitates the return of carbon back into the atmosphere. Decomposers, such as fungi and bacterial microbes play an important role in the carbon cycle. These organisms break down the remains of dead plants and animals releasing carbon dioxide through respiration back into the atmosphere.

The carbon that is stored in the roots of trees and in dead plant matter can be locked into the maintenance of that living organism for years, decades and even centuries. It is eventually released when decomposition takes place. No matter how long those carbon molecules are bound to their contractual arrangements they will eventually be released and become part of the carbon dioxide, which is all part of this great biospheric story.

Given the importance of water to human life and the fact that the earth is approximately 70% water and over 95% of that water is found in the oceans, a summary of the carbon cycle would be incomplete without some reference to the oceans.

Oceans have an ambiguous part to play in the carbon cycle. Wherever you find huge bodies of water the surface is cool and absorbs carbon from the atmosphere. This is mainly to be found in the colder regions and is particularly true of the north and south poles. In more tropical regions where the surface of the water is warmer, carbon is actually released into the atmosphere. From there plants will absorb the carbon and through the process of photosynthesis the carbon cycle keeps spinning. I will come back to the role and importance of oceans later on.

The carbon cycle explains the journey and transformation of carbon atoms as they move from our bodies into the atmosphere and through all living organisms back to the earth.

Avoid waste

The consequences of waste in terms of planet earth are staggering. Not only does it lead to the pollution of the biosphere, polluting air, water and soil, but it also generates a long list of negative consequences that impact us humans, leading to a multitude of health problems. The list of these health issues is far too lengthy to document here, but common examples are a range of respiratory disorders such as asthma and CPD, autoimmune conditions like rheumatoid arthritis, lupus and chronic fatigue. There are also countless skin disorders such as eczema, impetigo and psoriasis and many more diseases that are the result of a collapsing immune system. Irresponsible waste management is one of the key factors impacting on human health. The two cannot be divorced.

As environmental awareness is growing and the realisation that we are drowning in our poor choices around energy consumption and waste, the 4 Rs have been conceived as a response to this. They are, reduce, reuse, recycle and recover. Thankfully, this concept is slowly finding its way into the philosophy of more businesses who are moving increasingly towards higher standards of excellence... but there is still a long way to go if we are to prevent this liner from sinking.

Here is a summary of the 4 Rs. Firstly, seek to reduce waste wherever possible. Secondly, where waste is produced, find ways to reuse it if practicable. Recycling is the third option in waste management. It is important to point out that there are economic and environmental costs associated with recycling. So, wherever possible, reduction or reusing of waste is preferable. The fourth option is to recover materials or energy from waste, which cannot be reduced, reused or recycled.

The International Institute for Sustainable Development (IISD) has produced some very good information on how businesses can apply the 4 Rs to their particular sector. The Canadian government has also been persuaded to apply the 4 Rs to waste management having developed a robust policy that is increasingly being deployed. There are very good examples of the 4 Rs philosophy in China (small straw pulp mills) producing agricultural fertiliser. There are producers of cheese and other products in California who have reduced their solid waste disposal fees and generated tens of thousands of dollars a year from the sale of recyclable materials.

Another example of good practice in this area is packaging. This is where packaged items are received from one supplier, then the packaging is re-used and redistributed by the company receiving those goods - so rather than creating more packaging for their products, they're finding innovative and creative ways of reusing the same materials.

These examples signal the way forward and we need to encourage this movement by business so that the 4 Rs philosophy becomes an integral part of an organisation's culture.

We also need as individuals to be taking ecological action and apply the same philosophy to our lives. So, what does it mean to reduce?

Try purchasing products in bulk to reduce all the waste produced by individual packaging. When possible, purchase products whose packaging is easily recyclable. Avoid buying fresh food in pre-packaged containers. Avoid making purchases that you don't really need. There is a habit it seems to acquire goods not because they are essential but simply because we want them, which also adds to the burden of waste.

If you have a garden, then take composting and vermiculture practices (preparing enriched compost with the use of earth worms) seriously. There is so much capacity within a garden to reduce, reuse, recycle and recover - it's one of the best ways we can contribute practically to the environmental challenges we face.

Seek to reuse wherever you can. Easy adjustments that are growing in popularity are not using plastic bags in favour of paper and hessian/biodegradable ones. Reuse empty jars and bottles, where possible also reuse envelopes and other packaging. Hire, share or borrow items where you can. If possible, buy second-hand books.

Rather than throwing things away, have a garage or boot sale – your junk could be someone else's solution. There are many products for which you can now buy a refill, rather than a replacement. Rechargeable batteries are also a better option. There is so much we can do when we are mindful of the consequences of our decisions and choices.

Recycling is the most well-known of the 4 Rs but it should be noted that it takes a lot of energy and money to collect recyclable materials, melt them down and make new things from them. Recycling is not solely about the diversity of waste, taking what is described as rubbish and giving it another function. Arguably its primary benefit is the reduction of the amount of virgin resources that need to be harvested and processed for the manufacture of new products.

Look for items in packages and containers made of recycled materials. There is an increasing number of products made from recycled cans, paper, wrappings, cartons etc. Many of these items are available in grocery and other retail stores. Mail order catalogues, online retailers, stationers and print shops also may stock these and other recycled items. Support these options where you can.

Although recycling does come with a cost, it is nonetheless a valuable option in our attempt to live more environmentally friendly lives. However small, play your part.

Recovering is the final element in waste management where the item rather than being destroyed is recovered for an alternative purpose. When it is not possible to reuse or recycle objects, such as mobile phones, ink cartridges, unused paint, televisions and electrical devices, dead batteries and tyres, where toxic elements are to be found, then recovery may be a solution.

In many of these cases there are two tasks to perform. One, the careful disposal of toxic material which far too often is being inadequately disposed of, causing adverse consequences to the planet and human health. And two, extracting what is recoverable from these products. In some of the best examples, resources that would otherwise be thrown away are being converted into energy/fuel such as electricity, heat, compost and fuel using thermal and biological means.

There are good examples around the world where recovery of materials with little value is being taken seriously. Quebec in Canada is one such example. They have made the 4 Rs a central part of government policy and have produced a 231 page guide to help businesses and the community steer their way towards the 4 Rs.

Below is an extract from the foreword of that excellent document produced by the First Nations of Quebec and Labrador Sustainable Development Institute (FNQLSDI), making an impassioned plea for change. I've included it because it underlines where we are and what we must do:

"We are already experiencing climate changes. The inhabitants of the Great North, whose families have lived there for centuries, have been feeling its impact for a number of years. The ice is forming later in winter, and it is disappearing too early in the spring. Some animal species are adopting new behaviours while other behaviours are simply appearing.

In addition, extreme weather events such as heavy rain, tropical thunderstorms, heat waves, tornados and shoreline erosion occur much more frequently and more violently.

Climate changes may very well occur within a natural cycle, but one thing is certain: we are actively contributing to the global warming. We are perpetuating it. We are exacerbating it. We are simply making it worse...

The best way to alleviate the climate crisis is to change our habits, our actions and the way we live. We must remember that almost everything we do and everything we consume causes pollution, one way or the other. Individual and collective efforts are urgently needed if we are to re-establish our sacred bond with Mother Earth.

Mother Earth can certainly do without us. She would certainly feel better. But we cannot live without her. Let's restore the ancient respect that we once showed her.

Our well-being is at stake. So is our survival".

We all need a mission statement like this, something that drives us to actively create positive change where we can.

Understanding these four environments reminds us that they each need our on-going attention and respect.

I have attempted in this chapter to show the importance of each of these four environments, highlighting their individuality but also illustrating the culture of interdependence that exists between them.

There is a vast web of consequences we are all facing, as the planet struggles to find balance and harmony in the face of our arrogance, ignorance and neglect. We surely cannot expect to continue on our current course without condemning ourselves to further disease, famine, pollution, natural disasters and even more conflict. It's time for change and change begins with you and me.

I will keep referring to The Story of Health as we travel together, because I believe that it's the simplest and most valuable reference for creating a manifesto for personal change. The Story of Health puts responsibility in our hands. It enables us to become harbingers of change, not looking for someone else to do something but looking to ourselves.

The more we meet the needs of our minds, bodies, spirits and environments, the more we can live a better quality of life and enable others to do the same.

Hopefully the symbiotic nature of life and our part within that is even more clear and will compel you to find a way to cooperate in the silent revolution that is taking place right now.

"Personal transformation can and does have global effects. As we go, so goes the world, for the world is us. The revolution that will save the world is ultimately a personal one".

Marianne Williamson (1952 – present)

Points to remember

- There are four environments, each one separate and distinct but intimately bound together in such a way that optimum health cannot exist unless all four are sufficiently catered for. The more we understand these four environments and our relationship to each of them, the more we can resonate harmoniously with life.

- The environment of the self depends on creating a culture of introspection and reflection. It's a world that is nurtured by kindness, forgiveness, laughter and benevolence. The more compassion we have for ourselves, the more likely we are to meet life's challenges with grace and poise. By developing 'kind eyes', we expand our creative intelligence and unleash our hidden potential.

- The environment of the body requires copious amounts of water and a rich blend of nutrients in which our cells can flourish - and so we need to ensure we have a rainbow diet to underpin the brain and body's many diverse functions. We need to also ensure that our guts are healthy by thoroughly chewing our food, nourishing our microbiome, avoiding stress in all its forms and respecting the body's limits and capacity. The more we establish a love affair with our bodies the more we can be sure that they'll support our minds and spirits.

- Remember, prevention is better than cure, so rather than waiting for problems to turn up and then reacting, become proactive. Meet the needs of the mind and the body consistently. This will ward off most problems and if problems do occur you will find yourself in the best position to respond in the necessary way.

- Create a physical sanctuary. To have a space that you can regularly retreat to, where you can establish and build good habits and patterns will make your journey easier and more enjoyable – as a result you're much more likely to succeed.

- As the research clearly shows, clutter (via the visual cortex) unsettles the brain and stresses the mind, making most things feel more difficult. Clutter also lowers the spirit because it is difficult to create peace of mind, clarity and focus when one's life is full of mess. Consciously and proactively create order in every space and every area of your life.

- Develop a social conscience. Find ways to add value to all of your relationships. Don't be content with just doing this for your family. Find ways to do this for all the communities you're a part of. We need a 'we not just me' revolution. A world in which we all have a social conscience is what will save us from the rapid decline we are witnessing.

- By understanding the four states of attachment we can better understand ourselves and those around us. It also helps us to be more kind in our judgements. As a result, we can develop greater sensitivity and empathy. Wherever you can, create secure attachments.

- Conscious intimacy is where we seek to be kind in thoughts, words and deeds - we are kind to ourselves and to others. When we live in a way that truly connects us to this moment, this person and/or situation, we give a different quality of attention and love. This elicits something deeper and more meaningful from those we connect with.

- The environment of the planet is in a critical state and we all need to find ways to contribute to salvaging Mother Earth. Of course, trying to do big things where we can, is required, but it's the many small acts of conscious living that are most going to help the environment. Think of what you can do to help with the soil and the carbon cycle. Think of how you can avoid waste and become active in the 4Rs (reduce, reuse, recycle, recover). However small, there is always some contribution you can make.

- Our minds need a new diet. Focus more on what's good in the world rather than allowing the relentless assault on the senses of bad news to continue unfiltered. The good news culture needs our help. We need to find ways of thinking and talking more about the positive things that we see and experience, rather than allowing ourselves to be immersed in what's wrong in the world. This simply propagates more of the same. Actively become a part of the solution!

A meditation to remind you of the primary themes of this chapter...

I have come to understand that there are four environments... each one performing a different role with a unique set of functions... independent and yet intimately entwined... one cannot exist without the others...

The first is the environment of the self... the world of consciousness with all its different dimensions... its terrain is vast, varied and deep... made up of many different realms... it is bursting with memories, feelings, thoughts and ideas... it is the cauldron of creation... where creative intelligence is conceived... from here I can perform wonders... all I need to do is to learn how to focus and channel my energy...

Secondly, there is the incredible world of the body... the most amazing, complex organism... a life force producing miracles every second, every minute of every day.... a force of nature that works tirelessly to protect me and ensure further growth and well-being... it needs my love and respect and in return it offers me its support and fidelity...

The third environment is the social context in which I live... it includes the need for a physical sanctuary, a place where I can be at peace... it also encompasses the network of relationships I am a part of... my family, friends, colleagues and my community... in this environment one needs to develop healthy attachments and contracts of love... building a social conscience in the process... this is how I can add value to the world...

Mother Earth is crying out for my cooperation... it is pleading with me to find ways of reducing waste... nurturing the soil... making better use of the water and the natural resources on which all life depends... I am now waking up to the fact that there is so much I can do... and rather than thinking this is someone else's problem, I realise it is our problem... I no longer shy away from my part, my responsibility... the fourth environment, sustains all life and can no longer be taken for granted or be neglected...

Now that I understand the role of each environment, I connect with each one... forming an unbreakable bond with them all... I now use my mind to create powerful, kind thoughts... I use it to visualise being at peace... at one with myself...

and share that vibration of love... with my body, my cells, muscles, tissues, organs and brain... I see waves of light rippling through my body into the world...

This beautiful energy passes from the first environment, into and through the second environment... extending its reach beyond me... encompassing my family, friends and all those I associate with... I've become a transmitter of love, light and good energy and that inspires me and inspires those around me...

I now find both simple and creative ways to save the planet... I am part of the solution... I know that the responsibility to change the world doesn't lie with anyone else... it lies with me... and we...

I now stand up and am counted amongst the brave and true....

CHAPTER 3

PROTECTION AND GROWTH

"The individual has always had to struggle to keep from being overwhelmed by the tribe. If you try it, you will be lonely often, and sometimes frightened. But no price is too high to pay for the privilege of owning yourself".

Friedrich Nietzsche (1844 – 1900)

The more you are a student of life's complexity, the more the role of protection and growth is unveiled. These two giants are perpetually at work. They are the throbbing heart of the universe.

In this chapter I will provide you with an overview of their primacy and power. From the cell to the cosmos there is almost nothing this pair does not touch, shape and influence - and to ignore their role denies us access to our own potential and magnificence.

Protection enables growth and growth provides protection

From the moment life is conceived there is a protective force at work, shielding the organism from insults in order that it may grow.

In a healthy system protection and growth are always working cooperatively, but when for whatever reason their relationship is spoiled or undermined, then dysfunction and maladaptation begin to drive the process.

The ultimate energy contract is to be found in the relationship between protection and growth. Their pledge is to enable all life with its vast cast of characters to perform the roles each is designed to undertake. Their promise is to carry out their tasks faithfully to ensure that energy can express itself and flourish. However, when the agreement breaks down, then the drive for survival (protection) overrides all previous agreements.

You'll remember from earlier in the book I provided the illustration of the most common mental health issue, that of anxiety. In that example I explained how the limbic system (amygdala) wrestles away control from the neo-cortex. At this point the instinct to survive is no longer open to reason. In that moment, the threat real or perceived, has now taken ownership of consciousness.

In this example of anxiety, the instinct to protect has not been persuaded that there is sufficient evidence to overcome the threat (leading to growth). This calculation takes place within nanoseconds and if the evidence for growth is not clearly visible and accessible, then at that point the instinct of protection takes over, either temporarily or indefinitely.

Although these two forces are essential to virtually all energetic arrangements and transactions in the universe, it is protection that will dominate if sufficient evidence for growth is not present.

In a healthy system, both are equal. In an unhealthy system, protection takes primacy because without protection, there is nothing to grow.

There is a fascinating dialogue here that we need to understand, in order that we can be part of the conversation. The essence of the dialogue is this; we can grow out of any experience or situation, but to move into the growth state, 'evidence' of positive change is required. Without evidence the cell will not follow your intention only your actions. Without evidence the unconscious mind will not let go of the old paradigms in favour of new ones, no matter what we promise. Without evidence old habits will not relinquish any ground for new ones. The universe runs on proof.

Remember from chapter 1 that patterns are the DNA of actions. Patterns are the evidence, the proof on which future calculations and transactions are based. They are at the heart of momentum whether that be in a positive or negative direction.

If we are to rely on growth as our means of protection - which is a perfectly reasonable position to undertake - then an evidence-based way of being is required. Positive change cannot be achieved without it.

In the absence of evidence, it is important to note that the protection of the system will take precedence over its growth - and our experience of that may be positive or negative subject to the situation and context.

When anxiety kicks in it is protecting us from a threat, real or imagined and if there is not sufficient evidence that we are in control, in other words, have grown in the ways we need to in order to address that threat, then protection runs in like the arms of the mother, protecting the child from the dog that's about to pounce.

In that moment it cares about nothing else. This is because safety is nature's highest concern – without a safe, sensitive and supportive environment, very little can thrive.

Safety and security - nature's primary narrative

To further understand the primacy of protection, we need to understand that nature's first concern is for the welfare of all life, energy and systems and so safety and security are its highest priorities. This statement could be considered to be at odds with Maslow's hierarchy of needs (1943) as he, in his famous triangle, puts safety second, as he sees the physiological needs of humans being the highest priority.

Although it's indisputable that we need food, water, warmth, rest and space to flourish, I would argue that the need to belong and feel love should also be considered as the primary driver alongside those needs. To be loved and to belong would be considered the third need in Maslow's hierarchy. However, I believe this need is bound up with the physiological requirements. I don't think they can be neatly separated from what is essential to human development - they are in my experience always entwined.

It's true that the physical needs contribute to that sense of belonging, that sense of love. But no less important are physical contact, tenderness of touch, quality of eye contact and the harmonic sound of a voice that loves and cares. These make a qualitative difference. They add something crucial alongside the physiological needs - and as a result, feelings of safety and security are created. I think our emotional and psychological needs are enmeshed with our physical needs, which makes it a more complex picture when working with damage and trauma. I also believe we need to apply this understanding in a 'person specific' way. We have to take account of how these needs play out with different individuals and the contexts in which they find themselves.

Whether you study cells, animals, the environment or any other aspect of the human experience, you will find the pursuit of safety is nature's greatest concern because she understands that unless safety and security are maintained the organism or system cannot thrive and flourish.

As a psychotherapist, when I'm working with clients, whether that be individuals, couples or groups, my primary concern is to create a safe, sensitive and supportive space. This is because I know the individual(s) is much more likely to take the risks required to create their growth in such an environment.

I have yet to come across someone who is willing to risk all when they do not feel sufficiently held by the space and by me. I would go further and say that no matter how much experience you have and how skilled you are, no matter how effective your model, strategy or intervention, without creating a sense of security on which the therapeutic relationship can be built, little progress will be made.

There is overwhelming research in this area looking at family systems where we can see a clear correlation between a child's emotional and psychological development and the degree of safety and security they feel from their caregivers. I mentioned the role of attachment in the previous chapter, highlighting that where secure attachments exist individuals experience love and a sense of their own value and worth. Insecure attachments on the other hand leave the child/adult grasping for those things that will address their deficiencies and needs.

When children are surrounded by fear, uncertainty and mixed messages they are unable to create secure and positive attachments, so their sense of self is fractured. They end up with a poor self-image. Their primary concern is then to fit in in any way they can. Unconsciously they go in pursuit of an alternative family if the family they were born into does not provide the conditions they need.

It's in the pursuit of belonging, fitting in, that so many children and adolescents lose their way.

Without understanding the power of this dynamic, this core driver, we are unlikely to understand much of the dysfunctional and maladaptive behaviour we see in our society today. If we are to stem the tide of antisocial behaviour then we must do something about creating safe, secure spaces where positive, healthy attachments can be formed.

From my experience, working at the coalface, this has to start in families and primary school education. If we don't get this message to take root in families, we will continue to see the fabric of society unravel. If we don't adapt our educational system in a way that embraces these values and principles, then the next generation can only keep adding to the mistakes that have already been made.

A manifesto for positive change

As previously stated, protection is needed in order for there to be growth. So, when considering a personal manifesto for positive change, we need to bear this fact in mind.

This needs to start with self-care. In the prequel, Synergy, I discussed this topic at some length and those of you familiar with The Reach Approach will know it is a central character in the wonderful cast we have assembled. Its message is clear, optimal living and the fulfilment of one's meaning and purpose, is only really achieved when we are meeting our core needs.

This is how we protect ourselves from the ravages of negativity and from those urges and impulses that lead us to disrespect ourselves and others.

Once a culture of self-care is installed, it naturally spills into our relationships and our homes as an attitude of compassion replaces one of fear and criticism. The empathy and sensitivity that is generated makes the home a safe space, one where conversations of the heart can easily take place. Children can trust their environments because they are surrounded by kindness and love. They can feel and experience their caregivers being stable and aware. This connects them with their core nature as a virtuous cycle is created where self-care produces welfare, a space in which all participants are nourished and can grow.

We need an education system built on these principles, a system that values citizenship and teaches our children how to be the best humans they can be in their families and communities. Such an education programme also needs clear and consistent boundaries that create a sense of safety, enhancing the opportunities for learning and growth.

English, maths, the arts and sciences would remain focal points of any educational programme, but especially in primary school we need to lay the foundation of 'right action' – promoting the idea of treating others the way we wish to be treated. This would mean including in the curriculum something that encompasses an ethical way of living.

To create such a system, the focus would be much more on values, promoting the need for kindness, patience, friendship, generosity and equality. Only then will we create a world where teachers, midwives, scientists, electricians, plumbers, workers of all denominations have an ethical framework and a code of conduct that not only makes them better at what they do, but makes them better humans too, because they are driven by the need to do what's right rather than being right.

A society with these values would be inclusive, protective, offering safety and security. And if these values were taught at an early age the children of today would become kind custodians of tomorrow because they would understand that growth in every area of human life depends on such values.

For many this will seem like a Utopian idea or maybe the stuff of science fiction - where idealism has replaced the reality of how things are. But I would dare to say that if we took these concepts seriously and if we began to create a culture where humanity came first, where kindness was understood to be beneficial to all, then we could literally change the landscape.

But for this to be the case, we first of all need a small group of committed people who are keen to begin by changing themselves, their physical spaces, their relationships, the way they live and act, and who quietly campaign through their example for a better world.

If we all keep thinking there's nothing we can do, then nothing will change. No effort sincerely made is ever in vain. Stop finding reasons to opt out and look for reasons to opt in.

A manifesto for positive change is a three-dimensional concept and this brief sketch is only illuminating one tiny corner of what is needed – but it is an important cornerstone. Five hundred years before Christ, Confucius advocated a culture built on Ren. Ren is a position where one's actions are steeped in love and that love is bound up in the very fabric of our governments, institutions and families and this enables the self to flourish. This is a 'we, not me' system. We now need a culture based on Ren.

Until we are prepared to commit ourselves to something much bigger than any one of us, the cycle of protection and growth will spin out of control, creating much of the chaos we see around us. We need to understand that if we don't put in place those conditions that generate safety and security then we become victims of chance and circumstance.

So, in closing, look for ways to create safety and security in your life, so that the overwhelming power of the survival mechanism does not prevent you from growing.

I would like to take you further into the protection and growth story in order that you might form a healthy relationship with them both. Here are some examples of this formidable duo and how they affect every aspect of human life.

The cell

There are two types of cells, prokaryotes and eukaryotes. Prokaryotes refer to bacteria and eukaryotes are a large classification of cell into which animal and plant cells fall.

There are significant differences between the two types of cells, one being that prokaryotes do not have a nucleus structure holding the DNA. The DNA simply exists in the interior of the cell, whereas in the eukaryotes there is a nucleus, surrounded by a lipid membrane, which contains the DNA material.

Both cells contain a variety of organelles - suspended in a jelly like material called cytoplasm, which protects the organelles and provides structure to the cell. The organelles each perform different functions. This is much like the human body, which has organs performing a range of functions for us such as the heart pumping blood around the body, the liver playing its part in detoxification, the lungs absorbing oxygen and expelling carbon dioxide. Every function found in the body is mirrored in the cell. Let us now take a look at those various organelles and their functions. I will start with the eukaryotes.

The cell has a membrane whose job it is to control what comes into and goes out of the cell. With the onset of the epigenetic revolution, this membrane has come to be described as the brain of the cell (for those of you who are interested, take a look at Bruce Lipton's research in this area). This is because of its important regulatory function. In addition, the membrane also separates the internal and external environments of the cell.

Another important organelle, the Golgi apparatus, has a significant role with regard to the use of proteins. It repackages them in preparation to be either moved out of the cell, for redistribution around the body, or to remain inside the cell for its use there. In either case it is supporting the growth process.

Mitochondria are pivotal organelles known as the powerhouses of the cell. They are only found in eukaryotic (plant and animal) cells and are involved in the metabolism of food. Mitochondria take in nutrients that enter the cell, break them down and convert those nutrients into energy. This energy supports all the many functions in the eukaryotic cells.

ATP (adenosine triphosphate) is the energy-carrying molecule produced by the mitochondria through a series of chemical reactions. ATP provides the energy to drive many processes in living cells, such as: nerve impulse, muscle contraction and chemical synthesis. ATP is also known as the molecular unit of currency because of its role in the intracellular transfer of energy.

Glucose and other carbohydrates produced by plants during photosynthesis are broken down by the process of aerobic cellular respiration - this too takes place in the mitochondria. This sequence of activities and reactions which are involved in the production of ATP is known as the Krebs cycle.

The lysosome is the organelle of detoxification. It is found in both cell types and contains digestive enzymes, which enable it to digest decaying or dead organelles and other waste in order to clean up the cell and facilitate its healthy functioning. Lysosomes play a vital role in the health of the cell, which is reflected in the wider functioning of the body.

A critical function of the cell is division or duplication (mitosis). The organelle called the centriole is the part of the cell that assists in this process, making sure cells are separated out equally.

Although both plant and animal cells belong to the eukaryotic family, there are some key differences between them. There are three organelles that are specific to plant cells, which do not exist in animal eukaryotes.

The first is the cell wall, which allows it to hold its shape and protects the cell – this is in addition to the cell membrane. Secondly, plant cells have a large central vacuole whereas animal cells contain several smaller vacuoles. This is an organelle, which performs different functions according to the nature and the characteristics of the cell. These include, holding waste products, getting rid of what the cell doesn't need and housing water and enzymes.

The cell wall is made up of polysaccharides and peptides. Within the wall there is a lipo-protein cell membrane. There is also another layer, the capsule, sometimes described as the slime layer. This is only present in eukaryotic cells where there is no cell wall. This slime is made from various starches and glycolipids and its role is to prevent the cell from drying out (desiccation) - it also protects the cell from other environmental assaults.

The slime layer which is also present in prokaryotic cells (bacteria) can prevent detection by the immune system and protect it from attack from antibodies and antibiotics, such is its ingenuity and instinct for survival. It also helps bacteria adhere to certain surfaces, which is very helpful in terms of its survival in different environments. The deeper one looks into the cell, the more the relationship between protection and growth is evident.

Let's now move on to the prokaryotes...

Prokaryotes are single cell organisms and are very important to our ecosystem. Many of them are well known in terms of diseases we may suffer such as E. coli, staphylococcus, streptococcus and cellulitis but remember even a healthy human body has a significant amount of bacterial material essential to life. When the aforementioned conditions afflict the body, the bacteria have proliferated to such an extent that they are now a threat to human health.

Prokaryotes, because they don't have a nucleus, have an area called the nucleoid where the DNA is located. These cells come in three different shapes, spherical (cocci), rod shaped (bacillus) and spiralled (helical/spirilla). They have the ability to live in extreme environmental conditions such as very high or low temperatures, or very acidic or alkaline environments. One of the most important functions of bacteria as far as the ecosystem is concerned, is that they are responsible for the digesting and breaking down of dead and decaying materials, returning nutrients back to the environment ready for reuse. Here we can see their ability on the one hand to protect themselves in challenging circumstances and on the other hand to participate in rejuvenation and growth.

The prokaryotic cells don't have any membrane bound organelles. Some of them do have an infolding membrane, which increases their surface area, and it has been postulated that this is in some way involved with respiration (because these cells don't have any mitochondria which produce energy) and so they have to source glucose to produce energy. More latterly it's considered that these membranes may have more to do with photosynthesis.

Plasmids (which are largely to be found in bacteria although they exist in some eukaryotes) are described as extrachromosomal DNA, also referred to as extranuclear DNA. They house DNA material, which lives outside the nucleoid, performing important biological functions. They can transfer genetic information between bacteria (conjugation) via the pili (a hair like appendage found on the surface of bacteria) carrying specific genetic traits to other bacteria. The pili aid reproduction and facilitate communication between bacteria. This is how they ensure their survival and further growth.

So, what have we learned? There are countless contractual arrangements at this microcosmic level and the more closely you look, the more you see that the two primary drivers are constantly working together.

The protective membranes are a good illustration of this symbiotic relationship and they exist in all cell types. They exist in different forms dependent upon the cell type. With the eukaryotes, there is an outer membrane holding all the contents of each cell in place. Cytoplasm within the cell further supports the cell's structure and the organelles within.

In the plant eukaryotes there is a cell wall, a less flexible membrane protecting the cell, its contents and functions. In the prokaryotes, these cells have in addition to a cell membrane, a further membrane or capsule which acts as another layer of protection enabling the cell to attach to other cells or surfaces to protect it and promote its survival.

We saw with the prokaryotes, that they have the ability to survive and indeed thrive in environmental conditions characterised by extreme temperatures and where there is excessive acidity or alkalinity. This is an adaptation that ensures the protection of the cell, which not only promotes its survival but enables further growth.

There are other activities which I've not covered here concerning the nature and functioning of the cells, that illustrate my point further. What I've offered is just a sketch that gives some idea of this eternal ebb and flow.

I believe that nature's activities and innate wisdom are teaching us many of the principles needed to build a more sustainable life. We just need to pay attention and listen more keenly to hear those messages.

I'm now going to take a look in some depth at some of the bodily systems and the disease process, because there too we can see how this wonderful arrangement enables all things to achieve optimal functioning. The more we understand protection and growth, the more we can live richer and more fruitful lives.

The bodily systems

There are twelve major organ systems within the body. These are: the digestive system, immune, central nervous system, endocrine, circulatory, lymphatic, integumentary, skeletal, muscular, respiratory, urinary and reproductive systems. Each one performs a unique and essential role. The name for each system essentially summarises its tasks and functions, probably with the exception of the integumentary system which is the set of organs that forms the external covering of the body, protecting it from the threat of abrasion, infection, UV rays and other radiation as well as chemical insults to the organism.

The skin is part of this integumentary system (also known as the exocrine system). The wonders of the skin are many. It is the largest of the organs and its functions could be summarised as offering protection against extremes such as infection and temperatures, it maintains balance within the bodily fluids and synthesises vitamin D.

The skin produces melanin to protect the body from the carcinogenic effects of the environment. It also has a keratinised epithelium, which is a multiple layer of cells leaving us largely impervious to water.

The skin is made up of three layers - the epidermis, the dermis and the hypodermis. The epidermis is what we can see and would normally refer to as skin. It has a protective quality as it serves as a guardian to the dermis and the more vulnerable underlying tissues, protecting them from desiccation (drying out). It has no direct supply of oxygen and so its nutrients and oxygen are acquired through diffusion (a physical process that refers to the net movement of molecules from a region of high concentration to one of lower concentration). In this instance, this means its oxygen supply is coming from the dermis.

There is a relationship between these two that wonderfully illustrates the protection and growth story. The epidermis could not do its job of protection without the oxygen and nutrients provided by the dermis. The dermis also provides a rich source of immune cells that rise up to the epidermis, which in turn offers it protection from the environment.

The dermis on the other hand could not keep the circulation going, managing the production of waste and the production of the keratin cells that are continually required to renew and repair the epidermis if the epidermis were not both holding everything in place and keeping out the external threats. We lose millions of skin cells every day and so the dermis's task is a relentless one in its support of the epidermis – and so we can see that the one dermis cannot do without the other.

The sweat glands are another important character in this system. In the Reach Approach we often use the term 'the secret of health is the removal of waste'. This is true at every level in human health and the sweat glands excrete a variety of waste products, which enable the system to function in a more optimal way. They also are involved in temperature regulation – essential for maintaining the body's temperature at 37 degrees Celsius (98.6 degrees Fahrenheit), although this may vary according to time of day, lifestyle and age, ranging from 36.1 to 37.2 degrees.

Within the integumentary system there is a variety of somatosensory receptors (sensors in skin, muscles, tendons and joints) and nociceptors (a sensory neuron that responds to threat or damage). These receptors detect the external stimuli and in the face of potential threat or damage - from thermal, chemical or mechanical stimuli - send signals to the brain and spinal cord. They serve as a warning system prompting us to take evasive action where necessary. Inflammatory mediators (prostaglandins, cytokines and serotonin) are released by any damaged tissue or infection, which in turn triggers the nociceptors.

Here we see another aspect of the co-dependent relationship between protection and growth. When there is a threat from the environment, the signals detected via the epidermis cause the dermis to respond by producing the necessary biochemical response. The nociceptors warn us to take evasive action through the sensation of pain. Any inflammatory response, which is triggered by the damage to the organism also causes the nociceptors to register pain. Both the inflammatory response and the pain are signals demanding that the body protect itself.

There is much more activity taking place in the integumentary system, which is bound up with health. There is the production of oils and how they are used to protect the skin and their role in healing and rejuvenation. There is the incredible network of nerves sending an enormous amount of data around the whole body all of the time, ensuring that each appendage is cross-referencing with the other body parts, which is critical to coordination and balance.

The data stream taking place at this level which is then being interpreted by the dermis and distributed to the billions of cells bound up with this organ/system, is unimaginable but in every action and transaction we can see that the system is always protecting itself to ensure growth.

With the hypodermis, which is essentially where the fat resides in the body, it provides insulation, padding and storage. We tend to think of fat as bad, especially in this time of increasing obesity and of course when there is too much fat, this is the case. However, the hypodermis exists to protect us from the outside world. It also attaches the skin to the muscles and bones supplying them with blood vessels and nerves ensuring body-wide communication. This is one of the ways that the different systems speak to one another.

We can see here the overlap between the circulatory system, the respiratory, the skeletal, muscular and immune systems - and supporting these is the digestive system, providing the energy and nutrients for these activities to take place. The more you look at all 12 systems, the more you can see that there is multilevel communication taking place between them all the time.

This is something I referred to in Synergy as The Story of Light. Billions of activities are being coordinated via an electrical, bio-chemical and mechanical system, which constantly communicates via countless informational dual carriageways in the body. Data is being taken in via the senses and decisions about what actions should or should not be taken are produced.

All the time the conductor, protection and growth, is coordinating the orchestra of life. This state is described as homeostasis – the point of equanimity and balance, which the brain and the mind interpret as well-being, producing feelings of peace, joy and bliss – which of course is the primary objective of life.

Let's delve further and take a look at another system...

The lymphatic system

The meaning of the word lymph is 'clear water'. Lymph is a fluid, which flows through the lymph vessels and nodes.

There are three primary functions of the lymphatic system. These are: the surveillance of the immune system, assisting with keeping infections at bay, returning fluid back to the heart to maintain fluid balance and to protect this critical organ from infections. Thirdly, it helps larger molecules like essential fats and hormones to enter into the blood where they play a crucial role as messengers to the other organs and glands.

Each day a significant amount of fluid and proteins seep out of the vascular system through the slightly porous walls of the tiny capillaries. Most of this fluid gets reabsorbed again by the capillaries but that which is left behind forms the interstitial fluid (a sub-category of extracellular fluid - the other sub-category is blood plasma) around the cells.

This fluid must find its way back to the blood in order to keep the blood volume and interstitial fluid volume constant over time. A lowering in blood volume has an impact on the heart as this raises blood pressure, which in turn makes the heart work harder pumping blood around the body. It is the lymph vessels that collect the interstitial fluid and return it back to the blood. Once the interstitial fluid is in the lymph vessels it is called lymph.

Lymph vessels don't have a pump to move the lymph around the body. The smooth muscle of the lymph vessels responds to the pulsing of nearby arteries, acting like a pump. Then the skeletal muscles contracting during the course of everyday activity exert pressure on the lymph vessels, which likewise continue to push the lymph through the system, travelling from capillaries through to vessels, trunks and finally ducts. At different points via the trunks and ducts the lymphatic fluid can be distributed where needed.

As previously stated, lymph plays a vital role in getting hormones and nutrients such as essential fatty acids into other parts of the body via the blood, where the molecules are too large to travel via the capillaries. This is a critical function because those hormones and fats would otherwise not reach their destination.

Along with this important hormonal and nutritional role, comes arguably the lymph's most important role, which is supporting the immune system. It's a vigilant observer, identifying foreign bodies and preventing them from entering the blood stream where they would become a systemic threat, therefore not only affecting one organ or system but having the potential to threaten the whole organism.

The lymphatic system's virtues do not end here. It works hand in hand with both the digestive and respiratory systems. In both instances diffused lymphoid tissue can be found lining the gastrointestinal and respiratory tracts. There are also lymph nodes, which are balls of lymphoid cells bound together with protein in key areas of the body, such as the groin, the neck, armpits and in the intestinal wall.

When an infection gets into a tissue it can move into a lymphatic capillary and then a lymphatic vessel, to be drained into a lymph node. Here, dendritic cells continuously examine the lymph identifying pathogens and pass them on to other immune cells (B cells) which make antibodies in response to the nature of the pathogen.

Once the B cells experience anything that is foreign or a threat, they turn them into plasma cells and start to churn out antibodies, which travel from the lymph into the blood. Running parallel to this, there are also circulating T cells, another kind of lymphocyte, which move between the lymph, lymph nodes and blood also on the lookout for infected or abnormal cells and pathogens that have been marked by antibodies for removal.

As if the lymphatic system weren't amazing enough in the countless tasks it performs, it has amongst its cast two other incredible organs that help to protect us even further, the spleen and the thymus.

The spleen is about fist-sized, found on the left side of the body, below the diaphragm and above the stomach. In its interior there is white pulp and red pulp, both having very specific and distinct roles. The white pulp is where antibody-coated bacteria are filtered out of circulation and antibodies are made by B cells.

The white pulp essentially works like a huge lymph node except that it receives blood rather than filtered lymph.

Old and defective red blood cells are destroyed in the red pulp of the spleen where their constituent parts are either broken down or recycled. Another valuable function of this lymphatic organ is that it holds in reserve red blood cells and platelets which can be called upon at times of emergency.

The thymus (located above the heart, about where the average necklace might lie) is responsible for the production of T cells and enabling the body to fight infections. It also produces several hormones and as a result it is involved in the endocrine system and the immune system as well. Here we see again the intertwining of activities and functions - different organs and systems playing multiple roles, all busy protecting the system they are a part of and yet being integral to the other neighbouring systems.

This is why it is ludicrous to think of talking about these twelve systems as if they are separate and distinct when nowhere in the body is this true. Protection in one organ or system is facilitating growth somewhere else.

The final lymphoid organs I want to mention are the tonsils. They form a ring of lymphoid tissue around the throat, acting as gatekeepers to the pathogens that are imbibed either via the food that we eat or the air that we breathe and are another example of the protection and growth dynamic.

What this brief overview illustrates is the intimate relationship between the lymph and the circulatory system, the immune system and endocrine system. The lymphatic system has a critical role in maintaining blood balance, a task the circulatory system could not perform on its own. It needs the lymphatic system's cooperation because the lymph is able to travel through capillaries which blood molecules are simply too large to travel through. Vital nutrients take advantage of this facility too. The lymph's waste management system is absolutely vital to the health of the organism. With the lymph's cooperation blood pressure is kept down and the heart is protected from working too hard. At every step we can see that it offers the body valuable protection, which leads not just to our survival but enables us to thrive.

Wherever we find protection, growth is never far away and wherever we find growth, protection is its most loyal suitor.

Let's take a look at one more of these amazing systems that work tirelessly to keep us alive.

The digestive system

The digestive system essentially comprises a long tube (gastrointestinal tract) through which food passes. This begins with the mouth, then the pharynx, oesophagus, stomach, small and large intestines and anal canal. Along the tract there are some essential organs, critical to the digestive process, including: the teeth, tongue, salivary glands, liver, gall bladder and pancreas.

There are four main tasks that the digestive system oversees. These are ingestion, digestion, absorption and excretion. Ingestion refers to the intake of food, digestion to the breaking down of this food into nutrients. Absorption describes the passing of nutrients into the blood stream and excretion the removal of waste products.

What's critical to understand is that digestion begins in the mouth. This makes chewing probably the most important part of this process because when we don't chew our food properly the digestive system, at each of the subsequent stages, has to work much harder to deliver the potential of the food that we've eaten. This is why we shouldn't underestimate the value of chewing. There are so many health problems that begin in the mouth.

During the eating process, the teeth, tongue and the hard palate or roof of the mouth against which the tongue presses food, work together to break down the food and shape it into a bolus ready for swallowing. The uvula (flap at the back of the throat) acts like a valve to make sure the food goes down, rather than into the nasal cavity. During this mastication process the three sets of salivary glands secrete amylase, which is essential for breaking down carbohydrates as well as lubricating and compacting the bolus.

Once swallowed the food passes through the pharynx and on to the oesophagus. At this point there is a spoon shaped flap called the epiglottis that seals the airway so that food moves down into the stomach rather than into the lungs. This is protective action by the digestive system, which protects the respiratory system from possible invasion of food matter, which would cause infection.

The gastrointestinal tract is made up of four layers of tissue/muscle and due to nature's ingenious design a wave like motion is created, making sure that food is propelled in one direction only. This process is called peristalsis.

This wonderful event would not be possible were it not for the contribution of the circulatory and muscular systems as well as the central nervous system.

At different points along the gastrointestinal tract there is a thickening of the tract and at these points there are six sphincters - and each of these is crucial in protecting the rest of the body from the negative consequences of food being displaced. They ensure proper transit of the food and offer an additional service in the process.

Here's a brief summary of the six sphincters:

The upper oesophagus sphincter:
The primary role of this sphincter, as stated earlier is to prevent food from being aspirated into the lungs, which can cause a whole host of health problems.

The lower oesophagus sphincter (also known as the cardiac sphincter):
The primary role of this sphincter is to facilitate food being passed from the oesophagus into the stomach and to prevent acid from finding its way up into the oesophagus, which can have a detrimental effect on the heart.

The pyloric sphincter:
This is located where the stomach meets the duodenum (the small intestine). It opens to allow partially digested food into the small intestine for further digestion and absorption of nutrients.

The sphincter of Oddi:
This is located where the bile duct and pancreatic duct meet the duodenum. This opens when food has been eaten to allow for digestive enzymes from the pancreas and bile to assist with absorption.

Ileocecal sphincter:
This sphincter is located where the small and large intestines meet. It allows partly digested food (chyme) to pass through to the large colon and it is theorised that its other role is to prevent small intestinal bacterial overgrowth.

Anal sphincter:
This is located at the end of the gastrointestinal tract and its role is to facilitate the expelling of faecal matter. There are two aspects of this valve; the inner sphincter is not under our conscious control and it prevents faecal matter from leaking out. The outer sphincter is under voluntary control allowing for the individual to control their bowel movements.

As we look more closely at these transactions, we can see the numerous energy signatures forming energy contracts - each one promising its assistance and cooperation based on the unconscious belief that it will receive what it needs from the other systems.

Let's conclude this section by looking at how the digestive process goes on to provide the energy and nutrients for the whole network – literally nothing would work without its tireless contribution.

Within the four layers of the tract, which I referred to earlier, is a dense layer of tissue known as the submucosa. There you will find a network of blood vessels, nerves and lymphatics ready to lend their support to the miracle of digestion.

There is also buried in the submucosa the submucous plexus, which secretes digestive juices to ensure the proper breakdown of food stuffs into the relevant micronutrients. The submucous plexus also controls the size of the blood vessels.

There is another mucosa known as the intestinal mucosa. This is the part of the gastrointestinal tract that comes into direct contact with food. The three layers facilitate the breakdown of the food and the secretion of digestive enzymes and mucus, which manage the absorption of food. Blood and lymph vessels are found at this point too because the lymph is charged with the task of dealing with any potential threat or infection and the blood with carrying the digested food to its many and varied destinations.

The stomach has a pivotal role. The oblique smooth muscles within the stomach contract and expand helping to further churn and digest the food. There are millions of gastric glands within the stomach and their secretions include hydrochloric acid, which ensures any pathogens that have made it this far are destroyed. Pepsin (an enzyme) has the responsibility for breaking down proteins. Mucus is produced at this point to protect the stomach. Water turns the bolus into a liquid-like pulp making it more readily absorbed.

From here the food moves on into the small intestine, which is where most of the digestion and absorption takes place. The pyloric sphincter opens to allow its passage. The name 'small' intestine is a little misleading, given that it is about 35 feet long (10.5 metres), so hardly small!

There are three parts to the small intestine, the duodenum, the jejunum and the ileum.

The small intestine along its length has a corrugated appearance and so has many ridges and grooves and on each of these grooves there are small protrusions called villi. On each of these villi there are tiny microvilli. This feature of the gastrointestinal tract increases the total surface area of the small intestine hugely (making it approximately 250 square metres – about the size of a tennis court) and this greatly enhances the absorption of nutrients.

The absorption of nutrients however cannot take place without the input and cooperation of the organs I mentioned earlier, which are partners in this process of digestion – the liver, the pancreas and the gallbladder.

The liver, the large organ sitting on the right side of the body beneath the diaphragm, amongst its many other vital roles, synthesises bile. The bile is stored in the gallbladder which is a small organ sitting immediately beneath the liver - ready for any demand made on it. When the small intestine detects fat content in the partly digested food, it releases a hormone-secreting messenger into the blood, which then travels to the gallbladder signalling it to secrete bile from the bile ducts into the small intestine to help with the digestion of the fats.

At this point the emulsification of the fats takes place. This is essentially the breakdown of the fat globules into smaller droplets (micelle) making it easier to digest.

The pancreas now performs one of its vital roles providing the necessary digestive enzymes to further break down the chyme. The enzyme amylase is used to break down carbohydrates creating oligosaccharides. Protease breaks down proteins, creating peptides and lipase continues the breakdown of fats, creating fatty acids and glycerol – all of which helps with our uptake of nutrients.

At this point, to protect the intestinal mucosa from the hydrochloric acid in the stomach, the pancreas is stimulated to secrete water and bicarbonate, which neutralises the acidic content. By altering the pH in this way, the digestive enzymes are able to work more effectively. Bicarbonate is so critical to this process that it is secreted from numerous glands in the submucosa of the duodenal wall.

Absorption is now reaching that critical point. The fatty acids and glycerol are able to make their way from the small intestine into the lymphatic system, which will play its part in carrying these nutrients to the blood, but the carbohydrates need to be broken down further to ensure their absorption. The enzymes in the small intestine responsible for making the oligosaccharides into monosaccharides are called maltase, sucrase and lactase - creating simpler sugars, glucose, sucrose and galactose, ensuring they can be better absorbed and utilised in the best way by the body.

Running parallel to this, peptidases break down the proteins into amino acids, which are more readily absorbed into the blood stream making their passage easier to whatever tissue, organ or system needs them.

What isn't absorbed in the small intestine (such as fibre) passes through the ileocecal sphincter into the large intestine, the colon, which surrounds the small intestine. The bacteria contained within the colon, known as the gut microbiome, as you may remember is especially important in relation to mental health.

There are literally trillions of bacteria that rush in at the point the undigested food enters the colon. We know that the bacteria colonising the colon help to produce vitamins B and K. A variety of gases are also produced in the process, such as methane and sulphurous compounds.

Peristalsis again drives the chyme through the ascending colon, the transverse colon and the descending colon, en route to the rectum. This process, subject to the nature of the matter and the health of the colon can take hours, even days to complete. Along the way the colon absorbs water from the chyme to help shape and produce the faecal matter, which we will eventually discharge with the aid of the parasympathetic nervous system and the brain, which manage this defecation reflex.

I hope you haven't felt too bogged down with the physiology and anatomy, but I do think some understanding of the process, which involves the naming of organs and systems involved, is necessary if you are to understand the synergistic nature of what's taking place inside us. Nothing is happening in isolation.

As you reflect on this journey of digestion, think about how many organs and systems have been involved in the process. Think about all the protective activities that have enabled growth and think about how growth underpins and ensures that those protective activities can continue.

It's fascinating to note that the more we understand what's really going on at the microcosmic level, the clearer the picture is at the macrocosmic level.

The disease process

You will hopefully remember the terms quantum dissonance, which relates to disharmony within the body and quantum coherence which relates to balance, harmony and coordination. Obviously, we're aiming for quantum coherence, which in brief means all the bodily systems are working in sync, no system is acting with dominance and so there's a spirit of cooperation and equilibrium running through all of the systems and their processes.

When there's neglect of any kind to any organ or system, it moves into protection. In other words, it tries to protect itself from any further malfunction or harm. The problem when a system moves into the survival or protective mode is that functions in other parts of the organism will be undermined and as a result various activities and tasks will not be able to be performed optimally and in some cases not at all.

It's at this point that the disease process begins. A tension now develops, where one organ or system is pulling against the other. One is pulling in the direction of protection and the other organs and systems are pulling in the name of growth, as those systems demand the energy that they need to complete their tasks. It may appear to the unknowledgeable eye that the body is working against itself, but this would be a short-sighted interpretation. What is in fact happening is each organ is doing what it's designed to do, which is to protect its community in order that it can grow. There is not a war but rather an attempt to survive. This tension puts the body into a state of anxiety and once the body moves into a state of anxiety, the mind is pulled in that direction too, so we don't simply have dis-ease in the body, we also have dis-ease in the mind.

It's actually important to point out that this process also works in reverse, where the mind has dis-ease as a result of a trauma, a bereavement, some other distress or anxiety, depression etc. These emotional states create a despair and/or dis-satisfaction in the mind, which causes the brain to produce the corresponding hormones and neurochemicals to try and alleviate that suffering. But in that process, the body is producing a range of toxic substances and when there is a continuous flow of these chemicals and neurochemicals entering the bloodstream, they alter the body's pH and biochemistry. At this point there is an undermining of the bodily systems.

And so, it's not simply a question of the body pulling the mind down, the mind can also pull the body down, such is the intimacy of their relationship. If one side is not fulfilling its obligations to their lifelong contract, then at that point the negative consequences are reaped somewhere within the system. This is where quantum dissonance begins to prevail, and quantum coherence is lost.

So, dis-ease left unchecked, whatever its source, will eventually create disease(s) either of the mind or body – or both. Everything covered in this book and its predecessor is designed to help you minimise this and where it exists manage it in a better way.

One of the Reachisms we use a lot in our work, and I believe will be helpful to you is 'the problem and the solution live in the same place'. This is why, if we understand the aetiology of disease, we will find many of the answers we need to create/restore health and well-being.

Let's look now at the social aspect of the protection and growth dynamic...

Social protection

Much of the debate around social protection focuses on the relationship between economics and the environmental context in which people live. Social protection is defined by the United Nations Research Institute for Social Development as: preventing, managing and overcoming situations that adversely affect people's well-being. In other words, seeking to alleviate poverty and hardship with the understanding that if we improve the mental and physical health of a group of people, using the appropriate programmes and legislation, they can become positive contributors to society, therefore adding to the economic prosperity, not only of their own families but also the wider community.

There is mounting evidence especially in developing countries, that where policies that are designed around social protection are implemented, there is a positive upturn in both the housing and labour markets. The ODI (Overseas Development Institute) is an independent, global think tank, which focuses on using evidence and research to encourage movement towards a more peaceful world in which every person thrives. They have, alongside other commentators, been trying to spread the message that in order for a community and society to grow, it must protect its most vulnerable parts.

The ODI has produced numerous articles on how to create sustainable livelihoods, address the consequences of natural disasters and climate change and the impact of migration. The organisation since the 1960s has sent its researchers, economists and statisticians to more than forty countries in Africa, Asia, the Caribbean and the Pacific regions, all with a view to gathering the data to support the need for a policy of protection, promoting economic growth by enhancing the well-being of the world's citizens.

The World Bank is probably the most notable organisation actively investing in social protection. They have what they describe as a unique global partnership with over a hundred and eighty-nine members from a hundred and seventy different countries. They are busy combining their creative intelligence, research, political will and resources all in the name of creating sustainable solutions, particularly in developing countries.

Their brief is clear, they offer financial, practical and technical assistance to those communities and organisations that are struggling to develop strategies for coping with their economic and environmental challenges. This is not about hand-outs, it's about empowerment through education, targeted investment and the sharing of experience.

The reason social protection is important is not purely because of the economic advantages it creates. It goes much deeper than this. The most important thing I've discovered through my work is the need for people to have a feeling of meaning and purpose. The more useful and valuable people feel the more they want to contribute in a positive way.

If they are handicapped by inequality, poverty or any other kind of disadvantage, then the innate desire to be the best version of themselves is diminished, leaving them feeling marginalised, having little or no value and therefore unsure of who they are and where they are going. This can lead individuals to find their way to making inferior choices such as turning to self-harm in all of its different forms and a whole host of other mental health problems emerging as a consequence. For others it can be the precursor to a life of crime, born out of their feelings of neglect, low self- worth, exclusion and anger with a society that doesn't seem to care.

I'm certainly not excusing the behaviour of those who pursue a life of crime, I'm simply explaining that in all of the organisational environments in which I've worked, including prisons, schools, hospitals, private sector organisations, colleges and universities, I've seen a clear correlation between the person's sense of their own value and usefulness and the lifestyle choices that they make.

We need to be encouraging social protection, starting with our own families, ensuring that we root out any inequality and unfairness in terms of how our relationships and family systems are managed. This needs to extend to our neighbours, colleagues, friends and wider family. If we can all make a difference in our personal universes, we become positive contributors to a better world order.

We can't complain about what we're seeing happening in the world if we're not trying to do something about it. Social protection is kindness in action... compassion.

To be compassionate is to actively be kind in a way that starts with the self and reaches out to every area of our lives. Then we, our families, our communities and our world will flourish and grow. Find a way to become part of the social protection movement.

In this chapter, we've looked at the need for a manifesto for positive change and how safety and security are part of that picture. We've explored the cell, bodily systems, the disease process and social protection and I'd like to complete the chapter by looking at the role of the oceans.

On the face of it these subjects may not seem related and yet I hope you can now see the far-reaching influence of protection and growth - and its primacy in every aspect of the human story.

The pivotal role of the oceans

This is not meant to be a meteorological lesson because there are many publications and tutorials that will do a better job of explaining this subject. However, I think looking at the oceans and some of their critical dynamics and functions is another very useful way of illustrating some of the concepts we've covered thus far, such as: energy contracts, meeting the needs of the four environments and protection and growth.

70% of the earth is covered by water (mainly bound up in the seas and oceans) and so it is imperative that we maintain the health of the seas and oceans given their pivotal role in shaping our climate and influencing the weather patterns.

One of the most important facts is that the oceans produce more than half of the world's oxygen and kindly absorb fifty times more carbon dioxide than our atmosphere, a function they do not get sufficient acknowledgement for, because if it were not for the oceans, we would all suffocate and die. It would not be an exaggeration to describe the oceans as our main life support system.

The oceans' currents are like a huge dual carriageway transporting warm water and precipitation from the equator toward the poles and in the opposite direction, taking cold water from the poles back to the tropics. This constant to-ing and fro-ing of the currents helps to regulate the global climate, dealing with any uneven distribution of solar radiation by transporting it around the world.

The seas have a slightly different impact on the climate as they tend to affect specific geographic locations. Coastal areas are much more likely to be wetter and cooler than inland areas. This is because of the winds bringing that cooler air from the seas. The effects of the seas in relation to the land will vary subject to which part of the world one examines, as there are huge differences between coastal areas in Europe when compared to Africa and Asia.

The bigger the land mass such as with continents, the greater the range of temperatures, but the primary principles of how the climate is affected remain the same.

Here's a brief synopsis of how water travels around the planet. It provides us with many insights about the vast number of factors involved in creating the climate and weather systems.

Firstly, it's the heat from the sun warming the land, seas and oceans that generates water vapour, which is gas that then rises up into the atmosphere. As you look up at the sky, there are literally millions of gallons of water vapour hanging in the air above you.

As the air rises it cools and its ability to hold the water vapour decreases. The higher the water vapour rises the cooler the air and as a consequence condensation is formed. The condensation process is unable to take place without the presence of dust, pollen, smoke or sea salt particles onto which the water adheres. These particles are known as condensation nuclei. When enough vapour condenses around the nuclei a cloud droplet is formed. These droplets are incredibly tiny but when combined, make a cloud - some cumulus clouds can weigh as much as five hundred tonnes.

The droplets, when loosely connected, form clouds. According to the way the droplets congregate, different kinds of clouds are produced. They are generally categorised into three groups. Cloud classification is usually arrived at by the height the cloud is from the ground and its appearance and texture. In addition, the positioning of the cloud brings different kinds of weather.

The three main categories are: cumulus, stratus and cirrus.

Cumulus clouds develop vertically. These clouds have flat bottoms and rounded tops. They are the white cotton wool looking clouds, which are usually only a few thousand feet from the ground. At this point they are known as fair weather cumulus. The more they develop vertically the more they are subject to the atmospheric changes. When there's sufficient instability in the atmosphere, they become thunderstorms, which means cloud electrification occurs (the colliding of electrically charged water droplets), producing lightning and heavy, even violently heavy rain in the process. The tops of these clouds can be as high as sixty thousand feet from the ground and it's at these much higher levels that thunderstorm activity is more likely.

Stratus clouds are grey, blanket formation clouds and they form horizontally, at varying heights – but they are usually formed at low levels. They don't generally produce any precipitation although they can produce drizzle. They typically indicate that rain is on its way. When they are close enough to the ground, they produce fog. When these clouds become even denser and have a more threatening appearance they are referred to as nimbostratus clouds (some would describe nimbus as the fourth category of cloud). Nimbostratus clouds bring with them significant precipitation – steady and heavy rain and snow.

Cirrus clouds are the thin and wispy clouds. They form at higher levels, which is why they are known as 'high-level clouds' - usually beyond twenty thousand feet. They are formed by the super-cooling of the cloud droplets which turns them into ice crystals. They are often the first sign of a warm front, usually meaning fair to pleasant weather is on its way. By watching them one can generally see how the weather is moving.

Whatever form the precipitation takes, ultimately the water returns to the land, seas and oceans and the water cycle begins all over again.

The oceans try desperately hard to stop the planet from overheating and distribute the radiation from the sun more evenly around the globe, trying to regulate the temperatures. Furthermore, their absorption of carbon dioxide is helping the atmosphere to maintain the quantity and quality of oxygen, therefore benefiting plants, animals and humans.

Unfortunately, our interference in the water cycle has and is still having a significant impact on the oceans' attempts to protect the ecosystem in order that growth can continue.

Those who specialise in water management and study rainfall patterns, in order that we can make best use of our reservoirs and our water consumption are quite rightly worried about the way we are polluting the seas and oceans.

We cannot talk about the oceans without also including the marine environment because the inhabitants of the oceans are also suffering, due to our environmental choices.

Somewhere between 65% - 80% of the pollution impacting the waters of the globe and the marine environment comes from the land. This 'runoff' from the land is known as nonpoint source pollution. Nonpoint source pollution comes in two categories. There are those that are described as small sources, that which is generated by buses, cars, trucks, boats and septic tanks and there are the larger sources which include: badly managed landfill sites, industrial waste and spillages, forests, farms and ranches.

To understand nonpoint pollution, we need to take our minds back to waste products and waste management, which we discussed in chapter 2. Here are some examples of how seemingly unconnected actions and events can impact on the wider ecosystem and the quality of life for all species.

When topsoil or silt runs into the waterways, if there's no appropriate slope management, which includes terracing or contour farming, the soil/silt harms the fish, other wildlife and their habitats are seriously affected. Poorly managed construction sites have a similar consequence as the runoff and air contaminants again find their way into the marine environment.

Our cars and other motor vehicles drop small amounts of oil each day finding its way onto roads, parking lots, in fact anywhere where those vehicles travel. There is also the air pollution generated by all forms of engines and a host of manufacturing plants. This air pollution, by virtue of the winds and atmosphere, finds its way into the seas and oceans.

This does not take into account what is happening with plastic, which has now taken the developed world by storm because it has become such a crisis in its own right. In fact, many parts of the world whose people are less guilty of the mismanagement of plastic and its by-products are suffering greatly.

The Great Pacific Garbage Patch is one example of this heinous crime. At the time of writing there is an area estimated to be twice the size of France where the ocean currents come together creating a whirlpool and as a result of the energy generated by the movement of those currents, the plastic debris is pulled into its vortex. The oceanographer who made this discovery (Charles Moore) has predicted that in the next decade it could double in size unless there is a radical change in behavior, underpinned by the political will to create change, not just at the individual level, but at the organisational level. He described it as 'a ginormous plastic soup made up of confetti-like fragments of plastic'.

Can you imagine the impact on whales, fish, dolphins, seals, seabirds and their habitats? It's not just these animals that are affected, it's the wider oceanic community that is being poisoned by the plastic. Some mistake it for food, whilst others get entangled in it. Either way the consequences are catastrophic. There have been numerous autopsies on birds, dolphins and whales where the evidence of the throwaway plastic mindset has been found in the guts of these animals – having ingested plastic bags, labels and other such debris.

The Great Pacific Garbage Patch is a warning that we must take this crisis seriously. For those of you who want to look at the impact of plastic on the planet and play some part in reversing the negative trend, there are numerous ways to get involved. A quick Google search throws up a list of options.

The evidence of the impact of nonpoint pollution is growing daily. Over a third of the shellfish growing waters in the United States are now so affected by coastal pollution that those industries are struggling to maintain their livelihoods. The National Ocean and Atmospheric Administration is working with the US Environmental Protection Agency, the Department of Agriculture and many federal agencies, trying to mitigate the effects of nonpoint source pollution.

Many scientists and environmental experts are turning their minds to prevention as well as cure as there is increasing recognition that to resolve the problem, both aspects need equal attention. Millions of dollars per year are going into coastal management programmes in an attempt to stem the tide. There are similar initiatives happening around the globe, spearheaded in part by the United Nations and other environmental campaigners and agencies. In truth much more still needs to be done, because our very lives depend on it. Finding a way to contribute, however small, is imperative.

Below is an extract taken from World Ocean Review (2010). I believe that the conclusion of this review was so powerfully and eloquently written that I've chosen to copy it in its entirety. It summarises the state of our world climate and what our roles and responsibilities are for creating change.

World Ocean Review is an international collaboration of scientists who are passionate about the health of the ecosystem and are active in trying to engineer positive change. They are funded by several international institutions and organisations concerned about oceanic health and marine biology.

"Climate change will affect the oceans in many ways, and these will not be limited to just altering the currents or heat budget. Increasing carbon dioxide concentrations in the atmosphere are accompanied by higher concentrations in the oceans. This leads to increased carbonic acid levels, which acidifies the water. At present the consequences for marine animals cannot be predicted. Similarly, very little is known about how the weakening of thermohaline circulation or the Gulf Stream will affect biological communities, such as crab or fish larvae which are normally transported by currents through the oceans. The dangers associated with rising sea level were again stressed during the climate conference in Copenhagen in 2009. Specialists today largely agree that sea level will rise by around one metre by the end of this century if the worldwide emission of greenhouse gases by humans continues to increase as rapidly as it has in recent decades. This will be fatal for island nations like the Maldives, which inundation could render uninhabitable within a few decades. The fact that scientists cannot yet predict with complete certainty what the future effects of climate change will be is not a valid argument for inaction. The danger is real. Human society needs to do everything in its power to bring the climate-change experiment to an end as soon as possible. The climate system reacts slowly to changes caused by human intervention, so there is a strong possibility that some changes are already irreversible. This risk should provide sufficient motivation for forward-looking action to significantly reduce the emission of climate-relevant gases. There is no time to lose in implementing climate protection measures. There are many indications that the most severe consequences of climate change can still be avoided if investment is made today in low-carbon technology. It is time to act".

This is a powerful warning that continues to be ignored. Our tokenistic gestures will not suffice. We have to wake up to the fact that protecting our world ensures our own growth. The one cannot exist without the other.

This concludes the overview of the enormous topic of protection and growth. I hope through the different lenses I've offered you've been able to see the interconnectedness of the issues and how what is happening in one area of our lives always has a bearing on something else – and we are never excluded from the consequences of those actions and transactions.

If we can better understand the nature of protection and growth, we can become part of this cycle in a constructive way, properly evaluating the side effects and consequences of our choices and decisions.

We need to become more aware, responsible and active. Seek to protect the planet, the land, seas, air, atmosphere and oceans, by taking waste management seriously. We also have to actively nurture and nourish the planet if it is to continue to provide an environment in which we will flourish.

It's not realistic in the first instance for us to think we can have zero impact on the environment, but it is realistic to think we can drastically reduce our impact and work towards a position of positive equity.

I believe everything in this chapter can be summed up by this one statement: without protection there is no growth... and growth ensures better protection.

Let's now move on to the incredible subject of consciousness, in particular the mind.

"You are not here merely to make a living. You are here in order to enable the world to live more amply, with greater vision, with a finer spirit of hope and achievement. You are here to enrich the world, and you impoverish yourself if you forget the errand".

Woodrow Wilson (1856 – 1924)

Points to remember

- The ultimate energy contract is between protection and growth. These two forces are involved in some way in every contract that is made. In a state of health, they work cooperatively for the greater good of that system or organism. However, if for some reason that relationship is corrupted and spoiled then the survival instinct kicks in - at that point the systems 'appear' to be working against themselves as they fight to survive.

- In a healthy organism or system protection and growth are equal partners, but when an unhealthy, diseased state exists, then protection takes primacy to ensure not just survival but the potential for further growth when the conditions allow. This relationship is driven by evidence - therefore it is not enough for us to want things to change and grow, we have to create the right conditions and then prove through consistent action that growth is indeed our ambition. Remember the universe runs on proof.

- Security is nature's primary narrative. When looking at human cells, natural vegetation, animals, consciousness and family systems, you find a craving for safety and security. Nothing can truly flourish in the harsh winds of uncertainty. In Maslow's hierarchy of needs, he puts our physiological needs before safety and security. Although it's indisputable that we need food, water, warmth and space to flourish, I believe that what is equal in need for the child when it begins its journey is the feeling of belonging, the feeling of love. Security is not a purely physiological phenomenon.

- We need a manifesto for positive change. We need to create safe spaces and places, 'environments of trust'. This needs to start in our homes and in our schools. To create these environments of trust, it is vital that we understand how essential it is to honour and respect the need to be loved, to belong, to be safe and secure. The crumbling of our society cannot be averted until we address these factors.

- Remember how the cell and the bodily systems are bound up in the eternal conversation of protection ensuring growth and growth funding protection; both forces at all levels of life collaborating for the greater good. We need to consciously sign up to these contracts, which gives our bodies the best chance for healing, recovery and growth.

- The disease process needs our understanding and respect. The state of disease is where a state of misinformation and misunderstanding exists - for whatever reason the conversation has broken down. We can either be passive by-standers in this state of malfunction or become emissaries for positive change. To become emissaries of change we need to be aware that even our thoughts have an impact on the disease process.

- Find ways to help eradicate inequality and poverty. Help to create a system that fosters inclusion and removes alienation. Don't turn your back on what's going on in your homes, schools, communities and in the wider social context. By turning our backs on what is going on we become part of the problem too.

- When focusing on protection and growth the pivotal role of the oceans is worthy of special mention, as they produce more than half of the world's oxygen and kindly absorb fifty times more carbon dioxide than our atmosphere. They are our main life-support system, and we owe them a debt we could never repay.

- The oceans also try desperately hard to stop the planet from overheating. They distribute the radiation from the sun more evenly around the globe in an attempt to regulate the temperatures. This amazing function of the oceans, alongside maintaining the quantity and quality of oxygen, ensures all plants, animals and humans can survive.

- Follow the example of the oceans by pursuing a philanthropic life. Becoming part of the 'gift economy' is a very powerful way to do that. Think big but start small. Encourage others to become part of this new way of thinking. The 21st century needs a new philosophy... and giving should be at the heart of that - because when we give without counting the whole world prospers.

A meditation to remind you of the primary themes of this chapter...

Protection and growth are intimately bound together... they are the heartbeat of the universe... these two forces, work in parallel, influencing everything we see, touch, feel and experience...

Protection enables growth and growth provides protection... the nature of all life is to express itself and grow... but without the loving arms of protection, that growth would be short lived... and I would not be able to reach my potential... what I've now learnt is that when the system is confused, protection can get in the way of growth...

I have fallen foul of this on numerous occasions... it usually happens in the company of fear... at that point the brain and the mind are scrambled and common sense, along with my creative intelligence, seeps away... it's at this point that I need to understand that protection is doing its job... which is to ensure I am not hurt or harmed... but when protection overreacts, then I find myself in a position where I cannot grow... in fact, I am stifled... this is where anxiety and panic ensue...

The brain informs the body of the perceived crisis... and the energies no longer work collaboratively... there is now a cognitive dissonance which creates a quantum disturbance... the body retreats into a protective pose, awaiting the threat... it's in my power to switch off this response... because the longer I spend in this protective pose... the more there is biochemical confusion and emotional disturbance...

I now choose to make my mind a peace-palace... I now choose to flood the brain and the body with thoughts of peace and reassurance... I now choose to instruct every cell and system within the body to release all anxiety and fear... I can feel the body letting go of hypervigilance, I am filled with a warm feeling of relaxation... it's divine... I move into a tranquil, calm space... the light of healing and well-being reaches every corner of my being... I relax more and more...

I now understand that I need to spread this message of protection and growth wherever I go... I need to live in this awareness... supporting these two giants to undertake their extraordinary work... this journey for me begins with self-care... but it must extend out into the world...

I cannot change all that is happening around me... but I can make a positive contribution in my home, my place of work... with my family, friends and colleagues... I can find ways to be a positive contributor, protecting those things that nourish and support life... and helping things to grow wherever I can...

I am at one with protection... I am at one with growth...

CHAPTER 4

THE FOUR ASPECTS OF THE MIND

"Yoga is the settling of the mind into silence. When the mind has settled, we are established in our essential nature, which is unbounded consciousness. Our essential nature is usually overshadowed by the activity of the mind".

Patanjali (Estimates range from 200 BC to 400 AD)

Change is a process, not an event

Our 'must have it now' approach has found its way into every aspect of modern life. So much so that when we can't have what we want our irritation and impatience can easily evolve into anger. Our sense of entitlement has bred a misunderstanding about the change process. It seems that now many self-help gurus and spiritual commentators are offering a 'quick fix', the promise of immediate change with less and less effort. I believe this is doing a great disservice because it offers hope, even certainty, in what are often unrealistic time frames. There are many now professing to address the worst kinds of traumas in one session and if one is not aligned to this solution focused approach one is somehow out of date and even worse in some cases accused of incompetence – all because it is believed that one size fits all.

There is no doubt that there are some issues that respond well to short-term intervention, however, if one is pursuing sustainable solutions, trying to fix deep or life-long issues, trauma, significant mental health problems and addictions, then these are generally not things that can be fixed overnight.

The Reach Approach is built on various psychological traditions. However, it should be made clear that psychology as a discipline in its own right has only existed since 1879, when Wilhelm Wundt opened the Institute for Experimental Psychology at the University of Leipzig and so he is widely considered to be the father of psychology – although there are those who consider Sigmund Freud, his more famous contemporary, to be the founder. It's more accurate to say that Freud was the father of psychoanalysis. He began practising seven years later in 1886. Whatever side of the debate one stands on, my point is that psychology in terms of human understanding is a fairly young discipline.

Psychology is the progeny of philosophy and has grown out of more than two thousand years of philosophical thought. Those aspects of philosophy that put greater emphasis on the emotional elements of the human condition were formulated into this discipline. It's at this point of divergence that I believe something was lost – a dilution of some of the ancient, potent ideas and principles. This is why, in my work, I have put as much emphasis on philosophy as psychology in order to build a model that embraces both and much more.

Philosophical thought was the first to examine the mind and behaviour. This began in ancient India, China, Egypt, Greece and Persia. Many classical works were produced at that time – each country and culture presenting the human experience through vast texts, poetry, prose and beautiful story telling. With the creation of psychology as a separate school of thought, some of the esoteric qualities and wisdom have been lost as psychology became more and more scientific in its examination of human behaviour.

It was in 1920 that John Watson passionately argued that psychology be defined as the 'scientific study of behaviour' and not a discipline focusing merely on thoughts and feelings. This movement away from introspective examination and what many would call subjective analysis has led to a more seemingly objective and empirical approach to human behaviour. This is why psychology is much more focused on personality types, classifications and labels, using various questionnaires, psychometric tests and statistical analysis to work out and conclude where a human is positioned on the mental health continuum. Can we be so easily categorised? Are the complexities of the human condition easily labelled? Is the intricate and fluid movement of consciousness something that can be defined by applying often rigid and logical analysis to a system that's dynamic and ever changing?

Labels can be a useful point of entry when trying to enter another individual's world in order to help. However, there is a downside with labels. They can also have us prematurely drawing conclusions about a person when there is not sufficient evidence to do that, leading to many misdiagnoses in the process. This is something I have seen a lot of in my clinical practice.

I should point out that this is not an attack on psychology. Psychology has made valuable contributions to our understanding of what makes us tick. I spoke in the previous chapter about John Bowlby's extremely beneficial work in helping us understand the role and nature of attachment. I question aspects of psychology because, as it has developed in a more scientific way, some of the original 'soul,' which relates to introspective thinking, has been lost. Increasingly we talk with certainty about someone's personality type based primarily on a questionnaire or a test they've undertaken.

My experience tells me you cannot extract enough data from any test to do that. We can draw a useful sketch and that can be helpful in guiding the direction of travel, but if we are too wedded to the categories and labels, we stop seeing that person's idiosyncrasies and potential.

The model I've created draws on both philosophy extending back before Christ as well as the psychological traditions beginning in the late 19th century. Both have different things to offer and in my view are made richer through their amalgamation.

One of the primary things we have lost with the division between philosophy and psychology is that sense of respect for time and the healing process – something much more evident if you consult some of the ancient texts of Patanjali, Confucius, Lao Tzu, Mahavir, Buddha and the Sufi Saints.

The masters, teachers and sages of those times had a deep respect and reverence for time and its relationship to change. They knew both were perpetually influencing life's unfolding. They also recognised and applied the natural laws to their philosophy, because they understood those laws were the essential cogs driving the universe.

Since we've tried over the last century to 'improve' the psychological models and the interventions to achieve change more quickly, I believe we have increasingly disregarded the nature of change, which is reflected all around us.

The solution-focused traditions have conceived many offspring, each offering a quicker, 'better' route to healing and recovery, but how many of these are truly sustainable? Can we manipulate and manoeuvre our way around the natural laws? Clearly there is a school of thought that has emerged suggesting we can, but is there an overreaching, maybe an arrogance, that has found its way into some aspects of psychological research and methods? I believe there is.

I welcome some of the newer methods and techniques that have entered the world of psychology and therapy. Amongst them are NLP, CBT, EMDR, EFT and other solution- focused therapies. I believe they have for the most part made a valuable contribution. However, there does appear to be a 'panacea mindset' that often is aligned to these methodologies. In some quarters they are presented as the ointment for every ailment and unsurprisingly clients and patients expect immediate relief from these treatments – but their limitations equally need to be acknowledged.

My experience and research show that there are many people still ensnared by their nemeses even after such interventions. I believe that this is because these short-term treatment programmes do not always identify the underlying causes of people's issues, because the timeframes they operate within do not afford sufficient exploration for the causes to be illuminated.

If we use nature as a mirror, she presents us with many clues with regard to the process of change. The seasons tell us that she will not be hurried. Regardless of what we do, nature faithfully changes her costume every three months. This is of course reflected slightly differently according to the part of the world we inhabit. Nonetheless spring becomes summer, summer becomes autumn, autumn becomes winter... and the cycle begins again, each phase taking approximately three months. At every stage within each season a multitude of changes, largely unseen, are taking place but the process rarely deviates from the time-honoured contract.

The body has its seasons too. There are literally billions of activities taking place simultaneously, all working tirelessly to keep us alive. At the cellular level cells are busy producing energy to carry out countless activities, imbibing nutrition, excreting waste, all beautifully choreographed by light. Approximately every twelve weeks the direction and the destiny of cells change, as new cells emerge replacing old ones – the previous instructions passed on to the new generation of cells who obediently honour what has gone before.

This seasonal change at the cellular level is also mirrored in the global changes of the body. Every seven years, just as the snake sheds its skin, we too sit in a different skin by the time we are seven, fourteen, twenty-one, and on it goes – every seven years, the body is renewed at every level – cells, tissues, muscles, organs, all part of the promise of further life.

The cosmos reflects the rhythm and nature of change too. The earth travels round the sun over a period of three hundred and sixty-five days, which is something we are all familiar with and within that annual cycle are the cycles of days and nights, weeks and months. There is an order, a precision, a design and when we go against that we create tension, conflict and even chaos.

It would be reasonable to ask what this has got to do with the therapeutic process - and my answer would be, everything. Therapy and personal development are simply methods that are designed to help us better understand the human condition, so we can engineer change that is beneficial and resolve issues that limit our development. But how can we do this if we are not honouring the principles of the world we inhabit? Why do we believe we are above the natural laws? Even worse, why do we think we can improve on that which has not fundamentally changed – namely the way change itself works?

At Reach we do not believe we can improve on the governing principles of the universe. In fact, we would go further and say it is folly to think that we can, and it is this attitude that has brought so many of the unwanted environmental challenges to our door.

This is why The Reach Approach is more than a counselling or psychotherapeutic model because it embraces numerous traditions and disciplines. It recognises that history, philosophy, science, religion, geography and spirituality, all have something valuable to offer. And the migration of our species around the planet, spawning many languages, cultures and traditions has also much to teach us if we are to liberate ourselves from our many ills.

I do not believe that we can actually be free without slaying ignorance – which means embracing much more than the education we've had and the cultural contexts we have grown up in. It means surrendering what we 'think' we know in order that further knowledge and wisdom can be imbibed. This requires great humility because so much conflict is based on opinion and dogma.

Change is a process, not an event. This is not a sound bite or a catchy 'new age' phrase. It's a deep and eternal truth. If we are expecting to really transform habits, patterns and drives that are feeding our unconscious and subconscious minds, then we need to recognise it's only when we meet the primary needs of the mind, body, spirit and environment that we are likely to experience the change that we seek. A single intervention or moment in time will rarely erase that which has taken years to be created.

In my view, the therapeutic process is not just about fixing the presenting problem, it's about learning the skills to live more mindfully, living lives that are steeped in an understanding of how we as humans work and how we relate to our environments, because the two can never be separated, which is one of the reasons why nature offers many of the clues in relation to our own growth.

I have spent so much time talking about the intimate contracts we have with our bodies, their organs and systems and with the planet that we inhabit, the land, the seas, the oceans and the atmosphere, because there is a deep connection between all life that must be honoured and revered.

The Change is a Process concept needs to be coupled with what I believe is the basis of sustainable change. That is: knowledge plus application equals personal power. I would go even further than this: knowledge plus application equals everything.

In chapter six I will discuss the difference between information, knowledge and wisdom, but for now I will simply say that those who consistently apply what they know with a sincere heart become wise and are able to liberate themselves and others.

A summary of the four aspects of the mind

The mind is such an incredible phenomenon and as a result it is extremely difficult to classify its numerous functions and astounding complexity. Over the centuries there have been many attempts to define the mind and its role in our lives.

Psychology, since the time of Freud and Jung, has provided us with many labels describing the anatomy of the mind. Some summaries and definitions are comfortably aligned whilst others present diverging descriptions and classifications. This has led to a situation where different theories and models have formed different interpretations about the topography of the mind. These different approaches are well documented for those who wish to research this area further. This, however, is not the primary concern of this chapter.

I believe that the mind's functions are best classified under four headings. These are: the unconscious, the subconscious, the preconscious and the conscious. These labels are not new and are already widely used (although the preconscious is less well known). However, I believe they are not always used with clarity and subject to the context in which they are used, they often mean different things to different people. In fact, the terms unconscious and subconscious are often used interchangeably as if they are one and the same thing.

In this chapter I will attempt to bring a level of clarification to this topic, enabling you to relate with greater understanding to what is going on within yourself and as a result, identify and fulfil your potential.

The unconscious mind

Our deep-seated memories, drivers and patterns are housed in the unconscious mind. The activities of the unconscious mind are driven by its overwhelming desire to protect us in order that we can continue to grow.

Everything we've ever thought, felt, said and done is recorded here. This is the hard drive where all data resides. Nothing is ever forgotten. When we 'forget', what we are really experiencing is a lack of access to a memory, event and time. This is one of many ways that the unconscious mind seeks to protect us from hurts and pain. It calculates the emotional consequences for revisiting certain experiences and can and does deny access when it feels the organism of the self is threatened.

Imagine remembering absolutely everything you've ever thought, said and done... all of the time. It would simply bring you grinding to a halt. It would be impossible to process it all and go on to make the best decisions and choices. You'd simply be overwhelmed. This is why it's primarily the impressions of our experiences that we carry with us - and those memories and feelings influence our outlook and behaviour.

Another way to think of the unconscious mind is as a cellar, which for the most part is kept locked and is largely immersed in darkness. The cellar is rarely visited; however, it contains an incredible library of information with an accurate record of everything, good, bad and indifferent, that has taken place in your life. However, without making special effort, most of what's contained in the cellar remains out of reach. If we are to be masters of our destinies, we need to make the effort to go fearlessly into the cellar on a regular basis, illuminating what's there.

This means performing an honest audit to establish the 'truth' about the real state of your inner world and facing demons you've denied and/or hidden away. Without this courage and honesty most of the contents of the cellar remain inaccessible and continue to influence and shape your life without your awareness.

Introspective practices like meditation, mindfulness, hypnotherapy and darkroom work can take you into this cellar and enable you to make those life-changing discoveries. (Darkroom work is a discipline only Reach practitioners are trained in – if you're interested in finding out more take a look at our website).

The whole Reach philosophy is built on the principle of making the unconscious conscious. Those things that remain in the unconscious mind that have not been checked, understood and where necessary resolved, continue in the present to shape your decisions, choices and life. As a result, we make the terrible mistake of thinking these things are simply our destiny, which allows the past to be recycled whilst we mistakenly call it 'the now'.

The subconscious mind

The forces shaping our personalities largely emerge from the subconscious mind. The habits, attitudes and values that govern much of our lives are propelled from here.

The subconscious mind is much more accessible than the unconscious mind, nevertheless in everyday awareness it remains largely out of reach. This is because for the most part individuals are living at the surface of consciousness, acting out of the conscious mind. To access and experience the subconscious world, as with the unconscious mind, requires a special kind of effort. The previous activities listed (meditation, mindfulness, darkroom work and hypnotherapy) can all help with this adventure.

Most people access their subconscious minds and indeed their unconscious minds more typically in the dream state. They step out of the conscious mind and enter that realm of uncertainty, creativity and imagination. As a result, dream analysis is another way that the subconscious mind can be accessed in order to unveil its secrets and messages.

Sadly, far too many of us dispose of our dreams without proper care and consideration, which is unfortunate, because dreams do offer many insights and understandings beyond what is available to us through the conscious mind.

Trauma is another pathway into the realm of the subconscious – bereavement, loss, war, torture, accidents and anything that is sprung upon us, often when we least expect it, can throw us into the subconscious arena, forcing us to face and discover those beliefs, thoughts and feelings that for the most part are out of view.

Obviously, it is more productive to access the subconscious mind through conscious decision-making and choice and I would encourage you to embrace self-examination fearlessly; and should you need help with this, don't be afraid to seek it out.

The preconscious mind

Intuition, instincts, insights and what many refer to as 'gut feelings' are residents of the preconscious mind. This is very much a 'feeling' mind, influenced by much more than logic. Many individuals discount its nudges and urges, which are described as intuitions or instincts, whilst others rely on them far too much when making decisions and choices.

The more you understand the four aspects of the mind, the more you realise it is balance that should be pursued above all else. There is an intimate dialogue, which takes place between the four minds that helps us to value the contribution each one is making for the greater good of the whole – I will explore this dialogue later in this chapter.

Gut feelings and intuition are a vital part of our repertoire. They bring to our awareness that which might not be seen or understood as a result of the machinations of logic and intellect. They invite us to question our calculations about a situation, person or event. Gut feelings and intuition call on us to take account of the invisible and the metaphysical. It's important to understand that logic and the senses although valuable tools miss so much of the data presented to us in any given moment and as a result cannot be relied upon to tell us the whole story.

The fairly recent discoveries about the four forces that shape our world (strong nuclear force, weak nuclear force, electromagnetism and gravity) have taught us that if we are to rely on our primary sense, seeing (if we are sighted), we can only see the tiniest fraction of reality on the electromagnetic spectrum. It has been calculated that we can see as little as 0.005%, which could be described as being blind. This puts into context how little of the world we can actually see. So, what might we be missing?

Logic does help us to 'see' our reality more clearly – this is where science has been invaluable – but we need to be aware that it too is limited. Logic without emotion is lame and emotion without logic is blind.

So back to gut feelings and intuition... they are by no means the missing link, but they are another sense (a sixth sense) that do add another perspective that we would be foolish to ignore. There is a difference though, between gut feelings and intuition. Gut feelings are instincts, intuition is informed instinct.

Instincts are often right as many times as they are wrong, but we're very good at remembering the times when they are right. This gives us a false sense of their accuracy. Intuition on the other hand, takes instinct and aligns it to experience and context. It realises that we can be deceived when we don't pay proper attention to the context in which something is happening. Our intuition is more likely to be right some three quarters of the time and the more we refine the relationships between the four minds, the more that percentage grows.

As you develop your relationship with the different aspects of the mind, the preconscious part will be one you come to respect more and more - and avail yourself of its wisdom.

The conscious mind

The conscious mind is the arena in which thoughts, feelings, moods and willpower are most prominent. It is the most accessible area as it interfaces with our everyday reality. Much of the game of awareness is played out in the conscious mind and one could argue that therein lies our problem – that we spend so much time entangled in our thoughts, feelings and moods that we are denied the other gifts of awareness, leading us to see a very narrow view of reality and as a result we end up misusing and mismanaging our willpower.

That said living at the surface of the mind is part of the grand design. If we think of our cellar, with the books, files, albums and countless pieces of data stored there in the dark, would that be the most sensible place from which to act out and express our creative intelligence?

We do need the data stored in the unconscious mind but it's the experiences, impressions and feelings that we need most, not the raw data. Those experiences, impressions and feelings are what become the basis of our personalities, habits, attitudes and values (the subconscious mind). They also become the insights, intuition, gut feelings and instincts that arise in the preconscious mind.

As a result of this stream of consciousness flowing through the unconscious, subconscious and preconscious minds, the conscious mind then enables us to live influenced by what we've experienced before but with the option not to be defined by it – which is the role of free will. Unfortunately, because these dynamics have not been understood, many of us end up being defined by the past and lose the discernment required to act in ways that are valuable and beneficial to us now.

If we are to live positive and healthy lives, we need to ask soul-searching questions. We need to check and re-check our intentions and motivations. We need to question and challenge what we are presented with as facts and see if they stand up to scrutiny. Only by probing in this way can we move beyond the familiar and discover the true meaning of life - which is to be the very best we can be and to find ways of empowering ourselves without harming others and sharing that empowerment in kindness and with love.

The Four Aspects of the Mind is another important piece of the jigsaw puzzle. I hope you will use the map provided here to improve your self-knowledge and your inner landscape. The better your understanding of the subtle contract between these four energies, the more likely you are to make the unconscious conscious in such a way that you do not blame destiny for your fate.

How the four aspects of the mind relate to one another

Having provided an outline of the four aspects of the mind, I would now like to focus on their relationships to one another. It's by understanding both the functions and their relationships that I believe one can better navigate one's inner landscape.

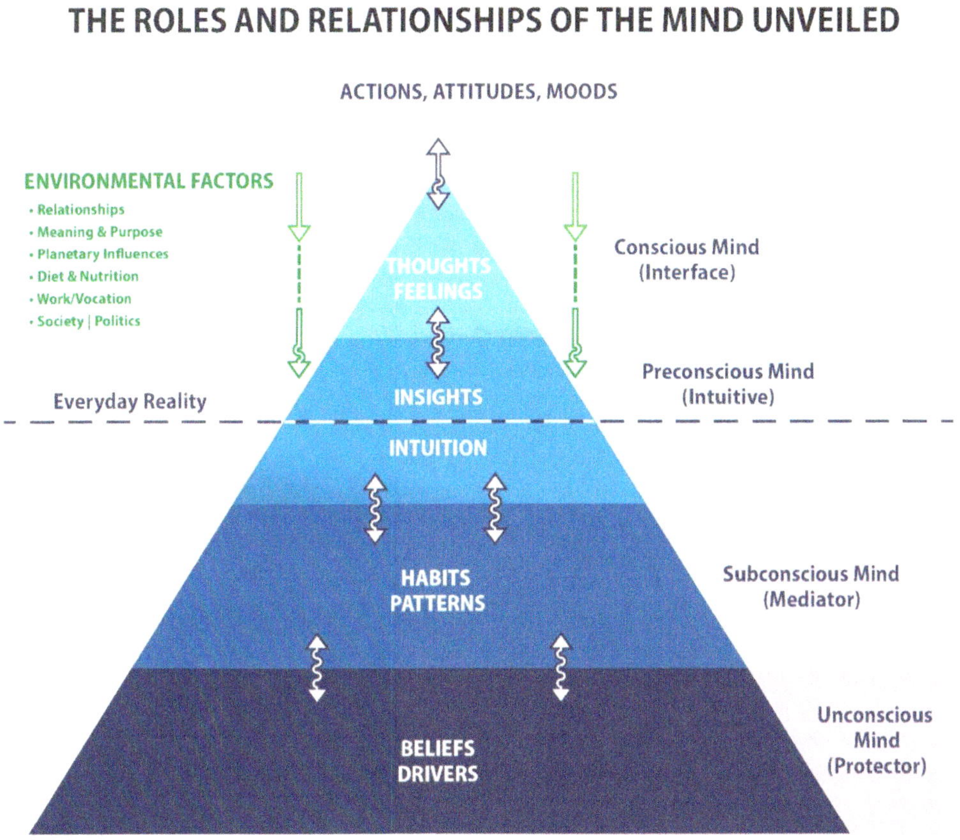

The unconscious mind

As described earlier the unconscious mind is the library where everything ever thought, felt and experienced is stored. It is vast and incredibly powerful. If we think of consciousness as an iceberg, the unconscious mind is the deepest point and in terms of influence and power, it contains somewhere between 40% and 50% of the overall capacity of the mind - although this figure can vary significantly according to one's experiences and personal evolution. In other words, this percentage could be much bigger, such as 60% to 70%, leaving one largely dominated by one's beliefs and drivers - unaware that the unconscious mind is essentially running the show.

The most accurate description of the unconscious mind's role and how it relates to the other three aspects is that of protector. This is its primary function. It is always using the evidence of the data it accrues to make what it 'believes' to be the best decisions and choices in the name of protection. This evidential characteristic of the unconscious mind means it is not persuaded by our hopes, intentions and dreams. It only believes what has been previously proven. It trusts nothing else because it retains substantial evidence of the promises and the pledges we have broken. Only actions and results that have been repeatedly played out make any sense to the unconscious mind. The whole culture of the unconscious mind is built on protecting those paradigms where promises have been kept. These 'promises' can either be positive or negative.

The way the unconscious mind relates to the rest of the mind is quite simple. Unless new data can persuade it to change course, it simply will not deviate. The unconscious mind is not fickle or gullible, and it will not be sweet-talked into taking a path it's not convinced is true and certain. There is however an unfortunate aspect to this characteristic; it often holds onto things long after they stop being useful. This is because the unconscious mind is simply 'data-matching'. It's not making value judgements - it is, after all, unconscious. The merit of the experiences coming in is not its primary concern - it's how they relate to the existing patterns.

The beliefs that are constructed in the unconscious mind drive all of human behaviour, feeding up their influence via the subconscious mind into the preconscious and conscious minds. It should be said for accuracy that this is a dual carriageway, so what is imbibed via the conscious mind will cascade down through the preconscious and subconscious minds too, eventually becoming part of the unconscious terrain.

The primary language of the unconscious mind is formed from our deep-seated beliefs and the drivers, which emerge from them. The best way to communicate with this realm is through repetition. Any activity that generates an obsession will find it has influence on the unconscious mind – whether it is healthy or unhealthy but since we are trying to change the internal dialogue, then of course we are concerned with healthy obsessions.

Activities that take the mind into trance offer a valuable inroad into the unconscious maze. Storytelling, metaphor, symbolism and imagery are also precious currency, which will help strike up a conversation at this level. There are also particular kinds of music that can take us deep into this realm. I will speak more about the influence of music (sound) in the next chapter. Aromas also have a special impact on the unconscious mind and so the use of specific fragrances can assist one in developing an unconscious connection.

In my view re-educating and aligning the unconscious mind to your highest hopes and expectations is one of the most important aspects of personal development.

The subconscious mind

The role of the subconscious mind in this intimate dynamic is best summarised as the mediator. It's in this arena of consciousness where an intimate dialogue between the unconscious mind and the conscious states takes place. The subconscious mind occupies about the same amount of territory as the unconscious mind – about 40%. However, if the unconscious mind has been left to dominate the inner mindscape, then the subconscious mind can find its role is significantly diminished as the unconscious mind then flexes its superior power in such a way that the subconscious mind's role of mediator is overshadowed and diminished.

Going back to our analogy of the iceberg, the subconscious mind is equally entirely submerged occupying the layer immediately above the unconscious mind. Its intimate relationship with the unconscious mind is the primary dynamic driving all human behaviour. But it's this critical role of being the mediator that we really need to understand.

If we are to carve out a new road of fortune, one that will serve us better in every regard we need the mediator to make the necessary representations to the unconscious mind. Sincerity is the key to the success of this conversation. It is the one with a sincere heart that can galvanise the powerhouse of the subconscious mind, which will then make a passionate plea to the unconscious mind for positive change.

This brings us to the importance of the preconscious mind in the establishment of a new contract, which will bring the paradigm shift that is needed if we are indeed to sit on the seat of self-respect and self-realisation.

Positive change depends on the preconscious mind being able to secure the services of the subconscious mind. Here we see again that it's the art of conversation that is driving the relationships between the different aspects, and when that conversation breaks down, we lose our way. This is the key to energy contracts – negotiating a mutually beneficial state of being where all parties prosper.

The primary language of the subconscious mind is shaped by habits and patterns and so if we are to communicate effectively with this aspect, as with the unconscious mind we will find that repetition, metaphor, storytelling, symbolism and imagery are wonderful media for achieving this. Sounds and aromas work well at this level too.

The preconscious mind

This aspect of the mind is best described as the intuitive. I would like to remind you again that intuition is not instinct. I find that they are often used interchangeably which I think is somewhat misleading. Intuition is 'informed instinct'. It has taken the gut feelings of instinct but has built a wisdom based on the additional experiences it has accrued. If we operate purely from instinct, we will be wrong just as many times as we are right. On its own it is quite a blunt instrument. We need the additional data that comes from experience and context for our instinct to become intuition.

It is the preconscious that is able to see beyond logic and the senses. Its primary interest is with the metaphysical because it realises this is where the magic happens - and being a slave exclusively to the conscious aspects of reality serves to deceive us. It 'knows' there is much more to the human story than what we can 'see'.

Other labels that have been used in different contexts to describe the preconscious mind include: sixth sense, third eye and ESP. They describe in different ways our ability to understand what is beyond the material world.

The preconscious mind unfortunately has for so many become redundant. The spiritual and the metaphysical aspects of reality are increasingly viewed with disinterest and scepticism. Although there appears to be a mini revolution surrounding topics like mindfulness and meditation, the truth remains that our overall interest in the deeper philosophical issues has waned as modernity has increasingly consumed our hearts and minds, with the growth in technology, countless 'quick fixes' and an expectation that our insatiable needs should all be met now!

It's not a surprise then that the 15% to 20% of influence the preconscious mind is capable of having when everything is balanced as it should be, can quite easily be reduced by two thirds – in some cases the preconscious mind is virtually non-existent as the unconscious dominates the inner terrain, reducing the influence, talents and capabilities of both the subconscious and preconscious minds.

When the preconscious mind is playing out its unique role, acting as the representative between the conscious aspects of the mind and the subconscious and unconscious minds, it seeks to persuade the subconscious that the new tendencies and traits being developed consciously are worthy of being considered as 'game changers'.

In my work with clients, it is primarily the preconscious mind that I am seeking to resurrect and develop. In our iceberg analogy, the preconscious mind is partly submerged and partly emerged. When in balance, that's about a 50:50 split. It is this unique role of straddling the conscious and unconscious areas of the mind that is critical for the negotiations that need to take place in order to bring about sustainable change.

All the personal development activities we promote at Reach help to develop the preconscious aspect. These activities develop our intuitive propensities, offering insight and the language needed to secure the subconscious mind's support.

The primary language of the preconscious mind is shaped by metaphysical concepts/ideology and deep-seated feelings – these are heartfelt, seemingly intangible murmurings emerging from the core. This is why introspective activities such as meditation, yoga nidra, conscious breathing, creative visualisation, mindfulness and prayer are all useful vehicles for communicating at this level.

The conscious mind

The conscious mind's primary role is best described as the interface. It's the meeting point between the external environment and the internal environment. It is where whatever transactions have taken place between the other three aspects percolate to the surface, shaping and influencing how we are in the world. Our way of being is visible through our moods, attitudes and behaviours. These, whether we know it or not, are symptomatic of the powerful relationships and politics that lie primarily below the surface, that bit of the iceberg that is not visible to the eye – somewhere around 80% to 90%.

The conscious mind is the least influential aspect at around 5% to 10% of influence/power. However, if the unconscious mind comes to dominate what's below the surface, the preconscious mind becomes largely redundant, thus allowing the conscious mind to double in size. This is not a good thing because it tends to mean that logic is dominating our behaviour and the emotional, subtler aspects that are of equal importance are diminished. It also means in these cases that we are much more likely to be wedded to dogma, caught up in the web of our own experience, perceptions and opinions. This is a dangerous position to operate from because we are unlikely to be listening and are less open to reason.

The primary role of the conscious mind, as it is 'front of house', is to receive data, information and experiences from the outside world and allow them to be vetted and sieved through our internal filters and respond accordingly.

The conscious mind is important in its own right and so its take on reality should also be respected, but when it is viewed in isolation, then a lot of reality is missed and misconstrued. It is important that the conscious mind is not overrun by the environmental factors. To that end, engaging in activities that slow us down, encouraging us to ponder and reflect enables what is happening at the interface to shape, educate and inspire us in the right ways – otherwise we simply become a set of reactions, rather than developing the art of being able to respond.

If we were operating optimally, although the conscious mind is the first point of entry, the preconscious mind would also be in attendance as the countless environmental messages pour in through our senses. This would lead to the best decisions and choices before the subconscious and unconscious minds step in to play their roles. It is here that we can achieve the momentum for positive change. If we nurture and cultivate positive activities, then the representations made by the preconscious and subsequently subconscious minds, are much more likely to succeed.

The primary language shaping the conscious mind is thoughts, ideas and feelings. It is much more likely to be persuaded by conversation, intellectual concepts, relationships and their impact on one's self-image and self-worth. Social conditioning has a big part to play in how the conscious mind receives or repels information.

Summary

Hopefully this overview will have helped you to understand the dialogue that is always taking place between the mind and its environment. There is a constant ebb and flow – messages making their way down from the conscious mind and in the opposite direction powerful urges, impulses and impressions emerging from the unconscious and subconscious minds which make their way to the surface.

The conversation taking place between the internal and external environment is arguably the most important conversation on earth and if we are not aware of it and so are not consciously partaking in that conversation, we become victims of circumstances.

We have seen that the conscious mind makes representations to the preconscious mind when seeking to undertake a new positive path and the preconscious mind when stimulated by introspective practices and positive pastimes seeks to persuade the subconscious mind - again through the art of conversation. At this point repetition, storytelling, metaphor, symbolism and invocation all become part of this dialogue.

If the subconscious mind is persuaded by the preconscious mind's representations it will go enthusiastically to negotiate with the unconscious mind for a new internal order and where there is sufficient evidence, it is the subconscious mind that has the ability and power to move the unconscious mind away from protecting the old paradigm and into protecting the new.

This is not an easy undertaking, because the unconscious mind only trusts and believes what has been laid down in action. This is why practice, patience and perseverance are most influential in bringing about lasting change. Intention and fine words carry no weight at this level, as the subconscious needs to provide evidence of change. Green shoots of promise need to be visible. Only then will the unconscious mind listen and become open to the new possibilities.

This is a subject that has many more layers, but if you can exercise in your own life what has been proposed here you can make incredible changes.

How to manifest positive change using the mind(s)

If you are going to manifest positive change in your life, getting your minds aligned is a very important part of the mix. And to do this, you will find it extremely helpful to establish some form of routine.

I would like you to think of discipline in its most helpful way – which is 'to become a disciple of' that which uplifts the mind, body and spirit. Discipline and routine are almost always aligned and what they promise, should we become disciples of their teachings, is power - not power over anything or anyone else but power which leads to absolute clarity, an unrivalled understanding and insight. A peace so deep that no storm can overturn, a contentment that is not reliant on anything external, because it drinks from the nectar of the soul - this is real power - unwavering and true.

This is a state of mind that seeks no acknowledgement because it is reassured by its own value and virtue. Please try to embrace routine and discipline. They will both protect you and ensure further growth.

I have spoken a lot about non-negotiables in my work. This is essentially about how to create a contract with yourself. It is around these non-negotiables that routine is built, and the single-mindedness of discipline will be required to actualise these non-negotiables.

The non-negotiables then become the engine of success because it is on the back of their momentum that your potential can be unveiled and then flourish.

What's the first step?

If you've understood the anatomy of the four minds, then you'll understand that each mind is concerned with its own primary function and is engaged in the activities that relate to that above all else. When there is clarity, health and well-being within the system, then the four minds work in unison.

Unfortunately, the way most of us live in the modern world means there is often tension and conflict between the four minds. The tension and conflict within the system leads to a wasting of our energy, our life force, leaving us often confused, living in unproductive ways. What is needed is an energy contract to bind all four together.

We need to educate the four minds, which is best done through introspective practices, because we need to set up a dialogue, which focuses on the merits of interdependence and cooperation. We need to spite the lie that autonomy will bring about contentment. This simply isn't true. It's only when the four aspects of the mind work collectively that we can find peace, clarity and joy.

How do we address this?

If you remember, in chapter 1, I spoke about the importance of identifying energy stealers, so you need to look at your life and work out what are your energy stealers, where are you wasting time pursuing activities that have little value? You'll find the energy stealers are also time stealers. They will account for you often feeling tired for what appears to be no reason at all. But what these time and energy stealers are good at is convincing you that what you're doing is so important you couldn't possibly be doing anything else, and they shouldn't be negotiated away.

This deceit keeps you going around in negative loops, which is what I've referred to in previous works as the 'hole in your soul'. No matter what you appear to be putting into your life, even the good things that you can lay claim to, there remains the feeling that you're not getting anywhere fast, and this is because you have numerous holes through which your life force is draining away. Therefore, task number one is to find these culprits and re-negotiate your contract with them.

Once you've identified the time and energy stealers your next task is to seek to conserve and consolidate energy. Energy is probably the best description we have for a force being put to work, but if we are to make that force useful and efficient, we need to find ways of containing it and managing it. This is particularly true if we're trying to engineer positive change, which cannot be done if we don't find ways to take our energy and make it productive. This is why once we stop wasting energy, we need to find ways to conserve it in order that we can focus it, in the direction of our choice.

This is where non-negotiables are vital because this is your pledge to yourself to use your energy in a particular way. All non-negotiables are conserving and consolidating. This does not mean that energy is not being expended because every action of any description is utilising energy. The state of absolute zero, which I've referred to in Energy Contracts, and have spoken about in The Story of Light is really a theoretical position, because there is never a point when energy isn't expressing itself.

What I mean by conserving and consolidating is that non-negotiable activities are creating a state of positive equity and so the net result is that one feels a sense of well-being and empowerment. We now have energy enablers, rather than energy stealers running the show. This shift aligns the four minds.

For the sake of clarity, it's important to say again what qualifies as a non-negotiable. Any activity, promise or pledge that we make and carry out at least 80% of the time can be described as a non-negotiable. It's unlikely that you can do anything 100% of the time. That said, making that your aim is what is most likely to help you to reach that magic 80% mark. Experience has taught me that those who aim for 80% rarely make it. You may find it helpful to look at Eight is the Magic Number which you'll find on the Reach website. It is an article that will encourage you to find at least two positive things you do consistently under each of the headings, mind, body, spirit and environment. It's a very useful map for those who wish to undertake this journey.

What next?

Once the energy stealers have been minimised and the energy enablers are in place what is needed most of all is patience. This is because as discussed at the beginning of the chapter, change is a process not an event. Understanding this liberates us from trying to force things to happen before the point of maturation. Our culture of immediacy is nailing us to the spot, preventing us from reaching our destination. Without acceptance and patience, we are unlikely to progress. This is where we need to master the art of living with our ambivalence.

Until we can accept those elements of ourselves that remain trapped, damaged, seemingly resistant to growth, the parts of us that are marching towards healing and recovery, will be halted in their tracks. We don't change in nice, uniformed ways, it's a far more ragged process, where some parts of ourselves can be highly evolved, even wise whilst other aspects remain immature, reactive, lacking insight. Dealing with this duality can be hard, which is why acceptance is needed as well as compassion.

Compassion is such a beautiful balm. It heals the most damaged parts of us through its unwavering kindness. It understands and accepts the change process, so never seeks to condemn or criticise because it knows change cannot be cheated. If we can accept that positive change takes time and parts of us are going to change at different rates, then instead of feeling self-loathing and anxiety we can enjoy the fruits of peace of mind and contentment.

With this attitude and approach the paradigm shift required in the unconscious mind becomes possible. This is because of the realignment of energy so the tension between the unconscious mind and the other three begins to change. The representations made by the subconscious mind are now heard with a different set of ears. The subconscious mind makes more passionate pleas for positive change because the consistency of right action and the more generous accepting state that has been developed by the conscious and preconscious minds carries the power of persuasion.

It's now difficult for the unconscious mind to resist these arguments. This position is the fruit of patience, acceptance, compassion and kindness. These qualities allow us to compose a new script, which forms the basis of a new drama and the old productions are discarded.

With a new production in place, each of the four aspects of the mind recognises that its optimum position only truly exists when it is aligned to the other three. Now progress can be achieved without fear of relapse, without concern about making mistakes. The journey can now be made with the understanding that we can't change the past, but we can change how we relate to it - and so positive choice is always available to us.

My invitation to you is to move forward with a kind and forgiving heart. Use your past and mistakes merely as tutors. Don't get stuck in the illusion of how awful you are because you will simply keep fulfilling past prophecies and deny the truth of how truly magnificent you are.

Help the four aspects of the mind by changing your internal dialogue... become part of the bigger conversation and your spirit will fly free.

"Knowledge born of the finest discrimination takes us to the farthest shore. It's intuitive, omniscient, and beyond all divisions of time and space".

Patanjali (Estimates range from 200 BC to 400 AD)

Points to remember

- Change is a process not an event. Our 'must have it now' attitude has found its way into every area of our lives, including counselling, psychology and psychotherapy. This is why there are now so many personal development and therapeutic models offering to address our issues in shorter and shorter timeframes. In fact, it's gone so far that if one dares to say it might take some time to resolve the problem, then clients/patients are disappointed and those who are part of the new solution-focused approach accuse such therapists of not being sufficiently skilled. The truth is that one size does not fit all and for many, where the issues are long-standing and complex, time is indeed required.

- Look to the natural world and you will see the seasonal nature of change is everywhere. Our bodies and their many organs and systems, the planet with all of its various eco systems: the water cycle, the carbon cycle, the oceans and the atmosphere - all are bound by the character and nature of change. Within its measured turning there are tens of thousands of activities constantly whirring around, holding life and the cosmos together, nonetheless it will not be hurried.

- Psychology is the progeny of philosophy. Psychology is more scientific in nature and as a result it has helped to create the more 'labelled' approach to diagnosis and treatment. We have become so busy in classifying people and their problems, through questionnaires, psychometric tests and statistical analysis that the individual has in many cases become overlooked. We cannot simply distill a person into our charts and classifications and treat them as if that is the totality of who they are. Labels can be useful, but we need to be aware that they can also be misleading.

- Understanding the four aspects of the mind offers you a powerful gateway into consciousness. The mind is immense in power and diversity and is a wonderful blend of simplicity and complexity. Remember the primary agenda with regard to positive change is to persuade the unconscious mind (the protector) to give up and let go of the old paradigms. In order to do this, we need to develop our preconscious minds as the unconscious mind is not easily persuaded.

- The unconscious mind is always acting in our best interests, but it does this in line with the 'evidence' of our experiences and actions. The habits and patterns we've created have brought about powerful drivers and those drivers only 'believe' what we do, not what we intend. To develop the preconscious mind (the intuitive) we have to engage in introspective practices. We have to calm and tame the mind, with reflection, with 'kind eyes' as we process our experiences, developing soothing, positive thoughts and by expanding our awareness.

- The subconscious mind (the mediator) acts as the representative for the preconscious and conscious minds. As we develop these new activities and skills and make promises (via our non-negotiables) it collects those files and acts as the barrister, making representations to the unconscious mind. The subconscious mind will only take up our case when it is persuaded by the evidence of our practice, that we are indeed passionately focused on becoming better versions of ourselves. Again, we see it's the proof of action (evidence) that calls all energy to respond favourably. It's not what we say, it's what we do that counts.

- The conscious mind (the interface) is the meeting point between the external environment and the internal environment. Remind yourself by looking at the diagram about the dual carriageway that is perpetually in operation between the unconscious mind and the conscious mind. Data is always percolating to the surface, influencing the subconscious, preconscious and ultimately the conscious mind. But equally what is being taken in from the world trickles down via the preconscious and subconscious minds and is ultimately deposited in the unconscious mind. To improve the relationship with the other three aspects the conscious mind needs to slow down and think before acting, and to remember that less is more.

- The four aspects of the mind can only be refined when we are aware of the energy stealers and actively avoid them. We need to form relationships with the energy enablers, this is the contract that will save us.

- To become masters of our destiny we need to understand the personality of each mind, its preferred language and how they relate to one another. Make time to refine your understanding of each. This is how you can become a responder rather than a reactor.

- Do not be deceived by relapses, they are part of the paradox of progress. Once we understand that making mistakes and falling short are opportunities to reflect, learn and grow, we no longer get caught up in the illusion of how awful we are and how awful it is. Develop a kind and forgiving heart and step into your most magnificent self... s/he is waiting.

A meditation to remind you of the primary themes of this chapter...

The mind is the most magical of places... it's a maze, a labyrinth of infinite possibilities... it offers us access into the known and unknown realms... because of its enormous capacity and its ability to retain all of our experiences, it can be hell or heaven... both can exist in this place... but I need not be frightened by this duality... because amidst this ebbing and flowing of infinite possibilities, lies the wonderful gift of free will... my capacity to choose whether I am victim or victor... my fate is not sealed... I can choose...

The mind has different levels each with its own role, capacity and functions... and what is clear is how I relate to each of these aspects, shapes my experience of reality...

The unconscious mind is the protector... it will go to extraordinary lengths to keep me away from harm... because it is governed by the evidence of my experiences, it will make choices that fit with what has gone before... this can be helpful but at times it can be a hindrance... it never knowingly tries to inhibit growth... but without persuasion its iron grip is not easily released...

The subconscious mind is the negotiator... that part of the mind that once persuaded is prepared to act as my representative for positive change... but it too needs the evidence of action to act on my behalf... intentions are not enough... only when it sees consistent application of a particular philosophy, will it go to the unconscious mind and invite a paradigm shift... when the subconscious mind is persuaded, my exit route out of the maze becomes clear...

The preconscious mind has been lost to awareness for such a long time... and so has not been treasured in the way that it needs to be... it's the place where intuition and insight coexist side-by-side... it's that part of me that can see what the senses deny... or is simply beyond their reach... it profits from relaxation, still time and silence... the more time I spend diving into the deep, immersing myself in the mind's many layers... the more the preconscious reveals its multitalented and resourceful self...

The conscious mind is where I have spent so much time... unfortunately missing out on the beauty of my inner world... I have been pulled and distracted by the external world... and so I have not made best use of the conscious mind... which is really my window into the world... only now can I see this... the conscious mind is the interface between the inner and outer cosmos... I explore my reality with an open mind... informed by my three other minds... enriched by their unique gifts...

Now that I better understand this inner terrain, I am no longer a slave to the mind... I'm no longer deceived by what's happening out there... I'm no longer handicapped by my shortcomings, or by my mistakes... this world of infinite possibility holds no fear for me any more... because I have realised that I can be the master of this world... simply by choosing to be that... and I do...

CHAPTER 5

DON'T FOLLOW THE STORY

"Creativity involves breaking out of established patterns in order to looks at things in a different way".

Edward de Bono (1933 – present)

Patterns – the DNA of actions

The journey of becoming (which I covered in chapter 10 in Synergy and can also be found on the Reach website) is a clear synopsis of the relationship between our behaviours (action) and our awareness (which is an expression of our consciousness). It illustrates how we each become the product of our behaviours and how our sense of self is constructed around that.

The journey of becoming offers a formula well worth remembering, which is: our behaviours become traits, our traits become habits, which lay the foundation for our personality. Those habits become patterns, which in turn set the foundation for our character. It is those patterns that then create the drivers, which lead to our nature. Our nature is the point in our life's journey when we have 'become' whatever has most dominated our thinking and inner world – good or bad.

Although it is accurate to say that it is thoughts and feelings that are the initial catalysts on the journey of becoming, it is actually what we 'do' that most drives the process. That isn't to say that our thoughts are innocent bystanders on this journey, because they certainly are not: they are arguably the 'things' that have done the most damage, often in a quiet, unassuming way, as they trickle their potent messages into the brain and the body. Equally, thoughts are the most powerful allies we have in the transformational process but only if they lead to positive actions.

Patternology is the term I use for describing the part that patterns play in our lives. The term simply means knowledge of patterns. Everything about human behaviour comes down to patterns. From the behaviour of the cell and the tens of thousands of actions carried out by each cell every moment we are alive, to the countless chemical and electrical actions and reactions taking place in the brain underpinning every thought and feeling – all are shaped and driven by patterns. These patterns become the sophisticated templates (based on past actions and learned behaviour) that establish ways of keeping both the mind and body surviving and thriving... or orchestrating their demise.

The power of patterns does not end there - everything taking place in the known world is influenced by patterns of one kind or another. Take a closer look at the disciplines of physics, chemistry and mathematics and there you will find laws, formulas and structures oozing with patterns, providing us with incredible insight about ourselves and the world. Patterns are why the world works.

Scientists and mathematicians are unravelling these patterns further - from the subatomic level to the macrocosmic level. These patterns create rhythm, movement and momentum, which is the heartbeat of life and the closer we look, not just through our microscopes, but using the telescopes of our minds, the more we discover that these patterns make everything around us make sense. Some researchers and students of this process are now referring to these patterns as 'The Code'.

The Code explains what appear to be random acts of nature. Conversely, it also explains the order and predictability we find in the world. It offers a description of a hidden mathematical world governing everything within our bodies, on our planet and beyond. The focus has largely been around a) numbers and how they influence literally every event taking place in life b) predictions about future events based on past data and c) how the many shapes and forms within nature are constructed. More research is needed but what is becoming clear is that everything from the invisible to the visible is governed by this code and the patterns inherent within it.

Patternology tells the story of how our past decisions and choices are literally making current and future decisions – assuming no other course of action is taken. The more we understand the power of patterns, the more we are able to extricate ourselves from the 'stuff' that enslaves us. Let us take a deeper look into the world of patterns and how they affect human behaviour.

Many are so entangled in the web of poor decisions and choices that they actually believe there is no way out. Freedom from their low self-esteem, destructive patterns and addictions seems like an impossible feat and so they sit in the place of doubt and disbelief becoming further entangled in this web of despair.

At this point they feel they have no choice and in fact decisions and choices are now being made on their behalf. They feel pulled against their will back into familiarity and further self-harm. This feeling of having no choice is very real and once we get to see how traits become habits, habits become patterns and patterns become drivers, we can, probably for the first time, understand why individuals can feel that choices are no longer available to them. It actually feels to them as if they are being 'chosen' rather than 'choosing' to continue down the pathways they are so desperate to leave behind.

Once patterns have been sufficiently installed, conscious thinking has largely been suspended as the unconscious and subconscious minds step into the primary roles of caretaker and decision-maker. The templates (drivers) that determine how we respond and react are housed in the unconscious and subconscious minds as we discussed in chapter 4.

The interesting thing to note here is that the unconscious and subconscious minds are not really making decisions at all, they are acting on those decisions that have been previously made and in the absence of any new evidence to overturn the templates, they continue to trust that those past decisions and actions are still serving the individual well. If we want to choose a different way of being, we must change those templates - and understanding how they are created gives us a real chance to do that.

However, this does not mean we have lost the right to choose, because we never really lose that right, it's more accurate to say that we lose the awareness of our option to choose and once that awareness is lost, we become victims. Victims of the past, victims of old relationships, ideologies, opinions and beliefs and before we know it, we are doing (mainly unconsciously) what we've always done - quite simply because we have not renounced the old scripts. It's now time to renounce those old scripts, it's time to create new patterns and in order to do that, we need structure, routine and discipline, coupled with compassion and empathy. This will help us to make new and better choices. In addition, we also need to cultivate faith and to learn to trust in our yet undiscovered potential.

To have faith means doubting yourself, the process, and maybe even those around you, and yet still taking steps of courage in the direction of positive change. For many on this journey, trusting means believing in nothing and no one, which includes oneself - and yet daring to believe in the possibility of personal transformation.

It is important to remember that when you begin this journey you are likely to be in the position of uncertainty and doubt and those feelings will, if you let them, sabotage any ideas and hope that you have that things could be different, better even. If you recognise and accept this as a likely starting point and try to embrace the possibility of positive change then magical things will happen.

Positive change begins with knowledge. Once we have a sufficient amount of knowledge, we need to take responsibility for our own lives. What you have hopefully learned so far is that if we do nothing differently, the power of momentum (generated by drivers which have evolved from old behaviours) will keep pushing us towards the old and familiar - and so we need to create a forward momentum. This begins with new thoughts, which we must ensure become behaviours, as it is those positive actions that will bring about lasting change by creating new drivers.

Start by making a plan to reach your desired destination. Identify the help that you might need for that and actively pursue it. Find those songs that make your heart sing. Seek out joy and laughter wherever you can. Celebrate your most meaningful relationships. Count your blessings, great and small and you will find new patterns will emerge and gently propel you to a peaceful paradise – a place of clarity and contentment where you are able to meet life with confidence and grace.

Let us explore The Code, the mathematical genius behind all that we see and can't see. It is helping us to make sense even of the nonsense and is well worth further investigation.

The Code – the real story

The Code explains the primacy and the importance of patternology; helping us to understand that there is a formula that explains everything that is happening in both the inner and outer universes.

In this section I will give a more comprehensive understanding of this fascinating subject and focus on the aspects that have been unveiled through a variety of disciplines and research, helping in the process to create a template, which explains many of the phenomena in the universe. This includes how nature performs her magic and how we as human beings have come to be as we are.

Uncovering aspects of The Code has helped us to see that the principles of mathematics are at the heart of literally every action, reaction and transaction. As I hope I explained well enough in the previous section, patterns are behind everything we do... good and bad. We can either work with them or they work against us.

They explain everything from the invisible subatomic world to far beyond the visual field, to the movement of the planets and the stars - there really is no such thing as chance or randomness. Chance and randomness are only the labels we have come to use when attempting to explain something that stands outside of our current understanding.

The deciphering of The Code has begun to lift the veil on many of life's so-called mysteries, offering us an insight not only into the marvels of the universe but also how we can change and move beyond our personal limitations too.

Some of the modern references in this section have been drawn from Professor Marcus du Sautoy's excellent work on The Code. The references from ancient civilizations and cultures are the by-product of the research I've undertaken over the last forty years, which has led to two books. The first is entitled Science the New God? - addressing science's rise to supremacy - arguably at the cost of our values and beliefs. The second book, Antiquity Comes Full Circle, addresses the ancients' contribution to the modern world.

I hope you will enjoy this unusual and fascinating voyage, so here goes...

Prime numbers – the key players

Prime numbers are the most fundamental characters in the world of mathematics and can be found in every equation that explains the phenomena of the natural world. I will explore some of these as the journey unfolds.

A prime number can only be divided by the number one and itself - they are the indivisible numbers that make up The Code. A unique characteristic of prime numbers is that they can't be formulated by multiplying other numbers together - and so if any prime numbers were to be missing, some other numbers just could not exist.

Non-prime numbers (composite numbers) can be created by multiplying prime numbers together - this is why prime numbers are being considered as the 'genes' within The Code.

Music and ratios

Music offers us a wonderful illustration of the rules of mathematics. It also clearly demonstrates our intimate relationship to sound. It's interesting to note that when the mathematical rules of music are broken, we intuitively know it. An oscilloscope produces a picture of a sound (note). This instrument has helped us to understand the role of ratios in music. Every combination of notes can be defined by simple ratios - when we are listening to something that sounds beautiful to us and moves us the oscilloscope actually translates those sounds into wonderful curves with gentle peaks and troughs, which we can readily observe.

The oscilloscope has allowed us to 'see' these ratios and their patterns and what we have learnt from this is that the more complex we make ratios the harsher the sound becomes - and the visual patterns that we observe via the oscilloscope match the sound. In other words, the wave formation has sharp, jagged edges and lacks the elegance and the sweeping curves of a beautiful melody. If it sounds ugly the wave formation and patterns will look ugly too.

The more I have studied this aspect of The Code, the clearer it has become that there is a beautiful symmetry between our brainwaves and the shape, form and patterns of sound that we see with the oscilloscope.

This is why the sharp jagged edges created by music that is out of alignment has such a negative impact on the brain. Because when you observe (via an EEG) brainwaves that are jagged with many peaks and troughs then the person is generally experiencing some kind of anxiety, stress and/or panic.

Equally when you see the lovely smooth rolling hill formation, which is pleasurable to the eye, the person is experiencing peace, contentment and is enjoying a balanced state of mind.

Our brainwave profile and our daily experience of the world are inseparable. When our brainwaves are out of balance, there are corresponding problems in our emotional and psychological and/or neuro-biological health.

Research has identified brainwave patterns associated with all sorts of emotional and neurological conditions, such as: over-arousal in certain brain areas is linked to anxiety disorders, sleep problems, nightmares, hyper-vigilance, impulsive behaviour, anger and aggression, agitated depression and chronic nerve pain.

Under-arousal in certain brain areas can lead to various forms of depression, attention deficit traits, chronic pain and insomnia. A combination of under-arousal and over-arousal is seen in cases of anxiety, depression and ADHD.

Instabilities in brain rhythms correlate with tics, obsessive-compulsive disorder, aggressive behaviour, rage, panic attacks, bipolar disorder, migraines, narcolepsy, epilepsy, sleep apnoea, vertigo, tinnitus, anorexia/bulimia, PMT, diabetes, hypoglycaemia and paranoid behaviour.

This is a wonderful example of how intimately we are connected to our environments and how our environments affect us. We mirror them and they mirror us. This is an obvious energy contract. It is another example of how the four environments are connected... another example of synergy.

Professor Judy Edworthy of Plymouth University has spent many years investigating the psychological effects of sound. Her work clearly illustrates the relationship between sound and mathematics. She has demonstrated that certain sounds can elevate or disturb us, as our brains decipher their patterns, and we are called to act in a particular way. These actions may be to dance to a song or to respond to a siren or to remove ourselves from a screeching sound, which is literally getting on our nerves. In each case what we hear and are unconsciously responding to are those ratios – in other words, the numbers that produce the mathematical formulae synchronise with our brains and impact on our hearts and souls.

Pi

One of the key players in The Code is Pi. It is such a powerful number and provides conclusive evidence of how circles play a fundamental role in the engine room of the universe. The discovery of Pi has been attributed to many different sources including: the Egyptians, Babylonians, Greeks, the ancient Chinese and ancient Indians. What is sure is that each of these cultures and civilizations added something to the refinement of this arguably most fascinating of theories.

India is the Mother of mathematics, because it is there that the number zero originated. Without the number zero, the world would be a very different place. In fact, none of the scientific wonders we now take for granted would exist. The decimal system on which the modern world also depends was conceived in India along with algebra, calculus and trigonometry.

This in no way negates what the ancient Greeks brought to mathematics, but for the sake of accuracy and balance, the Indian contribution should be equally acknowledged. Much has been written about the contributions of Archimedes, Aryabhata and Baudhayana. All three were brilliant mathematicians and astronomers who, given the roles they played in the journey of Pi, helped lay down the foundation for the world we now inhabit.

The relationship between the circumference and the diameter of a circle always equals the number beginning 3.14 (Pi). Wherever you look in nature, be it in the fields of human biology or astronomy, this principle is true and constant. Whenever you divide the circumference by the diameter you will always get a number that begins 3.14 (Pi).

Pi seems to be written into almost all the structures and processes of the planet - and like prime numbers, it can be found literally everywhere. Using The Code, you can calculate all manner of patterns and behaviour i.e. the weather, the tides and even human behaviour can be predicted based on The Code - Pi has proven to be a crucial piece of life's jigsaw. This is why it is an integral part of thermodynamics, cosmology, fractals, statistics and electromagnetism.

The normal distribution equation is one of the most important principles within mathematics. Normal distribution is an important component in statistics and is often used in the natural world and social sciences (those disciplines concerned with the study of human behaviour). It has helped us better understand the variations in the natural world - Pi is an integral part of that formula which further indicates that the geometry of circles can be found within all living organisms and systems.

Pi is known as an irrational number, which extends into infinity without ever repeating and it is postulated that every number you could ever imagine could be found within the Pi sequence. However, only the first 39 numbers in that sequence are needed to calculate the circumference of a circle the size of the known universe!

Imaginary numbers

There is a group of numbers known as 'i' which stands for imaginary and these numbers, first introduced by the Greeks, break some of the fundamental rules of mathematics. For example, when multiplying two negative numbers you always get a positive and yet imaginary numbers actually break that rule.

Imaginary numbers, also known as complex numbers, have taken a long journey before being accepted as valuable contributors to the world of mathematics. The term imaginary number was first used in the 17th century and it was René Descartes, often described as the father of modern philosophy, who wrote about them in what was initially a derogatory way. It wasn't until the 18th and 19th centuries that they acquired respectability and since then they have found their way into all aspects of modern life.

A good example of the practical application of imaginary numbers can be found in the use of radar - where sound waves are mirrored back from a stationary or moving object. Complex mathematics distinguishes between static and moving objects – for example, without the use of imaginary numbers, air traffic control would be useless. These 'esoteric' numbers, like Pi, can also be found everywhere.

The role of gravity

Gravity began to be more accurately understood when Galileo, in the late 16th century, undertook his famous experiment of dropping balls from the leaning Tower of Pisa. Galileo was arguably the first to demonstrate that all objects fall at the same rate regardless of their mass – which brought about a paradigm shift from the Aristotelian idea that the mass of the object altered its speed. However, it should be said that Robert Boyle, considered to be one of the founders of modern chemistry and more widely recognised for Boyle's Law (1662), in his research underlined the principle that the mass of an object did not determine the speed with which it fell to the ground. In his experiment, he placed a feather and a coin in a glass tube and removed all the air to create a vacuum. He then inverted the glass tube and was able to demonstrate that both objects fell at the same rate. Therefore, it is only the resistance caused by air that creates the illusion that two objects fall at differing rates.

So, anything under the influence of gravity is falling at the same speed, regardless of its mass - 9.81m per second squared (9.81 m/s2). Galileo's work set the stage for Sir Isaac Newton who is the scientist most synonymous with the laws of gravity. The number 9.81m/s2 is the foundation of Newton's Law of universal gravitation – and it's by understanding this mathematical theory that we have been able to put satellites in space and understand and predict the movement of stars and planets.

Since the time of Newton, much more has been discovered about gravity and its role within the universe. In the early 20th century, Einstein further developed the laws and insights around gravity with his general theory of relativity (1915). Since then, as a result of quantum theory, we've come to understand that gravity is the weakest of the four forces that underpin our world – the other three being: strong nuclear force, weak nuclear force and electromagnetism.

Although gravity is a key player in the visible world, in the invisible world, at the sub-atomic level, its role to date is negligible.

Conservation and efficiency

In nature we see further evidence of The Code, particularly in shapes and forms. What has become clear is that nature is always looking for the most efficient way to produce something or perform a task – its leaning towards efficiency has been described by some scientists as 'nature being lazy'. I think this is an insult and a misunderstanding of the wisdom of nature, which is always seeking a balance between creativity and conservation. Why use more energy than needed to fulfil a task when the energy that can be conserved offers the opportunity for further productivity? Is this not wisdom?

The hexagonal shape has proven to be a wonderful example of this efficiency - it underpins numerous structures in nature, honeycombs being arguably the best-known example of that, a structure that is so strong, uniform and practical that mathematics has helped us deduce that no other structure could ever be more efficient for the bees' honeycomb.

As previously stated, circles, spirals and spheres are other examples, like the hexagon, of nature's efficiency. This is why these shapes can be found everywhere. From the structure of plankton to the fabric of the planet, from cells to countless microorganisms - all provide examples of circles, spirals and spheres being the most efficient way nature has discovered for fulfilling an objective.

Although the sphere is the most efficient form for many tasks within nature, it's interesting to note (as revealed through the science of soap bubbles) that when spheres come together the geometry around what is most efficient changes, thus spheres can form pentagons, hexagons, tetrahedrons, dodecahedrons, all in the name of saving energy and improving output. This discipline provides a wonderful illustration of the rules of geometry, space and energy conservation - see the work of Paola Rebusco at MIT if you're interested in finding out more.

The story of light provides another wonderful example of this pattern of energy conservation and efficiency. Plants and natural vegetation imbibe photons (the sun's energy). We then consume the food, imbibing those photons, which provide us with energy. The foodstuffs that are good for us slowly release the energy, the photons, into our bodies, promoting health and well-being. Those foods we put into our bodies that are not good for us are like little infernos that release their photons quickly, disturbing the delicate balance of creativity and conservation. As a result, we have energy flooding the system too quickly, providing us with a surge of power, rapidly followed by a 'crash', which in turn affects our perception, personality and performance.

We can see in this example, that our bodies are seeking the most efficient way to meet our needs – but where we don't cooperate (with inadequate hydration and poor food choices - which provide the least efficient photons) it struggles to find health and well-being.

I hope at this point you can see how everything in the previous four chapters is connected - deepening your understanding and increasing your awareness not just of the physical dimension but also highlighting the metaphysical factors that are underpinning so much of what is taking place around you and inside of you.

Geometry and nature

As we've discovered, the nature of The Code is to conserve energy - this is clearly demonstrated by the hexagon, the circle and spirals, which are the cornerstones of our world. This same wisdom can also be found in the best of both ancient and modern architecture.

Frei Otto, German architect and structural engineer, famous for the 1972 Munich Olympic Stadium, began a revolution in modern architecture by observing the natural phenomena within nature and using that as a template to build wonderful, stable structures.

The Munich Stadium is a great advert for energy efficiency, illustrating the principle that by copying nature we can achieve the best outcomes. However, it would be a mistake to believe that Frei Otto 'discovered' The Code. It would be more accurate to say that he tapped into that wisdom, because in fact evidence of this understanding around structure and form goes back thousands of years and can be found in the ancient Chinese and Indian cultures. The Egyptians were also clearly working with the principles of The Code using mathematics to build the pyramids – wonderful monuments to shape, symmetry and order.

The ancient Greeks are the ones who first coined the term 'geometry'; they believed that this was a potential key to understanding the world we inhabit. They discovered, through this discipline, five basic shapes called platonic solids, named after the Greek philosopher Plato.

These shapes were believed to be the primary building blocks of nature. They are the tetrahedron with four faces, the cube with six faces, the octahedron with eight faces, the dodecahedron with twelve faces and most complex of all, the icosahedron, with twenty faces (these are the only perfectly symmetrical solids). The Greeks believed that these five shapes were the building blocks for the natural world.

What is fascinating about this premise is that these geometric laws have only become clear in the 20th century. So, the Greeks' calculation that these five shapes were solely responsible for all forms in nature was in fact a phenomenal discovery, clearly built on part science and part intuition.

It's on the back of the discovery of x-rays (Wilhelm Conrad Roentgen - 1895) that we have come to understand even more about the geometry and the symmetry of shape and form underpinning not only the world we inhabit, but also our bodies. As a result of x-rays there has been a paradigm shift in our understanding of biology and all living organisms – x-rays also confirmed that the Greeks were right.

With the ability to see inside our own bodies came further evidence of The Code but it was probably only when we began to x-ray crystals that we were able to appreciate the beauty and the efficiency of the atomic structures underpinning all things.

What was unveiled through the use of x-rays is that the five main shapes that the Greeks first identified are also found encoded within our bodies. Circles, hexagons and spirals again make an appearance. It's the neat, symmetrical patterns known as diffraction patterns, that have revealed how individual atoms have been put together, providing us with a better understanding of atomic structures and giving us an insight into the geometrical principles governing all life.

Professor Stephen Matthews (Imperial College, London) is amongst those who have helped us further understand that the structures and geometric laws discovered within crystals can also be found in the biological structure of humans – his work looks at how atoms are constructed to make living organisms. His research has highlighted how bits of protein come together creating wonderful structures and symmetry, underlining the fact that within the evolution of our bodies very efficient structures are always used to perform biological tasks. The study of pathogens and viruses has also illustrated that everything from the cellular level up to what we know of the cosmos honours the laws of geometry and symmetry.

Physicist Professor Kenneth Libbrecht (California Institute of Technology) through his fascinating work with snowflakes (the physics of crystal growth and ice formation) has enabled us to see that even the 'apparently' random phenomenon in nature, of snowfall, is not random at all. By producing endless permutations of snowflakes in laboratory conditions he's been able to see that no two snowflakes are alike - and yet they are nonetheless bound together by the laws of geometry and symmetry.

What's important to point out is that when a snowflake is first formed it could be described as geometrically perfect – certainly at the atomic level. However, on its long journey from the cloud to the ground, the many climatic changes it is subject to cause it to lose the perfect geometry and symmetry it originally had. And so, if we are to understand the complexity of the natural world and the part chaos plays in nature, then a more thorough examination of patterns is needed. Let's look a little closer at chaos and whether it is subject to the same rules.

Fractals – nature's fingerprint

Jackson Pollock - abstract expressionist artist – was declared artist of the 20th century, although he split the opinion of the artistic world, with some calling him a drunken lunatic, whilst others considered him a true genius. Professor Richard Taylor of the University of Oregon - artist and physicist – was the first person to demonstrate that the chaotic, random images for which Pollock was famous actually told a story that literally mimicked the patterns that we can find everywhere in nature.

These patterns found in the 'chaos' of Pollock's work are known as fractals. Fractals are how nature builds the world – using detailed, never-ending patterns that repeat themselves across different scales identically. These never-ending, repeating patterns can be found in rocks, mountains, clouds, coastlines and trees.

Pollock's work was examined by Professor Taylor and what he uncovered was a mathematical rhythm and symmetry that could be found everywhere in the world around us, suggesting that when something appears random or chaotic, there is in fact an underlying symmetry and pattern even when it appears not to be obeying any laws.

Pollock's artwork was and still is considered unique and Professor Taylor believes, evidenced through his research, that Pollock's contribution was more than paint on canvas. It gave us an insight into the true workings of nature and the principles that underpin chaos.

The fractal system is governed by one rule that can be found running through nature - 'grow and divide'. Everything in nature is striving for the optimal growing conditions, whether that be a seed, a leaf on a tree, a human cell, a pathogen, the brain - everything honours this one law in its attempt to survive and thrive. Based on what I said in chapter 3, I hope you also understand the critical role of protection in this equation.

The idea that fractals are inherent in every facet of nature was first pioneered in the 1970s - by French mathematician, Benoît Mandelbrot – famous for his creation the Mandelbrot Set. The 'grow and divide' principle explains the fascinating complexity of the world around us, a complexity largely governed by this rule - a rule that further illustrates that nature, in fact all energy, is always looking for the most efficient way of doing things.

Fractals give us an understanding of the mathematical rules that influence the visible and the invisible.

Where does chaos fit into The Code?

Chaos has been defined as: The behaviour of a system which is governed by cause and effect but is so unpredictable as to appear random.

As we can see from this definition of chaos, the idea that things and events appear random may at first seem accurate. However, the more you examine chaos the more you find that the randomness of things does indeed have a strange order and beauty all of its own – as revealed by fractals.

Chaos is a central part of The Code and applies to the entire universe, including humankind. The difficulty with chaos is that prediction is much more challenging because tiny variables, under the influence of the cause-and-effect principle (which underpins all life's dynamics) can be magnified into huge events; our weather being one of the best examples.

This is why weather predictions beyond five days become more challenging and speculative, as weather is dependent on so many variables. Therefore, to factor all those variables into an equation of prediction is almost impossible. How can we know precisely the pressures of all the different weather systems anywhere in the world and how they might interact with one another? How can we be sure of what the wind will be doing in a week's time? How can our calculations about temperature be absolute at any given point? The answer is we can't tie down those factors precisely, especially the further we attempt to project these predictions into the future. Scientific data demonstrates that weather predictions under three days have a high level of accuracy, but that our mathematical formulae and calculations break down when we start trying to calculate the weather beyond a week.

Hopefully you can see that chaos is an illusion only supported by our ignorance about The Code. When we see variations in the symmetrical order of the known universe, what we are in fact seeing is variables impacting on that neat sequential equation that can be best observed at the atomic and subatomic levels.

As discussed earlier, these variables largely generated by natural phenomena, create a disruption of The Code, therefore distorting the outcomes. But despite these onslaughts The Code remains intact, making it possible for us to predict so much about human behaviour and the natural world.

Human behaviour – the patterns of predictability

At the beginning of this chapter, I spoke about patternology being the DNA of actions, in other words both the predictable and the unpredictable aspects of human behaviour can be understood when we recognise that patterns are what are truly governing our moods, attitudes, perceptions and actions.

We are slowly beginning to see that The Code is in fact a simple set of rules, managing great complexity. Each rule managing one bit of the web of life and yet each overlapping and cooperating in such a way that throughout the universe there is seamless unison - I have tried to demonstrate at every step of this journey that everything is indeed connected!

There does appear to be one law under which all the others operate and that is the law of cause and effect. In other words, nothing ever happens without reason. We may not always be able to see it, understand it and therefore explain it but the world around us and the world inside us always respond to this overarching principle.

Professor Iain Couzin of Princeton University has studied the movement of living things, from microorganisms to human beings. What his study has shown is that with all these organisms, be they ants, fish, or humans the rules are essentially the same – each striving for order and efficiency, using protection as their means of ensuring further growth.

Professor Couzin, by studying and establishing the patterns of human beings within crowds - then using that data, has been able to predict all manner of things about human behaviour - like how people behave in shopping malls, supermarkets and railway stations; through to what is likely to happen during the evacuation of a building. The study of people in crowds shows that although things may appear chaotic, we are unconsciously following the innate rules of efficiency, always trying to improve and maximise output.

When we look more closely at the individual, despite the great complexity, patterns of predictability are still apparent, which is why subjects like sociology and psychology have been very helpful and for the most part have proved successful in helping us to understand human behaviour and in predicting how to get the best outcomes through a variety of therapeutic programmes.

Criminologists have drilled down into human behaviour to such a degree that they have come to understand humans are unknowingly addicted to patterns. This has helped in de-coding and predicting the behaviour of criminals.

One very clear pattern is that by understanding past behaviour, future behaviour can be predicted in quite precise ways, not just for an individual criminal but for all criminal behaviour – and so the drivers which influence their decisions and choices can be used to anticipate what a criminal might do next. By working out these patterns it is also possible to retrace the steps of criminals and calculate what else they might have done.

We saw how patterns work in the previous chapter when examining how the four aspects of the mind operate and relate to one another. And so, if we do not consciously change what are largely sub and unconscious influences, we are pretty much destined to keep doing what we are doing. When that's exactly what we want to do of course that is fine because it means we enjoy greater peace of mind, self-esteem and joy. However, when it is not what we want to be doing we are imprisoned by a set of habits and patterns that deny us clarity and peace of mind.

To further understand how criminologists are using the knowledge of patterns, see the work of Dr. Rossmo of Texas State University, who specialises in analysing the behaviour of serial killers. Through his research Dr. Rossmo has distilled the patterns of criminals down to a primary equation, which has been used to great effect in police work all over the world. This formula and the techniques and strategies that have emerged from it have come to be known as geographic profiling.

The wisdom of the crowd

The wisdom of the crowd is a term that statisticians use for asserting that the mind of the group is greater than the individual. This conclusion has been drawn by repeatedly observing what happens when you apply the mathematical formula for calculating averages. If you get a large enough group to guess something, they achieve a startling level of accuracy.

A typical experiment that demonstrates this phenomenon is placing a number of jellybeans into a glass jar and asking each member of that group to guess how many jellybeans are in the jar. What you will find is there'll be some who are extremely high in their estimates and others who are very low. Almost no one will get the number correct, although some might be close. However, if you add up all of those guesses and divide them by the number of individuals in the group, some interesting patterns emerge. Generally, that average will be very close indeed to the actual figure - within the 1% range and in many cases as low as 0.1%.

This is another example of the underlying principle of the seemingly chaotic being more ordered and calculable than we might think. Interestingly this is why organisations like the NHS, Apple, Google and other institutions interested in social patterns and behaviour have begun to use the wisdom of the crowd principle to predict all manner of things pertaining to human behaviour. On the basis of the data accrued, they make predictions around disease and health patterns, buying patterns, where we are likely to go on holiday, how we might vote, the cars we might buy and other social trends.

Physicist, Professor Geoffrey West of the Santa Fe Institute, who has spent his professional life trying to figure out different patterns in the universe, most recently has turned his attention to human life within cities. Through his research studying the evolution of cities, he has come up with an interesting observation, which presents us with another piece of The Code.

His claim is that there is a magic number, which is 1.15 and that this number is arguably the most important number driving human behaviour. Looking at the historical evidence and the evolution of cities as they exist today, this number continues to turn up and he believes it can accurately predict what we will do for as long as civilisation continues.

His definition is: "1.15 is the amount by which social and economic activity rises per capita when the population of a city doubles". In other words, there is an increase of 15% in every social and economic area of life. This calculation has continually stood up to mathematical scrutiny, wherever in the world he has focused his attention.

Here we see again that we are not living in a world of chance. Patterns are driving all events. We can either work with them fulfilling our potential in the process... or we unknowingly succumb to their unwavering force.

I hope this synopsis of The Code has gone some way to lifting the veil of mystery that surrounds so much of human life. By looking behind this veil I believe we can see that life's systems and events are governed by clear, precise and efficient rules – always striving for the greater good. I hope you will use these insights to strive for a better balance between creativity and conservation in your own life.

Living beyond your story

Something I am very passionate about in my work is encouraging those I have the privilege of walking alongside to live beyond their stories. Many of us without even knowing it are trapped in the role we are in, often playing a character that for the most part we have inherited and then subsequently build on that persona.

We then blindly and passionately profess to be this person, defending that sense of self as if our lives depended on it, often not even knowing what it is that we're defending. In addition to those protestations, we also claim not to care about how we are seen and perceived by those around us - but really these sentiments mask and hide the real feeling of vulnerability and the desperate need to be accepted and loved.

Although most people whilst making such declarations, say they don't care... they actually do care. They care so deeply that they have essentially become what they perceive the world has asked and demanded of them, all in an attempt to fit in, to be liked and loved - and without knowing it their sense of self has been lost in the process.

Having made every attempt to meet the demands and expectations of their audience, is it a surprise that when the world rejects their countless efforts to fit in, that the person feels deeply hurt, wounded, even enraged?

Those who feel these emotions find that their self-talk becomes negative, and they are unable to access the virtuous reservoirs of the soul, because they do not know who or what they are. They are like chameleons that change according to their environment.

I talked in chapter 2 about our needs (the three 'A's) in relation to attachment theory and the importance of being affirmed, attended to and experiencing the warmth and generosity of affection. Given the primacy of the three 'A's and how desperately important it is to attach to our significant others and environments, is it any wonder that we will do almost anything to be seen, heard and valued?

With insecure attachments we saw how we act in dysfunctional or maladaptive ways - I prefer to refer to this behaviour as 'acquired'. I believe the selves that we acquire when our core needs have not been met create an illusion that masks the truth about who we are. As a result, 'composite characters' (sub-personalities), based on our experiences, are superimposed on the authentic self.

It is these composite characters that form the supporting cast in our play. However, at some point there is a jostling for power, as the more dominant sub-personalities compete to take the leading role. This is often not a democratic process as the more powerful characters dominate proceedings and one or two claim the starring roles - demanding control and respect from the community of the self.

At other points, certain sub-personalities will make special guest appearances because they are better suited to a particular situation and moment in time. The more dominant sub-personalities recognise that that aspect is better equipped to deal with a given situation and temporarily stand down until the situation has been handled or the objective achieved.

Can you see yourself in this picture? One part of you that takes the lead in most contexts and situations - when it believes that it can get away with playing that role. When at other times (often to do with fear, shame, anxiety or guilt), another sub-personality is called to the stage and another dimension to your personality is now on show. In modern parlance this has come to be known as the public self and the private self.

There are many who would declare this changing of costume and role is normal, even healthy. However, when you play a role that you have essentially learnt and it is driven by the need to find love and acceptance, can this really be healthy? And could this persona be described as your authentic self... the real you?

Experience has taught me that those who can disentangle themselves from this web, even though they are often afraid of what may lie deep in their soul, discover something more beautiful than they had imagined.

In fact, I have never met anyone, when they managed to extricate themselves from the web of the sub-personalities and the drama that has been constructed around them, who does not feel a tremendous relief – and also discovers that they are more spectacular than they had thought possible.

How do we move away from the acquired selves and meet this authentic being? Well, as you're reading now, you're taking the first step because the problem and the solution are always entwined. The more that you understand the problem and are prepared to face it the more the solutions are unveiled.

I said earlier that there is almost always at least one dominant character around which the performance takes place, and this character may bully and dominate the others, calling them to task as and when it sees fit.

However, this is only one way that this sophisticated play is acted out. The dominant personality can just as easily be the victim, the poor me character that influences the play by getting the other sub-personalities to do what it wishes them to do by playing the part of being vulnerable, needy, even pathetic, knowing that these propensities can also give them the control that they seek.

Those whose inner world develops in this way often become martyrs. No one's ever endured what they have endured. Whatever version of events they report that's always been the worst version in history. No one would ever understand because only they have been into that abyss. Do you recognise this character and this play – either in yourself or others?

This is not a time for shame, guilt or regret. Great courage and honesty are required at this point in order that you can disentangle yourself from your story.

Think of what we have explored to date. Think about how much time, effort and energy is actually wasted when we become embroiled in these characters – and in the process we are alienated from the real story, the one that truly matters.

I want you to also think of this in the context of protection and growth. Can you see how the acquired selves are initially constructed as a protective response, which is about fitting in, in order that we will grow.

When we first come into the world, we come full of potential, creativity, primed for growth and we unconsciously expect those in our environment to support and protect us, enabling that growth. But when we are faced with a situation where our needs are not being adequately met and we don't seem able to satisfy the needs of those around us, we move into a protective position. It is at this point that our sub-personalities are conceived. They are a direct response to the deficits and idiosyncrasies of our environment.

It's many years before the child realises that its expectations are not going to be fulfilled, but until that point, it keeps seeking what it needs. Many do not have this realisation until well into adulthood and some may never have it at all – so they are unconsciously driven, trying to find their place in the world. Unfortunately, the culture of mixed messages and uncertainty maintains the dance of the acquired self, perpetually seeking attention and acknowledgement.

It's the 'evidence' that comes from our environment that persuades us that we have it all wrong, as we aren't receiving consistent affection, attention and affirmation. At this point the protective alarm system is activated and the sub-personalities are born. They quickly become confused because despite their best efforts their needs are not being met. These characters now try to work out the best way to compensate and survive - and with that another protective layer is created.

This is how the insecure attachments that I spoke about are conceived – anxious avoidant, anxious ambivalent and anxious disorganised. The individual then learns to cope within the circumstances and context they find themselves. It's really important to understand this is not the system working against itself, it is trying to calculate the best way to survive in the hostile environment it finds itself in.

What happens in the remaining years of childhood/adolescence is that the story is further compounded, and the characters become cemented in their roles. Unless this is challenged, which can come through one's own self-awareness, then most of us don't grow out of this position, in fact it usually takes some trauma, tragedy or significant life event for us to re-evaluate the course we are on.

And so, it is circumstances that tend to demand a new direction - and more often than not we obediently follow. Those who change course through self-awareness and choice alone are rare. It often takes a significant bump in the road for us to question the course that we're taking.

My invitation to you is that rather than waiting for the decision to be made for you by the unpredictability of life's unfolding, choose to rip up the old script, which is for the most part not yours anyway, and write a new one, based on your hopes, dreams and on the principles and values you hold dear. Take the risk to be the very best you, you can be. Find the courage and honesty to do that today.

Look carefully at your own life and examine your sub-personalities. See if you are giving licence to the most dominant part of you to run things in a way that is not necessarily considered and healthy. Find out who's in control? Look at the contracts you have formed both with yourself and those around you. Are you controlling, demanding and manipulative? Do you impatiently force your will onto life and those you have the most intimate connections with? Do you play the 'poor me' role as a way of getting what you want – realising there is power in victimhood? Are you afraid to look into the abyss and discover the truth about who you really are?

By answering these questions, you will find your contradictions and where you find your contradictions, you'll find the source of your dissatisfaction and unhappiness. You will also find your solution, your way out. You may need support or help of some kind to disentangle yourself from this web, but if you're brave enough to truly acknowledge your own faults and flaws and are willing to do that compassionately, then your emancipation is assured.

It's vitally important to underline that having contempt for your 'community of the self' is likely to keep you in bondage for the rest of your life. Remember that these sub-personalities were initially created to protect you to ensure your survival. This is nature's way. The whole point of protection is to ensure at some point there can be growth. Therefore, treat the characters in your play with respect, empathy, sensitivity and compassion, and then the journey of positive change can begin.

Writing a new script

In trying to make sense of your own story, I think it's helpful to see your subpersonalities as actors, coming together and creating the play that is your life. When we understand how these characters are conceived and how they are moulded by the context and environment, we can begin to make sense of who we are.

Our subpersonalities create a complex web from which our belief systems are established, and new paradigms are created. This is the stage on which the performance will take place. Until those beliefs and paradigms have been altered, nothing can change in that person's story.

I spoke earlier about the dominant characters – there could be as many as two or three – that tend to oversee the whole story. These could be equated to the principal actor, the producer and director – they really do call the shots. If we are to change how this drama unfolds, it's the dominant characters that need to be persuaded. How can this be done?

First of all, if you have undertaken the inventory of incongruence with unwavering honesty, you'll have identified at least three or four primary influences (which I refer to as the drivers in the Journey of Becoming and the Pyramid of Shame). These primary influences (there could easily be half a dozen) are the ones that push you along whatever path you are taking. These forces are so powerful that unless we are aware, they run our lives without us even knowing.

Amongst their number is control, one of the most potent of all the drivers. Control can be either healthy or unhealthy. When it has been formed in an environment of uncertainty and built on insecurity, it becomes an unhealthy force that bullies its way to its chosen outcome. This is a position that is often blind to the needs of others. Its primary agenda is to keep ahead of fear. If it can control people, circumstances and events it believes this is the best way to avoid the threat and domination of fear. As a result, it can easily cast aside those it loves the most without even recognising what it's doing - such is its blindness. There are so many indoctrinated by this force and have no sense of the impact and effect they are having on those around them; their self-awareness has been drastically diminished.

The irony is that the one who is controlling in this way is trying to escape the fear that it anticipates will devour it and yet in the process it can create so much havoc and harm, generating fear in others and the potential for greater fear for themselves in the future. A person caught in the grip of this character does not live a fearless life because their anticipation of fear means they are in a state of perpetual anxiety - unable to drink from the virtuous rivers of their souls.

Other leading characters you may find orchestrating events are the perfectionist, the know it all, poor me, the child, the pathetic one, the victim, the hero/heroine, the intimidator, the pessimist, the catastrophist, the martyr, the possessive, the manipulator and the egotist. In all these characters fear is lurking somewhere.

There are others I could name, but these are the most prominent, the ones I see turning up regularly in my work. They are very disabling and many who are occupied by one or more of these characters aren't even aware of their existence. They explain away their choices and decisions, offering sophisticated justifications and defences for their actions. And unless they have taken a journey of self-examination, they believe this persona is simply who they are. Nothing could be further from the truth.

These heavyweights are made all the stronger by our need to be liked, our need to be loved and our fear of not being good enough – and at some point, being exposed. These are drivers we all have in common. They are part of the unspoken social contract of belonging and fitting in somewhere... anywhere.

We are like islands, separated by seas and oceans, independent, divine organisms, connected by a common humanity and spirituality. We all crave that which makes us better, but if we are not aligned to our authentic selves, we become lost in the maze of the acquired selves.

William James, the American psychologist and medic put it beautifully when he said: "We are like islands in the sea, separate on the surface but connected in the deep".

Having established who some of the leading characters are, you now need to work out for yourself which ones are dominating your inner play? You may need help with this - if so, it would be best if it were a skilled helper. Once you have named your subpersonalities it's important that you set up a dialogue with them. You need to begin a new conversation - you cannot let the status quo continue.

Do not be afraid to name and own your characters because it's the only way to disentangle yourself from the story. If you want to be the best version of yourself then you are unlikely to find it by playing a part that's largely been written for you. It's now time to construct a new character, one that reflects the part you truly want to play.

When writing your script, ask yourself where you want to be; what form you want your life to take? Dare to envisage the role you want to play; the story you want to tell. Take the reins off your imagination, give it permission to roam freely.

Establishing your storyline can take time but please be courageous and adventurous. Think big. Even if in the first instance, you cannot see how you can achieve your highest aspirations, don't allow this to derail you. Probably the thing I've learned the most from working with a vast array of individuals and the unimaginable challenges that can befall us, is that there is no power that can rival our beliefs. We are literally shaping our realities by what we believe.

The epigenetic revolution has been a valuable asset to our understanding of the human condition. If you're interested in this subject, you can take a closer look, starting with the work of Candace Pert (The Molecules of Emotion) and including some of the current authors and researchers such as Bruce Lipton (The Biology of Belief) and Nessa Carey (The Epigenetics Revolution).

What has been clearly illustrated by epigenetics is that our thoughts and feelings (which emerge from our beliefs) are arguably the most significant environmental factors determining how our genes express themselves. This has debunked the nature versus nurture argument and replaced it with the more obvious formula of nature plus nurture.

The data stream and insights that have flowed out of this revolution have offered us such great hope because we now understand that we can influence which genes are switched on and off according to our beliefs. It should be underlined that beliefs are not the only environmental factors to have a say in our genetic expression. Diet, nutrition, hydration, relationships, stress, meaning and purpose are all factors that mould the way our genes express themselves.

That said, we need to respect the power of genetic influences, otherwise we're likely to fall into the trap of thinking we can force things to go our way, when what's needed is a relationship of mutual respect. A bit like life, we are able to significantly shape and influence our destinies but there are some factors we cannot control and the only influence we really have in those instances is one of acceptance. Through acceptance we learn to go with the flow, changing the things we can along the way and working with the things we're unable to alter. This approach gives us the best outcomes and leads to greater peace of mind and contentment.

Without changing your beliefs, you have little or no chance of getting where you want to go, which is why they are so central to the change process. To change your beliefs, you have to start changing your behaviour. To change your behaviour, you have to change your thoughts. To change your thoughts, you have to change the conversations you're having with yourself.

Start by writing out your heart's desire, clearly and concisely. This is the new narrative for your play. The more detail the better. It should include what your ideal day looks like, how you want to be spending your time, what the nature of your relationships will be. Focus on what the antidotes to your weaknesses are, what you need to do to turn them around. Also focus on the resources, time and support you'll require. Question all your contradictions. What could you do differently, to address these discrepancies? Identify who and/or what you're going to need to achieve your goals.

As you develop your new narrative, think of how you can use your dominant negative characters in positive ways. Each of them has a virtuous persona, so think of how they can become bastions for change and transformation, rather than remaining hindrances and obstacles. Remember these dominant subpersonalities have become the primary drivers, and so they can either drive you over a cliff or take you to safety. This is why making them the protagonists in your story is a very useful strategy.

Approach this task with optimism and enthusiasm. Know that deep within your being, even if the revised script feels beyond your reach, that somewhere within you lies the power and the resources needed to successfully complete this task. Promise yourself that you'll be kind and sensitive to yourself and your needs. You can't reach your desired destination by bludgeoning your way there. Compassion and care will be required at every stage.

As you formulate your new story and begin re-writing the roles of the key characters, a new fragrance of hope will emerge, hinting at something more beautiful and prosperous that awaits you. Inhale and embody this fragrance and the feelings inherent within it.

Remember to be specific, be clear. Then regularly spend time imagining the story unfolding exactly as you want it to. This should be a daily exercise. Consciously daydream about the best version of yourself being at the helm of your life. Include in your daily imaginings the rest of the supporting cast of characters playing their parts in helping this new drama to unfold smoothly and beautifully.

There will be some characteristics from the acquired self that you will take with you. There's rarely a wholesale ditching of what has gone before. It's much more a melting and moulding process, a form of alchemy, where something more precious is formed as a result of the heat and chemical activity. And so many traits will come with you on this journey of becoming.

The more you can surround yourself with strategies and aids that serve as a reminder of your goals and ambitions, the more your brain and the hundred billion neurons housed within it will conspire to create new possibilities and opportunities. We are all standing at the door of infinite possibility. We're not helplessly bound to destiny – unless of course we do nothing. So, in this new role as screenwriter of your own screenplay, find ways to bring your set and stage to life.

Things you will find invaluable in this regard are writing down on a regular basis inspirational thoughts and ideas pertaining to this new way of thinking. Keep a book of insights and whenever you have a positive thought that moves and stimulates you or you hear something inspirational, jot it down. The more you can gather ideas, quotes and useful references and regularly consult those insights, the more they will build a momentum that pushes you in this new direction.

Something equally powerful that I recommend is writing lines. There are many who have found this exercise life changing. The same principle applies – you need to gather inspirational thoughts, paradigm-shifting ideas and sentiments that mobilise you towards action. Make time then to repeatedly write these thoughts down, trying to be as mindful as you can when you do. It is interesting to note that something that was used to punish children has now been identified by the neuroplasticity revolution as one of the ways we can change the neuronal pathways in the brain. These pathways are the threads that keep us bound to particular thoughts, habits and patterns. Writing lines can change the negative webs that have been formed, creating a whole new tapestry of beliefs.

I mentioned the importance of conscious daydreaming. One way of engaging in this process is by imagining yourself sitting in your own private auditorium in front of a large screen - and unfolding before your eyes is the play you have written, with the new characters and their roles. Visualisation is good for the brain, mind and the soul. Using the eye of the mind, see your story with as much richness of colour, and as much depth and detail as you can muster. The more you can bring it to life the better. Spend time creating the right context, situations and scenery, all in an attempt to generate an atmosphere of hope and optimism. Doing this for just ten minutes every day will change your feelings, motivations, intentions and in time your beliefs.

Another valuable strategy is to create a vision board. There are so many ways to do this, so do what most appeals to you. What I suggest is to take a large piece of paper and to divide it into four and attribute one quarter to each of the key characters, the mind, body, spirit and environment. Then, having worked out your needs for each quadrant, gather images that best reflect what you're striving to achieve in each area of your life.

I encourage people at the centre of their vision board to have a picture of themselves, looking really happy and contented. It certainly should be an image that for you exhibits the best of yourself. Have fun putting together something that is colourful, inspirational for you and summarises clearly how you want your life to look. Once your vision board is complete, it is best put in a prominent position where you can regularly be reminded of its messages.

One final way of writing your new script is having written out your plan I would suggest that you record it on an appropriate device. For many that would be their mobile phone. Whatever device it is, it's best that it's portable because you want to listen to this recording ideally every day and doing that whilst you travel is a good way of making that time more productive. The ideal length of this recording is no longer than ten to fifteen minutes. If it's shorter that's fine, because the length isn't the most critical factor, it's whether it truly captures your vision that counts.

When making the recording, try to be as sincere in your delivery of the messages as you can. Sincerity is like an aphrodisiac to the brain and mind. It's so powerfully seductive that the messages that carry the vibration and quality of sincerity are more deeply imbibed. These messages can literally turn the impossible into the possible, the doubter into the believer. I often refer to sincerity as the architect of miracles because I've seen so many impossible situations change when sincerity has been introduced.

So, when you record your message in a heartfelt way and you hear it back, your brain will dance joyously to the messages contained within it. The four aspects of the mind will then work more synergistically to create what you are focusing on. Do not underestimate the power of listening to your own story in your own voice. The voice that is most influencing you every day is your own and subject to the nature of its commentary your life is either moving in the direction that you wish – or not.

It is good in addition to recording your vision, to also create some positive statements, affirmations and mantras that serve as reminders for the key points of this new narrative. They are best written as short, punchy statements that galvanise the thrust of your endeavours. They should elevate your heart, feeling like booster injections when you hear them... generating feelings of hope and inspiration.

You want about ten of these statements, which you would record, going through the whole list in its entirety and then repeating the process three times. When recording your affirmations, leave enough space between each one so that you can repeat the phrase in your mind or out aloud. Again, sincerity is key. Your mind (all four elements) will ravenously dine on these messages the more that it hears them. The paradigm on which your life is based will alter and a new performance will unfold.

It is my experience that these strategies and methods are all powerful agents for change when applied regularly. You know from the contents of this book so far and all the things I have previously produced and written, that I passionately believe in the formula: knowledge plus application equals personal power. In fact, I would go even further: knowledge plus application equals everything.

Everything is obtainable to a mind that is willing to commit to putting what it knows consistently into practice. That is the challenge for us all... consistency.

Before concluding this chapter on how to live beyond your story I would like to say something about transformation, or more precisely trance-formation. This is because understanding the role of trance is imperative to positive change. Furthermore, it underpins all that I've said in this section on writing a new script and will enable you to get the best from the new story that I hope you feel compelled to write.

Trance-formation

The siloed approach defines human evolution in narrow, separate compartments, as if the best way to classify our knowledge and experience is to keep the different elements of our discoveries separate. This has caused great confusion because we have now developed the strange idea that things are best fixed in parts. This means that we habitually pop off to see different people to help us fix our various ailments and concerns, removing the connection and relationship that exists between all the things that make us human. We cease to see how one aspect of our lives is impacting on another.

We are so busy chasing symptoms, looking for solutions and in the process missing the most important point, which is, that we cannot fix the mind whilst our bodies are ailing... and we cannot fix the body whilst the mind is riddled with fear, anxiety and confusion. Also, we cannot fix the spirit when it has no positive focus, no meaning or purpose. In other words, attempting to address the symptoms will never provide us with lasting solutions because the symptoms are not the problem, they are merely by-products of the real issue(s). So, what is the antidote for this? In a word, trance.

The more we step into the world of trance, the more we are able to find the power to disentangle ourselves from the web of the past and create a new web of positive possibilities, a web that ties us to virtue and positive change and weakens the negative influences that have kept us stuck.

There are a number of ways to enter the world of trance, such as: meditation, prayer, mindfulness, relaxation, hypnosis, communing with nature, listening to particular sounds and music. In fact, any activity that creates some form of introspection and contemplation can take us into the incredible world of trance. And at that point trance-formation is available to us.

Trance bridges the gap between the conscious aspects of oneself and the unconscious realms. Most of our choices and decisions appear to be taking place at the conscious level with very little consultation with the subconscious and unconscious minds. As you know, these two aspects of the mind have the most powerful impact on the way we see and act in the world. The sub and unconscious minds shape our beliefs and perceptions but because much of their involvement is happening in an anonymous and automated way, we rarely notice their input, failing to see how influential they are in our everyday lives. Trance gives us a chance to change the way this internal mechanism works.

How does trance take us from the conscious world into the unconscious, giving us access to real transformation? All the introspective activities mentioned above take our brainwave activity out of the gamma and beta wave ranges (where the brain is at its busiest) and lead us into the alpha and theta bandwidths (this is where the brain waves are oscillating in a way that leaves us feeling calm, relaxed and better able to focus). The alpha and theta states build a bridge between the conscious aspects of oneself and the unconscious aspects. If you've never experienced trance knowingly, you will certainly have experienced it without realising it - most of us think of it as daydreaming.

In that daydreaming state we are straddling two realms - the conscious and unconscious. If we can take advantage of this opportunity, then our daydreaming can become so much more. We need to learn how to improve the communication between the two realms... we need to learn the language of trance. Trance can lead us to lasting and positive change.

Although it is somewhat simplistic to only talk of the brain in terms of the left hemisphere (predominantly concerned with logic) and the right hemisphere (predominantly concerned with emotion) because both hemispheres address many more tasks than this, it is nonetheless useful to have this overview as it helps us to understand that if we are to resolve our issues, then we need to communicate with both the logical and emotional aspects of being human.

Although there is significant overlap, the strategies and methods for doing this are different for each hemisphere. The logical aspect of the brain responds very well to words, ideas, theories and concepts. This is because it has a more mathematical orientation and generally seeks to make sense of things in more linear, chronological and functional ways. The emotional part of the brain also works well with theories and concepts, but it is more interested in the abstract, metaphysical dimensions of those theories and concepts, working on the principle that just because logic has given us an answer, it doesn't mean that it is 'the' answer.

The right hemisphere has a more holistic approach to the human experience. It responds very well to metaphor, analogy, storytelling and those techniques that draw on imagination. Therefore, if we want to change things in the more tangible world of the conscious mind, we need to regularly enter the intangible world of the sub and unconscious minds. And to do that we need to learn to speak their language so that our heartfelt messages and most important desires will be heard. Only then can we change our existing paradigms to ones that are better suited to our ambitions and dreams.

To familiarise yourself more with trance and learn its vocabulary, spend some time each day undertaking an introspective task. Breathing is a good gateway activity into trance, mainly because we all do it, which means it's easy to access and given how portable it is there's never a reason not to take advantage of its merits.

There are so many very good breathing strategies and techniques, so find one that suits you and practise it regularly. Focused breathing will naturally help you to move into that daydreaming state. From there you can learn the art of conscious daydreaming which enables you to install new ideas, thoughts and feelings, using positive statements, affirmations and mantras. It's worth noting that you don't need complicated scripts to create a new, positive mindset. Short, simple statements are very effective, such as 'I deeply and completely love and accept myself', 'I am a self-healing organism and I am wonderfully well', 'every day, in every way I'm getting better and better'. Simple statements like these, repeated whilst in the trance state, can help us to more quickly overturn old ways of thinking and perceiving.

Visualising when in trance is an equally powerful way to bring about internal change. When you can see in your mind's eye your desired way of being, your ideal destination, the act of 'seeing' what you need or want acts as a catalyst to connect all areas of the brain. This triggers the occipital lobe - located at the back of the head. This lobe is responsible for most aspects of vision – and also provides us with the ability to visualise things we've never even seen before. This wonderful function engages the imagination and then draws on the amygdala (the seat of our emotions) and the hippocampus (which offers vital context to our emotional experiences). The pre-frontal cortex (which oversees the executive functions) is also pulled into this dance of creativity, forging outcomes that had not up to that point been envisaged.

Therefore, we need to spend time regularly immersed in 'positive' silence. It's not enough to be still because you might be quiet whilst a tornado is raging inside of you. This would not be trance. Periods of silence need a positive focus. You need to galvanise your energy and channel it using the vehicles suggested, such as: breathing in a focused way or meditation - whether guided or self-perpetuated. Practise deep relaxation or self-hypnosis, using music, candles or any other audio-visual aid. Become obsessive about positive affirmations and mantras, carry them wherever you go and whenever you get a chance to consciously daydream, grab it with both hands.

Choose an activity that appeals to you, as you can see there are so many to choose from. Most people fare better with a combination of activities, which stimulate and develop different areas of their being. If you feel you need help, don't be afraid to seek it.

Remember, by making trance an integral part of your life you will achieve real transformation.

"The level of our success is limited only by our imagination and no act of kindness, however small, is ever wasted".

Aesop (620 BC – 564 BC)

Points to remember

- Patternology (the knowledge of patterns) reminds us that everything in the known universe is influenced by patterns of one kind or another. The laws that support this can be found in subjects such as: physics, mathematics, genetics, architecture, biology, psychology... and the list goes on. Even that which has been described as random is underpinned by patterns.

- The studies into human behaviour tell us that unless we make positive adjustments to how our familial inheritances, cultural influences and conditioning have affected us, then we are bound to keep making decisions and choices in the present that are merely reflections of the past. The primary reason that many of us are unable to change is because the patterns of yesterday are still moulding what we are doing today. This is why we need to change the old templates.

- Positive change depends on knowledge being applied. It's as a result of this application that we can create a forward momentum, allowing us to be free of the historical influences that are holding us back. Identify what help you might need and then actively pursue it. Seek out joy and laughter wherever you can. Celebrate your most meaningful relationships. Count your blessings. Listen to beautiful music and commune with nature. New patterns will then emerge leading you to a place of peace, clarity and contentment.

- The Code has helped us to understand the mathematical nature of the world. The countless actions and transactions taking place are all being shaped by numbers, formulae and ratios. Nothing is happening by chance. There is a quiet resourceful wisdom at play, influenced by the primary drivers of protection and growth, ensuring the sanctity of life.

- Nature is constantly trying to find the most efficient way to perform its many tasks. Remember the examples of Pi, hexagons, spirals, spheres, fractals etc., each one proving to be the most effective way that the task can be performed - whether that be within the body, nature, or even in the construction of our buildings, churches and stadia. This example of conservation and efficiency reminds us that we too should be living our lives according to that code.

- Human behavior, as illustrated in sociology and psychology, is also subject to The Code. We are more predictable than we would like to believe. Of course, we are able to manage and channel our energy in line with our desires and intentions, but if we are not focused and systematic about this and do not obey the rules that govern all life, then we find that any changes we make are not sustainable. We too have to honour and respect the natural laws.

- It's important when examining ourselves not to get entangled in our stories. The more we become caught up with what has happened to us and the context of our experience, the more difficult it is to extricate ourselves from that web. We have to look at the story honestly and examine the characters in that play, including the parts we have played, but it needs to be done, as far as we're able to, dispassionately, otherwise we remain victims. It's now time to become victors.

- There is often a dominant character (subpersonality) within your story, there may be two or three and the more you understand their role in shaping your beliefs, attitudes and outlook, the more it is possible to persuade them to take a different course of action... to write a new script. These dominant characters will have been running things probably most of your life, all in the name of your protection, and trying to create advantages for you wherever possible. But they now need to let go of fear, which has driven most of their activities and embrace the language of love and kindness.

- One of the most powerful ways to bring about change at all levels of human consciousness is through trance. Trance could be described as consciously daydreaming. It's where we use our greatest resource, our thoughts, to go inward and meet the angels of our better nature. Activities such as mindfulness, meditation, chanting and prayer are all wonderful ways to meet those angels. The angels are love, empathy, compassion, forgiveness, tenacity, courage, strength, faith and humility. We know when we've met these angels because we always feel better in their company. They remind us that what we've become isn't who we are and that we have the power to do something about that.

- Transform through trance.

A meditation to remind you of the primary themes of this chapter...

I now realise that my story is not who I am... the journey I have taken is only one dimension of me... the story so far only tells me about the path that I have taken... which is a mix of circumstance and choice... I can either continue to be defined by this... or I can evaluate the journey so far and see if it reflects my highest hopes, dreams and aspirations... and if not it's time to write a new script...

It's so easy to get caught in the web of the past... and believe the worst about myself based on my upbringing, the beliefs, prejudices and the projection of others... it's also easy to get caught up in the countless mirages that the materialistic world offers... but as I begin to wake up, I become aware of what is true and can be trusted... and what has deceived me and made me blind... my own story has been a big part of the illusion... and if I am to be free, I need to see what belongs to me and what should be left behind...

I now leave behind the parts of my script that no longer serve me... I now leave behind the guilt and shame that has crippled and undermined me... I now leave behind the hurts and the pains that have quietly tortured me... denying me the peace that I ache for... I now leave behind all the habits, patterns and memories that keep stealing the present moment from me... I now leave it all behind...

Starting from today, starting from right now, I unwrap the gift of this present moment... and as I do, I'm greeted by the infinite stream of possibilities that are always at my fingertips... I can feel my spirit bursting with joy as I am free to choose the path most suited to my heart... I am free to choose that which is in alignment with my hopes and dreams... I'm free to choose the part in the play that I am best suited to... and I choose that today...

Living beyond my old story allows me to write a new one... I now have the courage to believe in my very best self... I know this is the part I am worthy of... the part I was born to play.... by letting go of the outdated past and positively embracing the present, a future I could never have imagined unveils itself to me now... I see a future full of promise... a future where I live in complete harmony with myself, with others and the environment... I am overwhelmed with a feeling of joy... a feeling of bliss...

This is a future that is created by my positive choices today... now past, present and future are beautifully woven into a blanket of peace... a blanket that comforts me...

I'm no longer threatened by the past, afraid of the future and missing the beauty of the present...

I am now using my greatest resource, my mind... and with a sincere heart and focus I have become the architect of my dreams...

CHAPTER 6

ALCHEMY: FROM IMPAIRED TO EMPOWERED

"The best portion of a good man's life is his little, nameless, unremembered acts of kindness and of love".

William Wordsworth (1770 – 1850)

The world is drowning in so much data and information. Information overload is being acknowledged as a genuine mental health issue. Our brains are almost permanently switched on with the constant external stimuli of request and demand. It's impossible to keep up with all the data streams, social media platforms are growing and expanding all the time and we feel compelled to keep up with them and their nagging requests - all because we're afraid of missing out; we are caught up with the illusion of what the modern world deems important.

In Synergy I covered the basics of metaphysics. In this chapter I'm going to expand on this vast and essential subject. It is my assertion that you cannot live a truly fulfilled life without understanding your relationship to the metaphysical realm.

Let me begin by clarifying some of the language I'll be using, so we're at least on the same page.

Information, knowledge and wisdom

There is a danger of thinking of information as the critical ingredient with regards to our understanding of ourselves and the world. This is a dangerous proposition because until we understand where the information is coming from and whether it is a source that can be trusted we are at the mercy of that information. Information alone is not sufficient to awaken our minds.

It's difficult to know which facts and statistics to trust, given the extent of misinformation and the culture of fake news we are immersed in. The SEO and Google specialists I work closely with and the community they are a part of, have calculated that about 58% of the data we're all accessing on the internet is either inaccurate or ill-informed and because there is no vetting or regulation of this information, we are exposed to millions and millions of words uploaded daily infiltrating our screens and devices. Unfortunately, most of us take this information at face value and as a result find ourselves at the mercy of that data stream.

This is how our minds are becoming infected by factoids (information repeated time and again which then acquires the status of truth in our minds) - and memes (ideas, concepts, images, behaviour or other themes that are spread using non-genetic means such as social media). In both cases the data takes on the characteristics of a virus, infiltrating our consciousness, twisting and shaping our ideas and beliefs then influencing the philosophies by which we live... what a frightening reality.

Endless data and information are being poured out of the different media outlets, straight into our brains and minds. No wonder poor mental health is the fastest rising condition in the developed world - as our minds are being polluted and we are now unsure what is fact and what is fiction.

It is crucial to our development that we don't make the mistake of thinking that information is knowledge. It is simply data. Knowledge is a more sophisticated system or phenomenon - it's where we gather information and formulate it into theories and concepts that enhance our understanding and insight of a given subject.

Knowledge provides us with a framework, which we can use to examine and evaluate the value of something; experience is an important part of that process. If we look at subjects like, science, philosophy and psychology we see excellent examples of information gathered and over time moulded into a system – whether that be through observation, research, data analysis, introspection, discussion and/or debate, and from there a concept, ideology or philosophy emerges.

This is in stark contrast to the bits of information people now cobble together, citing and quoting that which they think is knowledge because they've 'Googled' it. Is something you've read on-line, in your favourite magazine or extracted from some other social media platform, fact, factoid or meme? Do you actually have enough contextual information to even draw accurate conclusions?

So much of what we believe is built on such flimsy foundations, especially now in the modern world where data is flying around like sparks from a welding rod - enjoying a moment of bright intensity and then literally gone in the next... and before we know it something else seemingly more compelling, more attractive demands our attention.

We are now so easily impressed that we no longer see what is truly impressive. We spend so little time being still that the gifts and joys of introspection are rarely experienced. As a result, we are unable to assess the merit and true value of the information that is whizzing around in our personal universe. And so, information has no time to be properly processed and rarely becomes knowledge. Knowledge is something that has evolved out of considered thought, thorough examination, meaningful experience and is then embroidered into one's awareness, informing one's view of the world.

Until we slow down, the opportunity for information to become knowledge and knowledge to become wisdom remains elusive.

The dangers of knowledge

Although knowledge is worthy of some reverence and transcends information and the data junky culture that exists, it would be short-sighted not to highlight the trappings and illusions of knowledge.

I believe we need to be wary of those deemed to be experts. This term is often used incorrectly. The correct definition of an expert is one who is 'experienced in' - which is much more than someone who is knowledgeable. There are so many people who can clearly and eloquently describe a theory or technique and concept. In my opinion, these individuals are best described as pundits. They are indeed knowledgeable but that does not automatically translate to them being experts (those who embody that knowledge).

In fact, I would say, most people who are knowledgeable never truly become experts. They can be valuable points of reference and useful signposts on the destination of becoming more aware, but she who is knowledgeable is not qualified to take you all the way – unless of course that is not your objective.

The danger with those who are knowledgeable is that they may believe their position reflects the whole story. They have not worked out for themselves that the seduction of knowledge is not the same as the warm embrace of truth - one is a mirage, the other is an oasis.

Truth, whether that be the truth as you see it, or truth in a more objective sense, cannot be achieved by having knowledge without its essential companion - application. To know but not to do, is like being given the antidote for a critical illness and never cashing in the prescription.

There are so many who speak knowledgeably on a multitude of subjects whilst not living in alignment with their own discourse. When deciding on the best path for yourself, make sure in your own research that you're pursuing a path where the evidence of application is clearly visible. Do not be persuaded by theory alone.

It should be said for balance that I'm not undermining the value of any theory or knowledge; because wisdom can only be attained when a theory has been tested time and time again and has proven to stand up to the scrutiny of such analysis. All the great mathematicians, architects, scientists and philosophers began their work with a theory that they tested in the laboratory of their own lives and it's the experience that emerged out of that examination that helped them to establish their principles and philosophies and become true experts in the process. Many of those principles and philosophies have stood the test of time.

Try not to be easily impressed and what is truly impressive will announce itself to you, in its own beautifully unassuming way.

Wisdom

Knowledge plus application equals personal power. I have mentioned this already and will keep coming back to it. This is because it is simple, clear, honest and accurate. It's also the formula for how we can achieve our life's objectives. Those seeking personal power also have to understand that courage is required.

Knowledge takes us to the door of understanding, but it is courage and application that will take us through that door. Experience and wisdom will be waiting for us on the other side.

The more one is immersed in experience, the more wisdom illuminates the path. There is an unmistakeable grace and humility about wisdom - it's so wonderfully generous, it gives without counting. It wants and needs nothing in return. The one who is truly wise is like a tree laden with fruit. Its branches bow down, freely offering its bounty to each passer-by.

This is a journey very few undertake, because it asks for us to give up what we 'think' we know in order that we can truly know. Sadly, most of us are trapped in our conditioning, bound by our education, class, our public persona and prejudices. And so, we believe our own propaganda - and busily seek the information from the world that supports our hypothesis. Wisdom cannot be found in this place. Only ignorance and arrogance find comfort in the illusion of solely believing one's own doctrine.

This is why we have to let go of our acquired selves in order that we can find our true self. Those of us prepared to do this can and do become wise.

Please note, this is the road least travelled and so is not for the faint-hearted. It requires focus, tenacity, patience and compassion, but it promises you its undying support, deeper understanding and the strength that you'll need at times of doubt and weakness. Wisdom is an ally like no other. It promises you its unlimited resources. All you need do is to keep having the courage to do the right thing even when it would be easier to resign to the circumstances and give way to fear.

Wisdom does not seek fame, fortune or personal recognition for its achievements; these may come as a natural side effect of your chosen path, but these attainments are never pursued for their own sake. Truth is not found in that place.

As you take your journey towards self-realisation and personal enlightenment, that place where your spirit is most alive and flourishing, be aware of the glare created by the endless information, being imbibed via the senses. Much of this data is unvetted and lacks credibility but sparkles with promises that pull you towards another mirage.

So, carefully analyse and research what is on offer - and only if it stands up to scrutiny should you move in that direction, because only then will you find the experience, which is the bridge between the known and unknown.

Listening, the doorway to wisdom

I've provided you with an outline of the difference between information, knowledge and wisdom. I've also indicated some of the pitfalls to be found within information and knowledge.

Wisdom in this context is clearly the 'holy grail'; but how do we transition from wherever we might currently find ourselves to become sages?

The answer is simple, but the challenge is more difficult. We cannot become those who walk the road least travelled without listening. Listening is the gateway to the seemingly unknowable, to the language of the Gods, to the treasure trove of truth.

This simple act is more challenging than most of us realise. Although we can all learn this skill, be under no illusion it is not easily mastered without paying attention. To really listen means to get out of the way – which is to get out of your own way and the way of the one you're listening to.

We have to suspend our beliefs, we have to ignore our prejudices, we have to entertain the idea that we may be wrong, and we have to resist the impulse to interrupt when the other person is still in flow... not easy to do. Especially when your mind is spinning around thinking you have the most important insight that you need to share, or that your point of view will change the landscape of the conversation, or you know more than this person on this topic, so you must say what's in your mind now.

To put those urges to one side and really listen requires much patience, a great deal of humility and incredible insight. You are unlikely to steer the conversation in the best direction if you are not truly listening. It's by allowing the other to reach the apex of their thought that you can best make a contribution. Your interruption, which may well have value and may satisfy some need or impulse in you, can take the conversation and its content in a different direction and in doing so the real gem that further listening would have unveiled is lost.

A satisfying interaction may still have taken place but that thought, idea, feeling that may well have changed the landscape for good has gone, evaporated into the ether... all because you were unable to wait and to let the flow of consciousness reach its natural end point.

How many times have you sat with a colleague, a friend or someone you love and because of your need to speak, derailed what they were sharing? And when you have done that, how many times do you think you were able to retrace that conversation and reach the point that would have been arrived at, had you been able to wait a few moments longer?

My challenge to you is to practise actively listening. By that I mean resist the urge to speak when it would be better to listen. Try when you are listening to sit in the other person's position or walk in their shoes. Try to enjoy listening more than speaking. It's a very pleasant pastime and beautifies the mind. The more time you spend there the more you'll be drawn to it.

It is only the listener, the one who steps into the spaces between the words who can ever truly become wise. They are able to feel what else is taking place in the conversation. Those who are data junkies will find information is only retained for a short while until the next instalment displaces it. The knowledgeable are much more likely to find that the information that they've accrued has a longer period of residency before it too is replaced. That said, many pundits can remain stubbornly wedded to their theories and concepts - not able to entertain that there is a knowing beyond knowledge. And only by letting go of their perspective, can they make that discovery.

Those who are wise, through consistent application, become the embodiment of experience. They discover a knowing beyond logic and the senses. The insights they gather from going beyond the physical limitations, become permanent residents in their consciousness. These are individuals where knowledge seamlessly flows from their minds and lips. They appear to have miraculous recall, but the reason for this is that they are not going in search of that knowledge or information. It's resident within them, ever available, easily accessible. They also give generously from the treasure trove of their minds, never fearing that it will empty because they know the highest activity in life is to share what they have and that true giving always rewards the giver and the receiver.

Something only really belongs to you in terms of consciousness when you have listened with your whole being. At that point it occupies a part of you forever and will guide and support you on your chosen path.

This is why merely accruing data and information is a vacuous pursuit. Become one who offers a home to truth and wisdom. Then you will find whatever you need to assist you is never far away.

Beware of intuition

During my many years of practice, I have heard the term intuition used repeatedly to explain someone's evaluation of a person, situation or event. At times this has been helpful, but I have to say just as many times it's been destructive.

There are far too many who draw definitive conclusions, create a web of theories and make life-changing decisions, solely based on what they call their intuition. This can be a dangerous pastime because intuition is much more than acting on one's feelings.

Intuition casts a wider net, gathering data from as many sources as are available before drawing conclusions. It realises that our feelings can both be helpful and deceptive, if they are not cross-referenced with other important factors.

So much of what individuals classify as intuition is in fact instinct or gut feelings and as valuable as these are, they are only helpful guides on the road of thorough examination.

Instincts are largely driven by the limbic system (the emotional centre of the brain) and do not necessarily draw data from other points of reference, therefore tend to be a reaction conceived out of protection.

Gut feelings could be argued to be a little further along that continuum because they can be informed by some experience outside of one's purely emotional reaction. That said, gut feelings are not drawing from the same pool of data and experience as intuition and are not as forensic in their analysis of the situation. With both instincts and gut reactions, one is operating from a position as if one's feelings could or should be entirely trusted.

Intuition, on the other hand, is much wiser than this, it realises that if we solely follow our feelings approximately 50% of the time, we will be right, which of course means that 50% of the time we will be wrong. These are not very good odds if truth and personal growth are our goals, because gut feelings and instincts would have us believe we are right most of the time, unaware of when we have in fact got it wrong. It's interesting to note that with instinct and gut feelings we have a fairly good memory for when we've got it right and are less accurate in our recollection when we get it wrong. This gives us a false sense of our 'rightness'.

One who is truly intuitive first of all acknowledges the feeling as it rises and then actively goes in pursuit of the other relevant factors in order that s/he can see the bigger picture. This is because intuition recognises that context is everything.

The Three Aspects of Consciousness is another of the primary pillars within the Reach philosophy. If you're not familiar with it, you can find out more on the Reach website. It's a very helpful model of consciousness which encourages one to look at the world from different vantage points in order that one's own understanding can be further enriched. I believe you will find it a useful tool when it comes to evaluating life.

Back to the dangers of intuition... there is the position I describe as 'other' in the Three Aspects of Consciousness, a position of advanced empathy, where the observer or the listener steps away from their viewing platform and they examine the world from the other person's perspective – only then do they begin to draw conclusions. This way of evaluating an experience calls on both the right and left hemispheres of the brain – the right is primarily concerned with emotions, creativity and the present and the left primarily with logic, analysis and the past and future.

The position of other also engages the amygdala and hippocampus. You may remember that both of these are parts of the limbic system and are involved with our emotions. The amygdala records the raw data of our emotional experiences and then acts and reacts to future life events based on what has been recorded. The hippocampus has a more contextual role, evaluating the emotional significance of those events, helping us to recalibrate how we act in the future based on the contextual factors.

In light of all this, try not to draw conclusions prematurely. Even if you think you're right, before arriving at a definitive position collect as much information as you can before drawing any conclusions. The best way to do that is by stepping away from your own world view and really listening and feeling.

I've seen so much harm done by those who say, 'my intuition never lets me down', 'I should have trusted my intuition', 'I could feel it in my bones' etc. and at a later point they find they were wrong. As a result of their actions others have been wrongly accused and they've hurt the hearts of those they like and love, all because their evaluation of the situation was not thorough enough and their instincts and/or gut feelings misled them.

If you want to develop your intuition, be sure to make introspection and positive silence your friends. As I said previously, positive silence isn't about the absence of sound. There is so much sound inherent within silence. The anxious mind may appear silent and yet there's the hustle and bustle of many narratives, pushing and pulling the individual this way and that. It's important to understand that silence can be both negative and positive and it's through the regular practice of introspection that we have the opportunity to create positive silence, which in turn will help us to create the clarity from which the intuitive mind is born.

Alchemy - the story of the miraculous

The story of the pearl is such a beautiful metaphor for human potential and for personal transformation. It tells the story of how an irritant, often a parasite, is capable of creating one of nature's wonders – a pearl. We too are able to take our irritants and afflictions and make them into the most wondrous things.

What does the story of the pearl have to do with alchemy? Alchemy is the mediaeval forerunner of chemistry and is concerned with the transmutation of matter - in particular it is concerned with the conversion of base metals into gold.

That said the more you probe this topic the more you discover other interpretations. Other cultures such as: African, Arabic, Greek and Egyptian all presented their own definitions of alchemy long before it found its way into northern Europe. In these ancient cultures, alchemy took on much more of a spiritual significance and wasn't simply about matter and chemistry.

These cultures understood that alchemy was about personal regeneration and renewal – a journey where the human spirit could be transformed from a leaden state to something more precious than gold, a state where we could possibly be more than human... angelic even. It is this aspect of alchemy that I want to bring to your attention. I do not want to get caught up in the magic and witchcraft that alchemy has also become aligned to, which has led to many condemning its credibility and value.

The modern discussions around alchemy are also developing an esoteric dimension that is not confined to thinking of alchemy as purely a mediaeval science and a precursor to modern chemistry - but as a spiritual examination of the possibilities for the human condition. Therefore, it could be argued that alchemy has both a scientific and spiritual personality - and subject to your interest you're likely to go in one direction or the other.

From my research, exploration and reflection you're much more likely to find the truth (that which is of personal value) by focusing on alchemy's spiritual virtues. There you will find a very profound message indeed. I will, however, bring in the science where I believe it to be relevant because I am a synergist and believe that truth can be found in both dimensions, often at that point where they converge.

An interesting piece of information that tells us that some of the greatest scientific minds were not dismissive of the merits of alchemy is that in 2016 the Chemical Heritage Foundation bought a 17th-century manuscript on alchemy written by Sir Isaac Newton and it is postulated that some of the metaphysical elements of alchemy influenced Newton's scientific work. Over a million words on the subject of alchemy were written in his own hand.

Newton was not the only notable scientist to respect the attributes of alchemy. There is a long list of known and lesser-known scientists who believed alchemy had a place in helping us to better understand the world that we inhabit. Examples such as: Robert Boyle (one of the founders of modern chemistry), Paracelsus (Father of toxicology), Roger Bacon (one of the first advocates of the scientific method), Jabir ibn Hayyan (one of the great Islamic alchemists), Tycho Brahe (astronomer and astrologer), Sendivogius (a medical doctor and a pioneer of chemistry), Johann Friedrich Schweitzer (a physician and alchemical writer) and the list goes on.

These examples of great scientific minds are not meant to sway you in one direction or another - my reference to Newton and others, is much more to suggest that before you dismiss the relevance of alchemy out of hand it's important to keep an open mind.

Until we are prepared to suspend our beliefs, interpretations, perceptions and prejudices, we are unlikely to ever know more than we know now. So, please, as you read on, try not to lose your way by drawing conclusions about the text until you've reached the end and even then, I would invite you to go and test what's offered in the laboratory of your own life. Only then do I think you are capable of either including the principles of alchemy in your personal understanding about yourself and the world, or dismissing it as being irrelevant.

I would now like to come back to the story of the pearl. The parasite has worked its way into the clam, oyster or mussel and once it has taken up residency the defence mechanism of the oyster is activated, and it begins coating the parasite in a substance called nacre. It takes layers and layers of nacre over a period of about three years to create the beautiful pearl. There are three different types of pearl, but the two main types (natural and cultured) are both created along these lines. The third type is imitation – made from a glass bead dipped into a solution made from fish scales. Like all imitations it cannot be compared with the real thing.

The difference between the natural and the cultured pearl is that the cultured pearl is created using an irritant, a piece of shell, called Mother of Pearl (usually from mussel shells), which is then planted into the oyster. In these cases, at least three years is required to produce a gem-quality pearl. If that process is not honoured, and it is accelerated, then only a thin coat of nacre will be formed, and the quality of the pearl is significantly reduced.

During my work I've seen so many times the ability of the human spirit to turn the parasite (the negative experience), into something more magnificent than they could ever have imagined.

The pearl also reminds us that change is a process, not an event. When the pearl's maturation period is interfered with, something inferior is created. My experience has taught me this is true for us as humans too. The most resplendent version of who we are needs time to shape the jewel within.

The four phases of alchemy

There are many schools of thought that now argue there are seven phases of alchemy, however I believe the spiritual processes are best summarised in four phases. These are: deconstruction, detoxification, transmutation and perfection (which could equally be described as fruition, or the maximising of potential).

These four phases have significantly impacted on my thinking and my work and have proven to be valuable classifications and instructive guides for helping me to help those I am working with reach the pinnacle of their potential.

N.O.S.E is another pillar of The Reach Approach. If you're not familiar with it, you can find out more on the Reach website. It summarises the essence of the work we undertake with clients and is an acronym for: name it, own it, surrender it and empowerment.

I do not intend to revisit that aspect of our model in this work, but it is worth mentioning that these four phases are similar in their nature, enquiry and primary focus to the four phases of alchemy - that is, deconstruction (name it), detoxify (own it), transmutation (surrender it) and perfection (empowerment).

In other words, we can only effectively deconstruct our negative patterns once we have named them. How can we address a problem we've not accurately diagnosed? The detoxification process begins once we've owned those negative habits and traits; they cannot be cleansed from the system until we take responsibility for our part in the stories we tell - whilst we continue to blame others and life events for how we feel we are denied positive change.

The positive change that we seek becomes possible when we engage in the liberating practices of surrender. It is only by practising the letting go processes that empowerment becomes possible.

The final phase of empowerment or perfection should not be confused with the idea of being flawless. It is best defined as the point where we become the best version of ourselves. This is where the 'nacre of our efforts' completes the coating and we become human pearls - now able to fulfil our promise in the world, spreading our beauty and spiritual glow wherever we go.

This is the primary focus of my work, to help someone, who generally starts out feeling less than precious to feel invaluable... and ultimately priceless. This is the primary occupation of both alchemy and N.O.S.E.

Let us take a closer look at each of the four phases...

Deconstruction

Generally, when someone walks through my door for the first time their starting position is one of dissatisfaction, anxiety, fear, grief or a desperation of some other kind. They are certainly not happy with their current position. This is where the task of naming their issue begins. Within the naming process I'm interested in helping them to find out what is 'really' wrong because often the presenting position is hiding a multitude of sins.

Finding out what is funding the negative position and experience takes time, keen listening, patience, empathy and focus. It is at this point of enquiry that the deconstruction process begins - because to gain access to what is lurking in the dark recesses of the soul is not done without the moving, probing and sometimes dismantling of what stuff is there.

This, however, can be quite a challenge because if the individual is holding onto his pathology (and many are) whilst expecting positive change, then experience has taught me that everything remains the same.

This is why the individual needs to suspend their current thinking in order to stand outside of it, to see how much of it still has merit. It's only when we scrutinise ourselves in this way that it becomes clear what needs to remain and what needs to be discarded.

If we come back to the parasite and the pearl, nacre is the substance that the oyster creates which is its defence mechanism against the invasion. When a parasite finds its way into our consciousness, our mind's immune system seeks to protect us from that hurt or trauma.

It does this by compartmentalising our experiences, applying a protective coat, which minimises and masks the emotional intensity of that assault. This is done by the brain creating the neurochemicals that sedate us at the time of the emotional event, which in turn reduces the experiential 'feel' and the impact of the experience. This is overseen by the mind - the mind is the pharmacist, and the brain is the pharmacy.

This is wonderfully protective in the first instance and gets us through many of the things we might otherwise not survive. The mind and brain are trying to get us to the best destination so that we might fulfil our potential. They unconsciously know we have the capacity to become pearls.

Sadly, if we have had insufficient emotional nutrition provided by the three 'A's (affection, attention, affirmation), it then becomes very difficult for the brain and mind to complete the task of gathering together those experiences which when pooled create a more precious and priceless version of ourselves. This is why it takes effort, time and patience to create an incredible jewel, glistening with purity and power.

The protective instinct, as we saw in chapter 3, is very important to the healing process but it can also stunt our growth - the mind's protective instinct is the thing that gets us through so much in life. However, this can lead to parts of us being very aware and resilient whilst other parts remain delicate and vulnerable as too much protection can inhibit our development. When our experiences are not properly processed there is a lack of resolution and healing. As a result, an imitation pearl is created - something that may look like a pearl but below the coating there is just a bead of glass. Many of you may recognise this as you carry around feelings of shame, guilt and regret, which prevent you from becoming a fully formed pearl... something more precious and beautiful.

In the therapeutic process we have to both acknowledge the value of the protective system, but also focus on creating the conditions for growth. This is why we must deconstruct the issue in order that it can be properly seen, evaluated and understood. Only then can we move to the next phase, which is detoxification.

Detoxification

You may remember that one of the primary tenets of the Reach model is that the 'secret to health is the removal of waste'. I make reference to this concept in chapters 2 and 3.

The concept of detoxification is often limited to just the body. Detoxifying diets can be found in their hundreds on the internet and on bookshelves all around the planet. There's a detoxifying guide for almost every condition, season and personal challenge. But in the context of consciousness, we need to consider the mind and the spirit. This does not mean ignoring the body and the environment because all four are invaluable to recovery and healing and as a synergist, my detoxification list would always include body and environment. But in order to understand detoxification in this analogy, I want you to think of it as the removal of hurts, trauma, blockages and any psychic wound that keeps you in a place of doubt, self-loathing and self-harm.

Although there will be some common themes that could apply to all of us there will also be some that are specific to each person as a consequence of their predispositions, their family inheritances and their own personal experiences.

As previously stated, detoxification is most closely aligned to owning (in the N.O.S.E. process), the phase where we acknowledge our part in the disease and dysfunction that is afflicting us. This is not a matter of negative criticism or condemnation of the self, as it requires compassion, whilst taking personal responsibility. It's the point where we realise that we alone can change our fortunes. No matter how much support and help we have, without making the necessary effort ourselves then the transformation we seek is unlikely to occur.

Undertaking a journey of forgiveness is arguably the greatest detoxifier for mind and spirit. It is a detergent like no other. Forgiveness understands that it heals the forgiver and frees her from further self-harm. It is not letting anyone off the hook because in a cause-and-effect universe, the consequences of our actions will always find their way back to our door – it's just a question of how and when. Life is a system that is always seeking balance and all our actions are eventually audited and any outstanding debts will have to be paid.

So, if our concern is to be whole and well then detoxifying the mind and spirit is a priority and all of the introspective practices I've previously mentioned, will help you in this endeavour. These include but are not limited to meditation, mindfulness, deep relaxation, creative visualisation, mantra-mind thinking, conscious breathing and prayer.

In addition, one has to develop an attitude and culture of self-care. This always extends to the body and the environment.

For the body this would include: a rainbow diet, copious amounts of water, skin brushing, juicing, massage, Epsom salt baths, necessary supplementation, exercising, body work and of course deep restorative sleep – which cleans up so much of the muck acquired each day.

In terms of the environment, this is primarily about decluttering or maybe more accurately redesigning your space and how you use it – removing any extraneous items that are no longer useful. Improving ventilation, your use of colours, decoration and managing hygiene.

With regards to the environment, our relationships are vitally important. They need to be kind and supportive of our endeavours and where that isn't the case, we need to make the necessary changes.

Other things to consider are making time for fun, hobbies, socialising and reaching out to those in need or more vulnerable than yourself.

All of these activities will unblock you, clear the pathways and continue the journey from parasite to pearl.

The third phase of alchemy is that of transmutation/transformation

Transmutation/transformation

Now that detoxification is underway the building blocks from which we can begin again start to emerge. This could in alchemist terms be described as the filtrate, the valuable residue from which a new compound (a new script) can be created. This is the point of transformation or transmutation - where the energy can now be crafted into something new.

This is where surrender (lovingly letting go of the past and unwanted patterns) begins in earnest.

Let me be clear, detoxification is an on-going process, so as far as N.O.S.E. is concerned, owning your stuff does not end when your issues from the past have been adequately addressed. This is simply stage one. Once that has been established, owning becomes part of one's way of being, part of one's culture of self-awareness. Preventing your life from being repopulated with unwanted stuff takes focus, vigilance and honesty. This approach means there is little build-up of unresolved stuff because the individual does not wait for something to become rancid before acting.

Likewise, with surrender, employing introspective activities and engaging in acts of self-improvement is not something done today and gone tomorrow. It's a permanent attitudinal shift, one based on the realisation that a surrendering mind is perpetually growing and flourishing. This leads to the resolution of our issues and further coatings of nacre and with each coating our position is strengthened.

I spoke earlier about decluttering and redesigning your space but it's important to state that this too is an on-going process. Whether the changes are internal or external, sustainable solutions are not found by making something merely a fad or a phase. This aspect of your journey depends on routine and establishing healthy patterns. You need non-negotiables (those personal pledges and promises one makes to oneself) to reach your desired destination.

I have consistently found that eight non-negotiables create a positive tipping point, leading to stability and personal power. This is not power over anything or anyone; this is a significant degree of self-mastery - where the individual becomes the captain of their ship, making choices and decisions that are true to his or her philosophy.

These non-negotiables, as you may remember, are closely aligned to The Story of Health and so I would recommend as part of your personal manifesto for change that you make a Story of Health Plan. Start with at least two things in each of the four areas and form an unwavering alliance with each - this will create so much self-respect and self-belief, which will keep the momentum of transformation going and ensure your healing and recovery.

This stage of transmutation is where consciousness takes the filtrate and makes it into something priceless.

Perfection

The more we immerse the mind in healing choices and let go of that which no longer serves us, the more we become a pristine version of ourselves.

At this point the pearl (our true essence) moulded by our efforts emerges and its unmistakable beauty is there for all to see. What lovingly letting go helps us to achieve is a purity based on the acceptance of our ambivalence. Accepting our ambivalence means realising that we do not grow in nice, neat columns, where every aspect of our nature and personality is equal to all the other aspects.

In other words, one part of our being or consciousness may be at around 80% in terms of its evolution and capacity, whilst another has only evolved to 40% of its potential. Being able to accept these discrepancies enables the 40% bit of us to grow.

It's vitally important to embrace your ambivalence because only then will your perfection be obtained. I spoke earlier of the pooling of the hurts, traumas and pains, each one with its own protective coating. However, whilst they remain separate a fully formed pearl cannot be created. It is the collective nacre of these experiences that creates the priceless gem. This is a lovely description for ambivalence, where we pool the less evolved and desirable bits together - and through our acceptance of them, perfection is attained.

Perfection as far as spiritual endeavour is concerned is not about achieving a flawless state; it is about being the best version of yourself. Once we understand that perfection is our highest attainment, we stop looking at others and comparing ourselves unfavourably, instead we look into the mirror of our own souls and fulfil the promise we came with... which is much more than most of us realise. Perfection is where we meet our most resplendent selves.

Perfection is paired with empowerment in the N.O.S.E. process because the empowered position is not something we actually acquire, it is something that naturally emerges out of the clean, clear waters of consciousness. As we remove the waste and toxic debris of unwanted habits and patterns, as we remove the traumas that have built up over the years and decades and the negative inheritances from the families and systems that moulded us in our formative years, a fountain bursting with the joy of who we are rises up from the deepest recesses of our hearts and minds - and our authentic self stands proudly before us.

Perfection in this context is similar in that the nacre of our efforts has now coated the long-forgotten parasite and created a thing of incredible beauty and strength. When most individuals begin the journey of self-improvement it seems unimaginable that they could ever live a life not just free of their pain but a life where their pain has become the foundation of their transformation.

This is alchemy at its very best, where something less precious, with time and patience is moulded into something of greater value and beauty. This is a transformation we are all capable of, a perfection that can then be sustained by continuing to lovingly let go - preventing a build-up of toxicity in our brains, bodies, hearts and minds.

Alchemist – becoming a metaphysical magician

I hope by the time you've reached this point I've managed to illustrate that metaphysics is a conversation we are all a part of. It's not some strange ancient idea or new age phenomenon, it's the invisible dynamic impressing itself on our physical transactions and material world.

The more we understand its role and influence the more we are able to understand ourselves and our true value.

My invitation to you is to become an alchemist, a metaphysical magician, someone who engages in a conversation with himself, the unseen, others and the world. Don't be passive in your own life, watching circumstances and events dictating your decisions and choices. You may not always be able to make things better, but you can always be better, regardless of events. For this to be the case it's important that you adorn yourself with the divine cloak of special powers, that realisation that nothing can deny you the full expression of your beauty - and this begins by accepting where you are right now, faults and all. Acceptance is where alchemy begins.

Let go of negative judgement. We have all fallen short - at probably many points in our lives we have not been brave enough, wise enough, honest enough, determined enough. But relentlessly punishing oneself resolves nothing. It leaves us fragmented, incapable of positive change. Acceptance, on the other hand, forgives us for our inadequacies and shortcomings and gives us a chance to redeem ourselves and reach the zenith of our souls.

Make a promise as you read this now to start cultivating the art of acceptance. Promise to forgive yourself for what you could have done better, for what you haven't done and should have done, embrace yourself with kindness and then the process of healing can begin.

You may at first meet much doubt and resistance but keep coming back to the mantra 'kindness is good for the soul'. Keep coming back to the mantra 'forgiveness sets me free'. Keep coming back to the mantra 'I deeply and completely love and accept myself'. Keep coming back to the mantra 'I lovingly let go'.

Any thought that reminds you that your future and fortunes lie in the very next thought you have, will keep you focused on generating kind, self-forgiving, self-nurturing thoughts and affirmations.

Remember, acceptance is not letting yourself off the hook, it's the recognition that there is no gain or value in self-harm. This is the first step to becoming a metaphysical magician.

Running parallel to the need for acceptance is the creative art of experimentation. The mind is the most amazing receptacle - majestic, powerful, with limitless creativity. As was pointed out in the Four Aspects of the Mind, most of us are only using the conscious mind, which is about 5% of our capacity, 10% at best. Instead of the mind being used in accordance with its true ability, it largely lies redundant, an impotent force, often working against itself.

If you are to change your fate, and fortune, then you need to become the master of your mind and by experimenting with and exploiting its immense power, you can achieve wondrous things.

Pause for a few moments and try this exercise...

Using the eye of your mind, I want you to see a large jug. This is the jug of universal love. It is filled with golden white light. This light represents all that you need.

Imagine the jug has been lifted up and its contents are now being poured into the top of your head.

It has the consistency of molten gold and as the light is poured you can feel its warmth and gentleness coating the brain and seeping through its undulations and crevices. As it is passing through the brain there are feelings of warmth and power, feelings of peace and contentment. The light continues to make its way down through your neck, into your shoulders, slowly making its way down your arms into your hands and into your fingers. At the same time making its way through your chest and torso. It's the most wonderful feeling.

The light is cleansing, purifying as it moves through your body, unblocking all the pathways and ensuring health and well-being. You're feeling refreshed and renewed... The light continues down through your pelvis and hips, making its way into your thighs. You can see and feel the light as it moves down into your calves towards your feet, into your toes.

The feelings of warmth and strength continue. The feelings of peace and contentment deepen. From head to toe you are now a body of light and you sit or lie with this feeling for a while.

Now, imagine that light that has filled your body is extending into the space that you're in. Whether you're inside or outside, the light extends beyond your body and you can see it, using the eye of your mind, touching everything in and around you, spreading its warmth, its strength, spreading its peace and contentment and everything animate or inanimate is enhanced by the kindness, generosity and love of this light - and you have become a channel for spreading goodness in the world.

Practising something like this regularly will not only harmonise your mind, body, spirit and environment but by emitting such vibrations you will improve the resonance wherever you are. Remember, you have an energy signature and whether you know it or not, you're making contracts every minute of every day. If you ensure that your signature is the best it can possibly be then the contracts you enter into will of course be the very best.

At this point you become a positive contributor. You become part of the solution. There are many ways to experiment with the mind's majesty. You will find many such examples on our YouTube channel. These include: Ancestors and Angels,

Listening - The Jewel in the Crown, Who Are You Really? Change is a Process Not an Event, The Magic Waterfall, Asking for Nothing and Receiving Everything and Beyond Limitations. There are many more, but these are good examples of how you can exercise and expand the mind's potential.

Another way to be a positive contributor, a part of the solution, is to practise conscious breathing. This is an easy and accessible thing to do. When we breathe correctly, filling our lungs to their capacity and fully exhaling, we automatically trigger the parasympathetic nervous system, (responsible for the rest and digest response), which is very soothing to our organs and other bodily systems and with that our capacity to access the higher aspects of the self is increased. We are now in growth not protection. The interior shifts and changes that follow, allow us to become the architects of our own destiny, choosing what we want and letting go of that which opposes us.

Make it part of your pledge to yourself to experiment and exploit the mind's majesty.

Something I do a lot whilst I'm working with individuals is imagine them sitting or standing under a waterfall of light. I see the light cascading down on them and a bit like the exercise I described with the jug of universal love, I see the light cascading down around their body but also passing through it. Whatever their complaint, hurt, trauma or suffering, I imagine that light washing it away. I imagine the discolouration of their issue and pain being diluted and the more the waterfall of light cascades down on them the more they are liberated from that experience.

According to what I think they need I see the light changing. If it's healing, care and nurturing I see the light turning green, if it's peace and calm it becomes blue. Where I think healing is required, I will often move between green and blue. If I feel they need hope and joy I see it as a yellow light. The kaleidoscope of colour is something I intuitively allow to take place as I'm listening and connecting to their experience.

If I feel the need is for emotional or psychological resilience, then the waterfall becomes orange, sometimes red. If I'm trying to connect to their essence, the highest part of their nature it becomes purple. When I'm not sure exactly what is needed, I see it as white light, which contains the full spectrum of the rainbow, where nothing is missing.

This is one way I aspire to be a metaphysical magician. You could do this too when sitting with a colleague, a friend, your spouse, a sibling, your child. Really listen to what they're saying to you and wish them what you think they most need. This practice asks so little of you and yet gives so much in return. You'll be surprised, if you practise this, to notice how your focus and concentration improves, your ability to listen and really hear is increased and your humanity and self-mastery expands.

Being a metaphysical magician is easier than you think. I hope I've inspired you to at least give it a try.

Ancient concepts fit for the 21st century

In my second book, Antiquity Comes Full Circle I tried my best to do justice to the Eastern contribution to history, which is less well reported on in the developed world. One could be forgiven for thinking that the world as we know it stands on the shoulders of the great European civilisations, philosophers, explorers and scholars. But this would be to deny the huge contribution of China, India, Africa, the Middle and Far East. In fact, the foundations on which much of the European culture is built are a direct result of the great civilisations and teachings of the East.

I make reference to this as it is my belief that many of the ancient values are needed if we are to save ourselves, our planet and all we hold dear. We seem to be using the shovel of progress to dig our own grave. As discussed in chapter 2, we can see how all four environments are struggling. Our relationship with matter is arguably at its lowest point. Our intolerance and ignorance are creating greater divisions as our fears and prejudices are stockpiling around the world, creating more unease, injustice and conflict.

There is a need to re-write the personal and social manifestos and my proposition is that we should be looking to the ancient values that were less material in their focus. As I said earlier, this needs to begin with the way that we educate our children. We need to make these spiritual values part of the curriculum. I'm not talking about promoting particular faiths or religions - these are personal matters that each one should decide for themselves. I'm talking about universal principles and values that apply regardless of one's faith.

There are some great spiritual academics and commentators from the East who did their best to disseminate the message of integrating principles and values that would serve to enhance our conscience and humanity. I've chosen three such examples from the twentieth century.

Aurobindo (1872 – 1950): although he had been educated in England and went to Cambridge, Aurobindo became a radical revolutionary who wanted to end British Colonial rule and with that the racism and attitude of superiority that the British Empire lorded over India. He went on to become a politician, but he was so passionate about yoga, he integrated his yogic and spiritual principles into his political life.

He believed it was possible to combine meditative and other spiritual practices with a life of public service. He went on to create a system of yoga called Integral Yoga - a system that believes we have secret potentials, which lie dormant and are actualised by making sincere effort. As a result of these efforts, we are able to experience the truth about the cosmos and the divine and with that a natural spiritual evolution occurs. His teachings cover a broad spectrum of topics but could probably be summarised in this one statement: truth is one, but the paths are many. He spent the last 40 years of his life spreading this message.

K.C. Bhattacharyya (1875 – 1949) was another integrationist. He was a great student of the ancient Indian scriptures such as the Vedas and the Upanishads. He did probably his greatest work after retirement when he became a professor of philosophy at Calcutta University and the professor of mental and moral philosophy. He constructed a comprehensive philosophical world view, which was an amalgamation of Eastern and Western philosophy.

He didn't believe in an allegiance to a particular school and so one can find evidence of Kant and Hegel (German philosophers) amongst others, in his work. He wanted to demonstrate that Indian philosophy was not exclusively mystical and unscientific as it was often claimed. He felt intellectual debates on the truth became too preoccupied with the rightness of one's position rather than focusing on harmonising difference – which he believed was the true path to peace.

Sarvepalli Radhakrishnan (1888 – 1975) was India's most eminent 20th century philosopher and was well versed in European and Asian philosophical traditions. He was a professor at both Calcutta and Oxford Universities and went on to become the president of India. Although he was educated in colonial India where Christian missionaries proclaimed Christianity to be the only true religion and Hinduism was considered to be flawed and blasphemous, Radhakrishnan went on to champion many of the ancient philosophical principles, especially karma, which he believed gave one responsibility for one's own destiny.

He compared it to a card game where we each have the cards we are dealt and free will gives us the opportunity to play the game as we see fit. He believed that the highest path a human could take was one of selfless service and non-violence. His writings and accomplishments are too many to list as he went on to produce many pieces of work that crossed the Eastern and Western divide. Radhakrishnan believed that there was far more that bound the philosophies together, examining the work of Buddha, Plato, Aristotle, Jesus, Hillel, the Sufis and many more. He passionately believed in applying values to all one's dealings and living a life in pursuit of the highest conduct, avoiding dogma at all costs.

These individuals were exponents of respect and reverence. They were champions of non-violence and personal responsibility. They passionately pursued the art of introspection and appreciation. They lived by and honoured the metaphysical principles, believing that was the best way for us all to fulfil our potential. They believed in looking for ways for us all to kindly co-exist.

I believe these are some of the values we should be teaching in primary and secondary education. Our children need to understand the power and the value of kindness, compassion, applying empathy, acceptance and tolerance, pursuing cooperation and collaboration rather than competition. They also need to understand different cultures and perspectives in order to enrich their own.

These topics are every bit as important as teaching mathematics, languages, the sciences, history and geography. What is the point of preparing our children for the world if we don't teach them how to be proper custodians of it? Our current approach to these matters has our planet drowning in toxic waste, wars that in some cases are centuries old, many of which are about whose God or ideology is best - which has only served to create a more fractious world.

Our use of science and technology has brought us to the brink of our own self-destruction. Isn't this because we've been pursuing the wrong ideology, the wrong principles and values?

We need a curriculum for the 21st century. We need our educators to insist on a value-based education system. We need to become global citizens, not citizens of a country or continent, ideologically wedded to the religion, institutions and cultures we are born into. We are much more than this. Our identity cannot be purely based on geography. The more we become students of geography, the more we realise we have become its prisoners.

In Tim Marshall's excellent book, The Prisoners of Geography, he demonstrates how much of global politics have been dictated by the geographic landscapes we are born into. So many decisions have been influenced by the positions of mountains, rivers and other natural demarcations. These have influenced the way that countries have been formed, how cultures have developed, how languages have spread. These geographical factors have also been pivotal in shaping many of the wars and insurrections around the globe.

Tying our identities to the place of our birth and not thinking beyond the limitations of these geographical factors has supported and facilitated an attitude of 'my part of the world is more important than your part of the world and as a result my beliefs matter more than yours'. The tensions born of this have generated so much conflict and war around oil, precious metals, cotton, spices, information and other technologies and resources.

Our preoccupation with the external environment means we've neglected our own internal geography, we have not focused sufficiently on what is important in our inner landscapes – what needs our time, energy and attention and how to best use our resources to connect with the wider world through self-knowledge and self-respect.

It's time to liberate ourselves from the ignorance of our physical identities and the attachments, connections and historical factors that bind us to the illusion that we are separate. Where our differences exist, we can find understanding and union but only by putting our egos to one side and embracing both humility and humanity.

It's time for us to commit to positive change. We need to commit to being part of the solution. Work out the best way you can do that and become involved in creating a better world.

Why synergy?

At this point in the journey, I hope this question has already been answered and you can see for yourself that no one thing is going to resolve our issues. Whether we're looking at solutions on a personal, communal or global level we need a multifactorial approach. Think of the topics I've covered... they have all come under the heading of mind, body, spirit or environment. The more you examine the problems of the world, the more it becomes clear that any strategy we develop must embrace all four elements.

We need doctors, teachers, inventors, historians, environmentalists, sociologists, carers, mothers, fathers, representatives of every faith, politicians, scholars, academics, accountants, lawyers, retailers, factory workers, those on the front line, the first responders - we need representatives from every walk of life to find ways of reaching across the divide. We need to create synergy in our own lives, our own families and to try and find ways of creating that in our communities in order that our society starts creating strategies and policies that are designed around mattering from the inside out.

Where there is division, we need to find union, where there is disagreement, we need to seek reconciliation. Where there is difference of opinion and ideology, we need to look for common ground.

The Reach Approach is an attempt to build conversations across the many divides and establish a different, kinder conversation.

The more I have investigated and researched the many topics that underpin and shape the human experience the more it has become obvious to me that different disciplines are often talking about the same thing but using different language. If we could get the advocates of those disciplines to sit around the same table, I am quietly confident that they would discover that what binds us is more than what divides us.

There are disciplines like cognitive neuroscience, psychoneuroimmunology and epigenetics, all of which in their different ways have illuminated the role of consciousness and its importance to the world that we live in. Yet these disciplines have different names and labels for the same basic principle, namely that consciousness is an energy that impacts on the biological, emotional, psychological and social reality. And so, it cannot be ignored.

Each of these sciences has in its own way proved that thoughts and feelings impact on our biology. Our biology impacts on our psychology and those psychological factors shape the dynamics in our families, communities and society, which have a substantial influence on the quality of our lives, our sense of well-being and our mental and physical health.

In other words, the overlap in these areas is so significant, why are the epigeneticists, the cognitive neuroscientists, the biologists and social scientists, the environmental researchers and all those interested in the elevation of our world, not sitting around the same table trying to create a common language. This approach would make it easier for us all to see that everything is connected, inspiring us to become more involved in positive change.

At every step of our journey, I'm inviting you to become a synergist. Start with yourself. Where you can, involve your family, friends and colleagues. Become a part of this most important of all conversations. Become a pioneer.

"The great solution to all human problems is individual inner transformation".

Vernon Howard (1919 – 1992)

Points to remember

- Remember the differences between information, knowledge and wisdom. Just because something is repeated time and again, does not make it a fact. We are drowning in factoids and memes, largely spread through the internet and social media. These viruses are infecting our minds and, in many cases, have us believing things that are either false or barely true. It's time to become more discerning as the assault on our senses provides us with the illusion that we are thinking for ourselves.

- Beware of knowledge alone. Although we cannot become wise without first becoming knowledgeable, we do need to carefully vet the sources of knowledge on which we draw. Our global culture is such that celebrities and experts have become such important points of reference, telling us what is valuable and how we should think and act. In some cases, this is helpful but there is a danger of mindlessly following something because someone tells us it is so. We should at least be testing what we're being told in the laboratory of our own lives.

- Wisdom only comes through the application of knowledge. You cannot really know anything until you've immersed yourself in it. Being able to report on something eloquently does not make you knowledgeable, merely a pundit. When you apply knowledge, you discover a 'knowing' that's beyond any theory or concept. You make contact with pure, unadulterated experience - something that resonates with so much beauty, words are not sufficient to define it. This is why to really meet your best self you must repeatedly apply what you know and feel the bliss that emerges from that.

- In order not to be deceived by information and knowledge, and to find your way into the arms of wisdom, you must become an active listener. Listening is not a passive activity. It requires conscious engagement. It's both an art and a skill. It demands focus and attention. Listening at its very best is selfless, it is not trying to get the other person to be quiet in order that it can speak. It knows that many of its best lessons are learned by being patient, being still and absorbing the sounds within its environment.

- Listening is a two-way affair. Wisdom does require us to pay attention to our external world, so we can best decipher its messages, but it also requires us to listen in to our inner world so we can decode those messages too. Those who can master both realms become masters of themselves.

- Intuition is informed instinct. It does not simply act on gut feelings because it knows they can be wrong just as many times as they are right. Intuition knows the value of instinct, but it also knows its shortcomings. This is why when feelings rise up, before acting with certainty, intuition calls on the full complement of the brain, knowing that both logic and emotion are needed. It also knows that examining things through the lens of the three aspects of time (past, present and future) offers a much better position of evaluation. In addition, it remembers the three aspects of consciousness, which encourage us to look at any given moment from more than one vantage point. Only then can we say we are using our intuition.

- Remember the spiritual nature of alchemy. First, we deconstruct, then we detoxify, transmutation comes next, and perfection is the end result. These four stages are mirrored in N.O.S.E. (Name it, Own it, Surrender it, Empowerment). To deconstruct our issues, we must first name them. For the detoxification process to begin, we must then own them. Surrendering our self-limiting habits, patterns and trauma leads to transmutation and the positive change that comes out of this leads to empowerment. This is not perfection in the sense that we are flawless, perfection here means we are the very best we can be.

- It is impossible for us as human beings not to judge. We are judging all the time. In fact, it's necessary to our survival and growth. Judgement to the mind is like breathing is to the body. What we can do is make our judgements kind in relation to others and ourselves. So, stop judging yourself harshly, you need to embrace yourself with acceptance and compassion. Learn the language of 'I deeply and completely love and accept myself'. There you will find your greatest fortune and brightest future.

- There are many wonderful examples of synergy if you look to antiquity. We think of progress as belonging to the present but there are so many things that we need right now that can be found in the past. To make those discoveries we have to give up this arrogant idea that progress comes from only looking forward. We must live our lives going forward but we only really understand life when we look backwards... both perspectives are needed.

A meditation to remind you of the primary themes of this chapter...

Alchemy is the story of the miraculous... the journey of parasite to pearl... it's a journey filled with incredible hope and reassurance... it reminds me that anything is possible... in fact, I am only limited by my own mind...

Alchemy helps me to understand the four stages of change... if I am to be free of my limitations, I first need to face the truth about myself... there is no benefit in glamourising my reality because that self-deception denies me a solution... once I can honestly name my issues, the deconstructing of the old in order to make way for the new can begin... then detoxification follows...

Detoxification is where I own the truth about my old patterns and the consequences of my choices and actions... it's where the slurry of the unwanted toxic stuff is now able to exit my mind, body and most of all my spirit... this cleansing process allows me to change... I've learned that waste weakens... and so it's important to remove it in every way I can...

The transformation process can now begin in earnest... the removal of waste opens up new pathways... and with them come new opportunities and possibilities... that which seemed beyond repair is made good... that which was damaged and twisted is realigned and made useful once more... those feelings of doubt and not being good enough disappear into the ether... I watch them float away with such happiness and joy... a peace begins to descend and with that, a feeling of certainty about my own value and worth...

Then comes the final stage, where the pearl is perfected... strengthened by its journey... this is how I now feel... as I recognise my challenges have helped to coat my soul... reinforcing it... making it more resilient and capable of wonderful things... I feel a quiet strength rising up in me... there is no ego or vanity in this feeling... I feel self-assured... a quiet confidence... there is the realisation that I am a magnificent being... and acknowledging my magnificence is not weakness but strength... I am beautiful and sparkling with love, humility and all the other virtues...

Alchemy sums up the metaphysical truth that I can be anything I put my mind to... I am the one who was once impaired and is now empowered...

Change really is a process not an event... and I embrace it.

CHAPTER 7

THE FOUR PILLARS OF STRENGTH

"Kindness is the language which the deaf can hear and the blind can see".

Mark Twain (1835 – 1910)

At times of challenge, pain and misfortune it can be very difficult to maintain your poise and equilibrium. It's easy to say when everything is going well in your world that you feel calm, confident and positive. However, the real proof of the state of your inner world and mental health can only truly be known when your life is scrutinised and insulted by those things that oppose your peace.

We really know how far up the ladder of personal progress we have climbed when our world is shaken, and we are shaken with it. It's at this time that most of us discover that the theories and beliefs we live by are not always easy to adhere to. In fact, in many cases, we do the opposite of what we believe and intended, we find our conditioning, fears and drivers bully us into making decisions and choices that do not honour our hearts. Our truth and integrity crumble and we find ourselves acting and reacting in ways that disappoint and undermine us.

Is it really possible to achieve that state of serenity – a state described by the Taoists as peace amidst the storm? Is it possible for the mind to remain still and unaffected whilst everything in its environment is resonating with a negative vibration? Can we transcend those influences in such a way that our peace remains intact?

If we have the right method and apply it consistently, then the answer is yes. It is possible for all of us to find peace within the storm, but only when we apply the formula consistently. This is not magic, but it is magical. To be able to enjoy a state of equanimity when the world threatens our peace and stability, is such a wonderful feeling and it's a feeling we can create by patiently applying the following formula.

The four pillars of strength are certainly not the only way to achieve serenity - at the time of doubt, fear, conflict and when the mountain simply seems too steep - but it is unquestionably a very powerful way to overcome that which seems more powerful than you. The more you stand within the fortress created by these four pillars the more you will feel a quiet sense of invincibility emerging. It's a strength that is difficult to define in words. Only when you experience the breadth and depth of these four pillars will you fully understand.

What are these four pillars? Those of you familiar with the Reach Approach will recognise each of them, however it's the order and the relationship between these four attributes that really holds the secret.

The more you understand the mathematical properties of the world, and how those properties underpin everything we see, touch, hear, feel and experience, the more you will understand that everything always has an order, a formula that optimises the outcome.

The four pillars are: forgiveness, gratitude, integrity and kindness. Let us explore each of them and why their relationship to one another holds the key to accessing our incredible strength and resilience.

Forgiveness

So much has been said and written about the importance of forgiveness. It is a core principle of many religious and spiritual doctrines and it is a central part of The Reach Approach philosophy, but why is forgiveness the first of the four pillars?

A lack of forgiveness blocks the mind of the one who is unable to forgive. The mind cannot fully access its potential nor flourish whilst it is burdened by those things that remain unresolved - hurts, anger and pain. These negative events and emotions continue to cast a dark shadow across our spirits, denying us access to the light within.

It is often said that something is 'unforgivable' and 'I will never forgive them for that', but these sentiments are not a punishment to the one who has committed the wrongdoing or crime. The sad truth is that the ones who cannot forgive continue to be punished in their minds and their hearts and are often denied the freedom they ache for. Not forgiving primarily hurts the heart it resides in. It might for a time provide the feeling of justice and satisfaction, as promised by righteousness and indignation, but the reality is quite different.

I work with a lot of individuals who are trapped in the unforgiving mind - they are stuck, unable to grow and are denied the future of their choosing because for them the 'now' continues to belong to the past. They repeatedly relive the hurt, the injustice the anger and pain, which courses through their veins... but at what cost? Their minds are hurting, their hearts too and often their relationships and health are caught in the cycle of suffering. In fact, when you look at the landscape of their life, it's hard to find any peace or joy as the lack of forgiveness permeates into every area, creating a culture of bitterness - an arid land where beauty struggles to grow.

When we forgive, we are set free. It is our minds and hearts that are emancipated. As we are released from the shackles of the past the rivers of consciousness can flow clearly again. We are able to find peace as we are liberated from our pain. Contentment can find a home in our hearts once more.

Forgiveness begins with the self. Until we can forgive ourselves for our mistakes, those regrets, guilt and shame that we conceal deep within our beings will keep calling us to do their bidding. This is why it is extremely difficult to forgive those that have trespassed against us. How can we give what we haven't got? So, the journey of forgiveness needs to begin from where you are standing.

If you can look back on your life with 'kind eyes' and forgive yourself for all those times when you were not true of heart, when you betrayed your beliefs, when you followed even when you knew it was wrong to do so; if you can go back to those moments and forgive yourself for not being enough, then you can begin the journey back to yourself and find that place of serenity.

As you forgive yourself for those moments in time, which you are in some way still negatively attached to, you will feel a lightness of spirit returning. You will feel a joy and clarity you have probably never known emerging. It's at this point of clarity that the mind can really engage in the uplifting pastime of gratitude.

Many embark on the journey of gratitude and yet still find they are unfulfilled and disappointed; this is because they have not properly attended to the pillar of forgiveness. The more we forgive, the more gratitude in us flourishes. Forgiveness is the foundation on which gratitude is built.

Gratitude

Forgiveness clears the rubbish from the fields of the mind allowing gratitude to sow its wonderful seeds of ambition, hope and joy.

The grateful mind is such a beautiful place. It's a virtual paradise, rich with colour, joy and abundance. The grateful mind literally has no room for complaint. It's not that negativity does not try to enter that sanctuary - as blame, criticism and condemnation all seek to enter this beautiful world of blessings. However, gratitude is able to cast a spell on that which threatens our equilibrium, encouraging a change in perspective and offering creative solutions as an alternative to chaos and turmoil.

It's especially important when developing an attitude of gratitude to give thanks for those things you most take for granted. There is so much, especially in the developed parts of the world that is simply not appreciated. If we are to truly reclaim our power and remain unwavering in the face of adversity, then gratitude along with forgiveness are imperatives. They are non-negotiables that can't be applied only when it suits us and discounted when we're not in the mood. If they do not become part of the architecture of our beliefs, we will find that when our faith is tested, we are found wanting.

Undertake an inventory of your life and look at where your mind has stopped seeing the beauty that calls out for attention each day. If you stop regularly and really look you will see miracles everywhere – all of which are worthy of your gratitude and appreciation. There are so many gifts that could enrich our reality that simply pass us by.

Looking into the mirror of your relationships to see who you may be taking for granted is a wonderful exercise. There you will find examples of where you don't sufficiently express what s/he means to you and his/her value. It's so easy to neglect those that love us the most and so it's absolutely essential for our well-being and for our spirits to show heartfelt appreciation to those that we love.

As we count our blessings, great and small, we will feel ourselves growing on the inside. It is from that place of inner contentment that all other qualities and virtues grow. Anxiety is replaced with confidence - fear is replaced with courage. Self-doubt becomes faith and fosters a spirit of adventure. Old patterns are also replaced allowing new horizons to emerge, and with those internal shifts new paradigms are discovered.

The practice of giving thanks in this way, showing heartfelt appreciation where one's heart is perpetually bursting with gratitude, can only be experienced when the negative intoxicants of past injuries and insults have been forgiven and let go. Then we are able to climb out of the abyss, into the light and from there fly free.

The second pillar of gratitude makes it possible for us to be true to ourselves and not be defined by the ever-changing opinion of others, or the circumstances we find ourselves in. This is because the heart that is truly grateful is far too busy celebrating what is really important... and is not easily deceived.

Integrity - honouring your heart

The third pillar ensures that we never walk alone. Whatever it is we believe, whatever our faith is anchored to, we should walk hand-in-hand with that force, that presence. This offers protection like no other.

Our beliefs are arguably the greatest force in nature - and so if we can be passionate about our lives and how we should be living, then there is a power in that belief that can propel us to our preferred destination. To feel this force in our lives we need to live with integrity – to be true to our beliefs, whatever they are. To be free of our own hypocrisy and contradictions requires an incredible level of honesty and humility.

The honesty required means looking unashamedly at oneself and not making excuses for our behaviour and mistakes. The humility that is needed requires us to step down from the arrogance of needing to be right. It is only with this kind of humility that we can discover the truth about what needs to change in our lives. For this both a forgiving mind and a grateful heart are needed. To walk such a path demands focus and resolve, our intention alone will not suffice.

The word humility is derived from the word humiliation. It may seem odd to speak of humiliation in relation to humility but until we are able to acknowledge where we fall short of grace, and name and embrace our shame, we cannot know the true joy and power of humility – and this may require feeling some humiliation. It's often when we have got it wrong and are not seeking to defend ourselves that we are able to attain its wise counsel. Whilst we are busy defending what we've always done, defending our prejudices, dogmatic points of view and beliefs we remain blind.

Many of us are wedded to out-dated ideas and opinions and are prepared to fight to the death for them, even when they have no foundation in truth – such is our indoctrination and ignorance. Integrity demands a much higher standard of us all and the journey begins by being prepared to renounce what we have held dear, in order that our minds might become better educated.

So, be prepared to renounce what you passionately hold on to and have not adequately scrutinised, to see if it is worthy of the status and respect you have bestowed upon it.

It's when you interrogate your ideologies, patterns and drives with an honest heart, that you discover whether you are walking an honourable path, or simply walking the path of familiarity.

It's so important to work out the truth of your heart and to set your moral compass accordingly. Only then can you begin to live a life filled with integrity and truth.

Where you find your life falling short and the same old patterns keep knocking at the door, you can be sure that your professed beliefs are not your actual beliefs. In other words, what you say you believe in, does not match what you do. And until it does the gap between those two positions is where you will keep falling short.

Integrity is not best described as a place of absolute congruence, although that can be attained, integrity in this context is about being true to yourself, your principles and beliefs and when you fall short it's about forgiving yourself for what is missing and giving thanks for what is there. It's by responding in this way that you can be the best you can be.

Make a pledge today to find the song of your heart and to sing it each day.

Kindness

There is now a mountain of research concerning the topic of kindness. We now know kindness is a dual carriageway where both giver and receiver are enriched, emotionally, spiritually and physically.

The mind lights up like a Christmas tree when we think kind thoughts and express them as kind deeds. The brain and body too are flooded with a plethora of neurochemicals and hormones, which caress and heal and even enlighten. Even the observer of kindness is blessed with all these gifts and so there can be no doubt of the far-reaching effects of this most beautiful of qualities.

Although the research has confirmed the many benefits of kindness, we need not go beyond the chambers of our own minds and hearts to discover that kindness is one of the greatest pastimes. Those that give without concern for reward, find that their courtyard is never empty, their horizon is never bleak, and their perspective is ever expanding.

This does not mean that their lives are not at times blighted with misfortune and difficulty; it simply means that they find a way - or are shown the way out of the maze of their difficulties and dilemmas.

Kindness, like integrity comes easily to the forgiving and grateful mind. So, every day for no reason at all perform at least one act of kindness. Random acts of kindness are good for the soul, but they go further than that... they are good for our karma and shape our destiny.

We really do reap what we sow. We don't always know when the fruit of our actions will turn up but if you are a keen observer and student of life, you will see the fruits always do turn up in the fullness of time. It's important for us all not to be complacent in this regard so that we can limit the negative impact of our actions.

Kindness is the highest end product of our efforts, it's the ultimate outcome of a life well lived. A right-thinking person would only ever choose the path of kindness because s/he would realise that any other decision or choice was filled with destruction for all parties... including oneself.

Make kindness your way of being, your way of life - do not be content with performing only one act of kindness per day, aim to reach a point where there have been so many acts of kindness each day you couldn't possibly remember them all. There you will find your bliss.

Kindness is the fourth pillar of strength and it is the one that will help you to sustain the other three because forgiveness comes more easily to the kind mind. Gratitude grows out of the joyous appreciation for the great and the small - and kindness makes those things easier to find.

The courage and honesty required to walk the path of integrity comes more easily to the mind where there is no inclination to cause harm - kindness fosters such conditions. Kindness completes the circle, and it invites even the unwilling heart to take its hand and walk bravely into the future.

This is an overview of the four pillars, each one can be constructed more easily by the one that comes before.

If you try to be truly grateful when the heart and mind are burdened with a lack of forgiveness, watch what happens. See if you can maintain that gratitude and appreciation. Try being kind when you're having difficulty honouring your heart and following your truth and you will see it's not so easy to do.

When each pillar is honoured and respected in the right way and in the correct order, then you are able to build a fortress of peace, a fortress you can inhabit and when the storms of challenge and difficulty come, you will feel protected and strong, able to weather all life's storms. Then you will find that the serenity that the ancient masters of the eastern world eloquently spoke of will be present whenever it is needed.

Start building your fortress today...

Creating your fortress of peace

A fortress of peace is a sanctuary like no other. It offers you safety and security and as your awareness expands, you are blessed with incredible clarity. That which was once out of view comes sharply into focus.

What is the best way to create this most special of places? Firstly, sit quietly, alone with your thoughts and honestly examine your heart. Gather all your transgressions, great and small, those things that you feel most guilty about and ashamed of.

Remember, this is not about self-condemnation, so the purpose of the exercise isn't to feel worse by the time you've completed it. Equally it is not about justifying your decisions and choices. There's no value in making yourself right.

When you've composed a list spanning your life, having gathered the worst items you can recollect, then you must make time on a regular basis to converse with those times, events and periods of history. Speak to the version of yourself that existed then, the one responsible for those 'crimes' either against yourself or others.

This may prove emotional and challenging to do but I guarantee you, the more you do it the better you will feel.

Our karma and destiny are kinder to us when we face the truth about our own behaviour and actions and as we reconcile with our past in this way, each conversation in which we own our part in our mistakes frees us from the web of negative consequences. Our minds and hearts become lighter.

It is at this point that forgiving others for their transgressions becomes easier. We can then embark on conversing in our minds with those who have hurt our hearts, and in the process, set ourselves free from that negative web of consequences.

This path may take days or weeks subject to what's on our lists, and how many times we need to revisit a particular subject before its emotional consequences no longer remain.

I promise you, no matter how long it takes it will leave you feeling stronger, more resourceful and capable as you feel the depth of the eternal truth. The secret to health is the removal of waste.

When you have detoxified the mind in this way, you can more easily move on to gratitude...

To understand gratitude, we really do need to understand the power of thank you. Thank you is the best place for us to begin to generate the grateful mind. The more we practise saying thank you, for all things great and small, the more our minds' landscapes change.

Thank you is best employed as a mantra. The more we repeat it the more things to be grateful for gravitate towards us and a virtuous cycle is established. This is because a thankful mind easily identifies more things for which to be thankful. Then your mood is elevated by the positive energy that is generated and you are pulled into the orbit of the positive energies that already exist.

Thank you is not as powerful as gratitude - gratitude is a much more potent sentiment, a feeling that resonates deep within our beings. Thank you may not always see the full value of the object of its focus. Gratitude on the other hand is more considered and takes time to see, savour and connect with what claims its attention.

Practise saying thank you often and you will experience its immense power as it propels you to that elevated position of the grateful mind.

Beyond even gratitude is a more virtuous position, best described as appreciation. Appreciation has even more respect and reverence for what it focuses on. It dwells longer in that position of gratitude. You may spend all day just appreciating one person, one event, a thing of beauty, a moment... and that one day could easily become a week or much longer. Appreciation rarely fades, its where one becomes truly entwined in the gift of the experience.

Appreciation could be described as the pinnacle of gratitude. It's a heartfelt endeavour which strengthens your immunity. Not only is the body's immune system reinforced, but also the immune system of the mind and spirit are strengthened too.

This is how the second wall of your Fortress of Peace is erected.

'Living with ambivalence' is a Reachism that runs through every part of our approach. It became clear to me some thirty years ago that real progress cannot be made without acceptance of one's flaws and shortcomings. My own life was the most powerful mirror of this as I realised, I could not transform the things I most wanted to change without accepting who I was in any given moment.

Until you can find peace with your incongruence and contradictions the road to contentment is denied you.

I don't intend to recount all that I have previously said about living with ambivalence because the subject is covered fairly comprehensively on the Reach website and in the previous book. That said, it is worth underlining the connection between integrity and this subject.

Integrity, as stated earlier, is not a flawless position, a state of perfection. It is a truth, a transparency, where nothing is hidden from oneself. And even where some things may be hidden, the individual is not in denial because she actively walks the tightrope of self-examination. She becomes a keen student, seeking to better understand herself through her attitude, moods, relationships, decisions and choices.

Integrity is therefore an excellent description for a mind that is pursuing the truth about itself with an honest and courageous heart.

It's also a position that sits comfortably with its contradictions because it understands that change is a process, and so it takes time to become the best versions of ourselves. Acceptance and compassion are wonderful catalysts in the process of transformation and the one with integrity knows this and so does not sit in negative judgement of herself.

This habit also means she is less likely to sit in negative judgement of others as she views life's ebbing and flowing with kind eyes. So, the way to erect the third wall of your fortress is to lovingly accept where you are today and to recognise that through this practice tomorrow will automatically be better.

Integrity is a natural by-product of the forgiving and grateful mind because once your mind has been detoxified and then beautified, what follows is searing clarity, a mind that sees itself and everything else more clearly and that clarity breeds contentment. What flows from that contentment is a river rich with virtue and the greatest amongst these is kindness.

The kind mind may take some time to cultivate but if you consciously set out to sow the seeds of kindness, and feed and nurture those acts of generosity, you'll find your harvest will be abundant.

Kindness needs to start in your mind. You need to create a flow of kind thoughts that become part of your stream of consciousness. In order to do this, you need to put some time aside for introspection, time where you can acknowledge your qualities and virtues and celebrate the best of yourself.

This cannot be a phase; this pastime has to become a healthy obsession. You need to find some time daily, or at least every other day, when you sit, reflecting on the best of you and how you can improve yourself and make a greater contribution in your world.

Another wonderful way to develop the kind mind, as espoused by the Loving Kindness Meditation approach, is to spend a few minutes every day, thinking about someone you love or care deeply about. Think of their qualities, virtues and attributes and having spent some time doing that, with the feelings that are engendered, send that loving energy out into the world, wishing some good fortune or blessing to someone, a group of people, or even a place in the world that needs healing. This act of kindness has been found to be extremely beneficial to the practitioner in terms of blood pressure, brain wave regulation, improvement in perception, mood and numerous other health advantages.

In 2008, at Stanford University's Centre for Compassion and Altruism Research and Education, three social psychologists (Hutcherson, Seppala and Gross) embarked on a research project in which they wanted to measure the efficacy and emotional value of loving-kindness meditation (LKM). Loving-kindness meditation is quite specifically focused on achieving social harmony – cultivating positive regard for those we may know and care for, those who we do know and may not care for or trust, and who may not like us, as well as those that would often be described as neutral strangers.

The results were very interesting, as it was clear that even a brief seven-minute exercise in cultivating positive regard was sufficient to induce changes of small to moderate shifts in mood and feelings.

What was discovered is that LKM produces increased positivity, which was significant not only towards its target but also towards strangers. What was also noted was that there was an increased positivity towards the self too, which is consistent with loving-kindness meditation, where one of its primary tenets is greater acceptance of the self.

Although there is much more research needed, the evidence is clear that meditation that has a compassionate focus better connects us to others and the world – and also better connects us to ourselves.

Research carried out at Duke University in 2009 has shown that LKM is also effective when working with schizophrenia and those challenged by other significant mental health issues. This is promising for the field of mental health, which needs to become much more creative and imaginative, if it is to develop an adequate response to the crisis that is occurring in the developed world.

Once you've developed a mind that is kinder to itself, it's easier to extend that generosity to others.

Kindness does not seek acknowledgement or recognition. It has no desire for a reward. The act of kindness is the reward because kindness performed with good intention, as previously stated in this chapter, is highly beneficial to the one being kind, in terms of their own brain, mood and physical health. Think of kindness as a virtuous cycle... the more you give and do (without seeking reward) the more you are actually rewarded.

Particularly seek out the small things to do, the ones that don't appear to have much value and yet can be significant for the recipient. There is no definitive list and according to the context and circumstances in which you live the list will obviously vary, but for example, small acts of kindness may include: cutting your neighbours side of the hedge, especially if you know that's difficult for them to do, looking in on an elderly person who lives alone and sparing them a little time to have a cup of tea and a chat every now and then, picking up a newspaper or a magazine for someone you know doesn't always have the time but would welcome that consideration, inviting someone who may be alone to join a gathering and enjoy a meal with you – you might know someone who has difficulty sleeping and you buy them a bottle of lavender oil to see if this might help their predicament...

The list of small, random acts of kindness is never ending. When you look at the context of your own life, you'll be able to see what you can do for others. But starting from today, actively seek out these opportunities.

It's important to say that there isn't a kindness quota. One who is busy tallying up their acts of kindness is missing the point. One cannot perform too many acts of kindness. That said, you can, without appropriate discrimination apply kindness in the wrong way and at the wrong time. A concept I have covered extensively elsewhere is the valuable principle that virtues always travel in pairs. The essence of this concept is that any positive quality when applied without discernment and consideration for the context, can in fact cause harm. So, as wonderful as kindness is, if you're not also applying discrimination at the time, you may actually obstruct or limit someone's growth.

You need to measure whether your kindness is the best fit for that person and the situation. This often applies to repeated acts of kindness, where you keep doing the same thing over and over again, but little change has taken place. Under these conditions you are more often than not inadvertently causing harm and your own growth is impaired.

In conclusion, to erect the fourth wall in your fortress of peace, actively be kind to yourself, kind to others and respect the world we inhabit. This takes you a step closer to being a synergist, a pioneer in a world desperate for positive change.

"We must develop and maintain the capacity to forgive. He who is devoid of the power to forgive is devoid of the power to love. There is some good in the worst of us and some evil in the best of us. When we discover this, we are less prone to hate our enemies".

Martin Luther King, Jr. (1929 – 1968)

Points to remember

- We will undoubtedly be challenged by life. Peaks and troughs are part of any journey and life is no exception. Along the way there'll be feelings of doubt, inadequacy, fear, but equally there will be hope, joy, insight and peace. The real skill is to maintain our relationship with contentment whatever we are presented with. This is at times easier said than done and it takes focus and practice to find equanimity. The idea that serenity is not freedom from the storm but peace within it is a beautiful description but how do we achieve this? Applying the four pillars is certainly one way.

- There is a sequence that we need to follow when using the four pillars to construct our fortress of peace. Forgiveness is the first pillar, and it requires that before we can truly forgive another, we must first forgive ourselves. Whilst we are bound by our regrets, guilt and shame, it's not possible for us to meet those angels that reside within each of us. A lack of forgiveness blocks our minds, poisons our bodies and stifles our spirits.

- Forgive yourself for those moments when you have not been enough, forgive yourself for not having the courage of your convictions, forgive yourself for lying because it was easier than telling the truth, forgive yourself for your most unkind and despicable acts. Then you will find you can forgive those who have trespassed against you.

- Once forgiveness has cleared the rubbish from the fields of the mind, gratitude can sow its seeds of ambition, hope and joy. The grateful mind is such a beautiful place, a paradise rich with colour, abundance and joy. To create such internal splendour start by giving thanks for those things you have most taken for granted. The power of thank you creates a mind full of gratitude and the mind full of gratitude has little room for complaint.

- As we count our blessings great and small our weaknesses and frailties are deprived of the oxygen of complaint and so they wither. They don't die - they fall from the vine and on making contact with the soil they are nourished and transformed. This is how our vices become our virtues and our weaknesses become our strengths. Such is the power of the grateful mind.

- The third pillar is integrity. This requires us to be true to ourselves and our beliefs, which takes an incredible level of honesty and humility. Neither of these things is about impressing others. This is about facing ourselves, owning our stuff and where there's toxicity removing it from our lives. This level of transparency leads to feelings of inner cleanliness and respect for oneself, which brings with it courage and confidence.

- Those with integrity are passionately wedded to their beliefs. Whatever it is they believe in, is visible in their lives. They are not evangelical and so are not clubbing others over the head, dragging them down the path of their convictions. They share their message through their quiet, understated example and where it feels appropriate, they will walk with others along this path.

- Kindness like integrity comes easily to the forgiving and grateful mind. These two pillars give rise to the other two. The kind mind does not negatively judge itself or others. It's honest in its scrutiny of things and people but it does not take up the mantle of condemnation. It lives in the place of perpetual hope, wishing for others what it wishes for itself. Its primary preoccupation is making its inner world better and brighter so that its contribution in the world is more stunning.

- When each of the four pillars is honoured and respected and we embark on each in the correct sequence, building a fortress of peace that we can inhabit is relatively easy. This is a fortress that will help keep the storms at bay. When difficulty comes you will feel protected and strong. It's at this point that you will understand that serenity is a sanctuary like no other.

A meditation to remind you of the primary themes of this chapter...

I regularly spend time building and strengthening my fortress of peace... at its four corners are forgiveness, gratitude, integrity and kindness... these four pillars ensure that my fortress is strong and impenetrable... impervious to the storms of life...

Forgiveness reminds me that it can unblock every path... it can remove every obstacle... and transcend the seemingly impossible... firstly I forgive myself for all those things where I have knowingly caused harm to myself and others... I also forgive myself for those times when I have unknowingly negatively impacted on someone else... forgiveness reminds me that I am not innocent... I too have hurt the hearts of others...

I decide now to forgive all those who have hurt my heart... even that which feels unbearable... I do my best to let go of my anger and hurt... because I know that this is only poisoning me... I release myself from this curse...

Forgiveness opens the door to gratitude... and I develop the habit of 'thank you'... the power of thank you nurtures gratitude in my mind and spirit... heartfelt gratitude becomes appreciation, enabling me to benefit from the wondrous blessings of a grateful mind... I enjoy this beautiful harvest...

I feel integrity developing in me as these two pillars enable me to honour my heart... to become increasingly true to myself... forgiveness and gratitude foster feelings of self-respect and selflessness in equal measure... I am driven to take better care of myself and to stay true to my values and beliefs... and I do... but there is also a drive and a passion to lift others up along the way... and so kindness is born...

Compassion is kindness in action... and every day I look for an opportunity to uplift and support another... I am not content merely finding the answers that best meet my needs... I am equally driven to find a solution for all... because everyone wins in a charitable world...

Kindness teaches me that the 'we, not just me' philosophy creates a world where we are all winners... a world where we can maximise our talents, abilities and potential... a world that is mutually nourishing and rewarding...

The four pillars of strength help me to create that world for myself... and I reach out to help others create their own fortress of peace... which is blissful...

CHAPER 8

ALL THE THREES

"A man is not called wise because he talks and talks again; but if he is peaceful, loving and fearless then he is in truth called wise".

Buddha (563 BC - 480 BC)

All the threes

The number three comes up often in my work, such as: The Three Aspects of Consciousness, The Three Gatekeepers, The Three 'A's, The Three 'P's. They are each very important signposts on the road to becoming a synergist.

In this chapter I would like to say a little more about each of these - offering an added dimension to help with that transition from knowledge to practice. You can find out more about these 'threes' on the Reach website should you wish. I will also add a couple more to this list - in the opening and at the end (The Three Aspects of Time and The Three Realities).

My proposition is that if you want to be at peace with yourself, clear of mind and brimming with confidence and joy, then all these threes offer some valuable nuggets you will want to add to your collection.

I'd now like to introduce you to the three that connects all the other threes – and that is The Three Aspects of Time.

The three aspects of time

We're all familiar with the three aspects of time, so there's no real mystery here – past present and future are terms we use in our everyday language. My experience though is that very few of us use these terms mindfully. We are unaware of how time and consciousness relate to each other – which is vitally important to our emotional, psychological and spiritual health.

How I refer to them in my work is as the Memoried Self (which relates to the past) the Experiencing Self (which relates to the present) and the Anticipating Self (which relates to the future).

These three definitions describe the intimate relationship between consciousness and time. They summarise, in a way that I think is invaluable, the relationship you and I have with the moment we're standing in, the moment that has just slipped away from us and the moment we are yet to step into. These three mental positions make us aware that we can either have a conscious arrangement with time, one where we are the observer, the student and the conductor of our affairs. Alternatively, we can be passive participants who are enslaved by our pasts, anxious and disturbed in the present and crippled and fearful about the future.

Past, present and future are not three labels that merely explain time's passing; they provide us with the opportunity to form a relationship with time in order that we might make the most of its unique gifts. In order to do this, we come back to the gateway to wisdom – the art of listening, which I referred to in chapter 6.

Only the one who 'listens-in' to what is going on in their inner world and also 'listens-out' to contrast and compare their inner experiences with their external reality - only they are likely to see the opportunity for growth in each moment and make it count. Whether it's spending time in solitude, going for a walk in the park, time spent with family and friends, undertaking an activity at work, learning from some previous experience... whatever it is, only the listener is likely to find the pearl because they realise the past is bursting with revelations and so they do not fear its nudges and reminders.

When we live attentively in the present it nurtures and nourishes us. The future then readily whispers the best instructions about how to move forward – offering the gift of foresight.

The three aspects of time are like three adjoining rooms. The one in the middle is the present and the rooms either side are past and future. When our consciousness sits with calm and poise and we need to consult the past, we simply move into the adjacent room. We access whatever memory or experience, and we claim whatever understanding or insight that's needed. As a result, when we step back into the present we are armed with insight and wisdom – and so we are able to make the best decisions and choices.

Equally, when we need to consult the future, we open that door and step into that room and we listen keenly and wholeheartedly, because time is always willing to share its secrets with us if we are listening. Time is the holder of so many secrets and if we can be still and focus our attention, then those secrets move towards us. They can emerge in so many ways – through conversation, a dream, a difficult experience, listening to a play, a piece of music or they can turn up in the form of an epiphany. Whatever form it takes if you're open and accessible, time and the universe will speak to you. She who is in conscious contact with herself moves between these three rooms effortlessly.

From this point onwards, practise looking backwards when it's beneficial, never in ways that are negative or self-harming. Look back for the learning that can be had, for the opportunities to grow. Remember, there is only winning and learning. The concept of losing is very unhelpful and misleading. We only lose when our mistakes and misadventures are seen as things to be despised or denied. Every experience you've ever had has some form of winning or learning encased within it.

When you anticipate things in the future, although you need to take account of your past learning, don't be limited by the past, realise that the future is waiting to embrace you. It is eager for you to meet your very best self, because it already knows what s/he looks like. So, passionately present the future with a script of positivity and hope - then it will unveil that very best version of you, inspiring you to be all you can be today.

By interfacing with your past and your future in this way, the present will feel like the gift that keeps on giving – creating opportunity for growth in every dimension of your being.

We have approximately sixty thousand thoughts a day. 5% of those have been calculated to be new thoughts, waiting to be ascribed meaning and purpose. If none is given, they fall under the seduction of familiarity, repeating those thoughts, habits and beliefs that are already well enshrined. Whether these have basis in fact or not matters little. Such is the power of the patterns of familiarity, that they will drag us to unwanted destinations.

This is why those three thousand new thoughts each day need to be accosted by your will and determination and then channelled in heartfelt and constructive ways. Fostering a healthy relationship with the Memoried Self, the Experiencing Self and the Anticipating Self, will make this task much easier, as a healthy relationship with them eliminates waste, allowing you to spend more time in self-care and self-validation. This enables you to fulfil your meaning and purpose and express your energies in loving, thoughtful and kind ways – all of which leads to greater self-mastery.

The lesson here is simple, respect time and time will respect you. By respecting the three aspects of time you will flourish. Practise being a time traveller.

The three aspects of consciousness – another dimension

The Three Aspects of Consciousness provides us with a map of awareness. The three positions 'self', 'other' and 'lovingly detached' help us to better understand ourselves and our position within reality and they also provide us with the opportunity to change that position if we are dissatisfied with where we find ourselves.

Optimum mental health can be achieved by learning how to move between the three positions. The natural starting point is self. You have been offered in this book lots of strategies so far for how to create a healthy state of self, which means creating your own internal paradise. All the introspective activities I have introduced you to, as well as all the other Story of Health components, clearly illustrate how a healthy sense of self can be achieved.

If you are dissatisfied with your reality, don't sit around waiting for it to change. Practise being mindful, change your self-talk, meditate regularly, change your environment if it's unsatisfactory, ensure your relationships are positive and healthy. Seek a life of meaning and purpose, eat a rainbow diet, drink copious amounts of water, make exercise part of your daily and weekly regime. Pursue activities that bring joy, practise being kind and compassionate in all your dealings. Find balance in all things and the position of 'self' will be positive and empowering for you and others.

When you create a world that supports the position of healthy self you will find moving to the position of 'other' becomes increasingly effortless. Be under no illusion, to cultivate the position of other does take practice and time, so do not think that this will just happen. Regularly adopting the position of healthy other is a very worthy pastime.

Having cultivated a healthy self, we have a clearer lens to step into and see another's world.

What this looks like in practice is when you are talking to a senior citizen and she's sharing her stories, heartaches and her joys, you are listening as if you are that eighty- five-year-old who's passed through those experiences. As best you can, listen from her frame of reference and appreciate what her journey has been like. Listening from 'over there' is a completely different way of interacting with another. It gives you a perspective and access to feelings that can't be gained from passive listening. Passive listening is almost always 'waiting to speak', waiting for the next gap, so it can express its point of view, because it believes its thoughts, opinions and ideas carry greater importance.

The position of healthy other does not fall into this trap. It really listens and really hears what is needed and so it can respond in the most valuable ways. So, when that adolescent boy, sharing his feelings of insecurity speaks about his self-image and feelings of inadequacy, the one anchored in healthy other listens with pure attention, with empathy and sensitivity and this is best achieved by 'becoming' that fourteen-year-old boy, by immersing oneself in his world, connecting with his fears and concerns. From this position, one does not seek to diminish or explain away how it feels to be him. That is replaced with 'complete awareness' a heartfelt connection to the moment – being present in this way means that teenage boy feels valued and heard and the intimacy of that connection helps to diminish the intensity of his concern as he no longer feels alone in his plight.

Professor Keysers, head of the Netherlands Institute for Neuroscience, has done a great deal of work in the area of empathy. His book The Empathic Brain (2011) for many is seen as the seminal piece of literature on the neurobiology of empathy. His work has highlighted a specific type of neuron, that have come to be described as mirror neurons, which are located in the anterior cingulate cortex (ACC). Although there is more research required in this area, what is clear is that these mirror neurons are what are triggered in us when we observe someone else's distress and feel distressed ourselves. It's why we laugh when we see others laughing and equally cry in sympathy with another. This capacity to feel what another is experiencing is an automatic response – one could say a human response. We are not making a conscious decision when this happens, we feel ourselves naturally pulled into the same circle of experience.

What I'm inviting you to do is to actively and consciously engage the mirror neurons. Listening in a highly focused way and having the desire to do that from 'over there'. This means sharing in the other person's world view and experience, which enhances our empathy. It also enriches the position of self because we begin to appreciate that seeing the world only through our own eyes is to be short-sighted. There is so much we miss by sitting purely in self. The more you are willing to surrender your own perspective and look at the world through the eyes of others, the more you are able to be your best you.

The next time you're in an interaction, see if you can find the awareness and the humility required to step away from your view of whatever situation you find yourself in. See if you can really listen to what the other person is telling you. Try to really step into their shoes or sit in their seat. Give up the idea that your view of reality is the most important. Surrender to the idea that there are numerous views of reality and yours is simply one of them. If you're open to other perspectives, your own perspective is automatically enriched. You will be surprised how much clearer things are when you move into this position and away from the notion that you have the best seat in the house.

Once you've developed advanced empathy and are applying it consistently, you'll feel as if you've been watching a movie in black and white and now for the first time you can see all of the events in colour. It is a wow moment. You'll find it surprises you. Every so often it will take your breath away. Long after the first moment it continues to remind you that life is at its best not taken for granted. Every scene, every interaction will have some opportunity for growing and learning, some moment of enrichment and blessing.

It's at this point that you can really experience the marvels of the lovingly detached position. This is a position free from unhealthy attachment. This doesn't mean a position where one does not care. To the contrary it's where one cares very deeply but because of the secure attachment it has formed with itself and others, it is now able to drift beyond the pull of people, situations and events and experience the uncluttered perspective offered by the bird's eye view.

Let me underline at this point that the position of detachment has been achieved through secure attachment. When we have established secure attachments, we can actually let go as we feel secure enough to do so. It's insecurity that has us holding on in fear, not knowing what comes next. Security provides us with the promise that all will be well and gives us the feeling that we can go and truly explore. You will remember in chapter two I spoke about safety and security as nature's primary narrative. Well, consciousness depends on the same foundation in order that we might reach the zenith of the soul – and so loving detachment is truly reached when we feel secure.

Loving detachment is the position of awareness that incorporates the best of self and other. It's also the position that takes complete account of the time and context within which all scenarios are played out. Its dexterity is such that not only does it see things from the position of self and other, but it can equally peel away from both those positions if needed and see the true nature of the transaction. Its specialism is that it factors in all the other variables realising that in any one moment a multitude of things are shaping what's happening, for example the nature of the space, whether one or both parties are tired, the climate, the hidden agendas that are at play and the many other dynamics that are part of the complexity of the now.

How can we possibly take in so much data and be present? Isn't this level of consciousness purely a theoretical concept beyond our attainment? One could be forgiven for thinking the answer to this question is yes. However, if you really become a synergist and pull together all the primary principles that have been explained in this book, the lovingly detached position will emerge in time. It cannot be hurried or forced. So be relaxed about it.

At first you will only get a glimpse of it from time to time. As you progress those glimpses will elongate. You may then feel you've cracked it, but you then wake up one morning and it appears to be gone. Do not be disheartened, it's gone nowhere... but it does need to be tended to, cultivated. When you understand the lovingly detached position ebbs and flows and are prepared to sit patiently at the shore, you will find increasingly when it turns up it spends longer and longer periods with you. It will become a true ally and will point out what you're missing, what you're taking for granted and how you can enhance a given situation.

The lovingly detached position is like being in a stadium, sitting in all the different positions simultaneously, enjoying every dimension of the game or event you're observing. You feel like you are watching each moment in slow motion, as if your respect for time has given you longer to process and evaluate things in real time. This allows one to see the context as clearly as the content - it's this ability to see both that enables us to make the wisest decisions. Remember, the lovingly detached position is not concerned with being right, it's only concerned with what is right. Its primary occupation is identifying the patterns, as that's where one finds the truth.

Although moving between the positions of self and other is the primary way to experience the lovingly detached state of consciousness, there is another way to reach those giddy heights.

To do this, practise looking in on an interaction that you're having with another person(s). Rather than standing or sitting in the position that you're in, take up a third-party position, where you're observing both yourself and the other person. It's as if you are watching the film, rather than being an actor within it. When you 'look in' in this way you need to apply kind eyes. Remember, we are judging all the time and there's no sin in that. It's a central tenet of being human. What we can do and is highly beneficial to do, is be kind in our judgements. This gives us a much better understanding of what we're seeing and experiencing.

Practising viewing the scenes of your life by taking up the position of the witness and assessing what you're seeing from outside of the constraints of your own point of view, enables you to see yourself and the other person more clearly. It also allows you to see the greater context in which the interaction/transaction is taking place. You'll find the more that you do this, the more you will develop the lovingly detached reflex, giving you the best seat in the house.

If you want to really immerse yourself in this position, i) create a set of non-negotiables and master self-care ii) actively listen and develop advanced empathy and iii) build secure attachments, only then will you find you can truly let go.

I hope these practical examples of the three aspects of consciousness in action will lead you to a position of awareness, where you can better see yourself, others and the world.

Make it part of your daily practice to move between all three positions according to the person, circumstance and moment. But to do this, you must embrace the different personalities and virtues of self, other and lovingly detached. This will strengthen your internal resolve and enable you to better navigate life's ups and downs.

The three gatekeepers – how to maintain vigilance

When I have previously spoken about The Three Gatekeepers, I have made the point that an individual who is not fiercely intent on transformation is unlikely to change.

The Three Gatekeepers are Truth, Kindness and Benevolence. If you are going to incorporate The Three Gatekeepers into your way of interacting with others, you need to be vigilant, patient and tolerant - because if you want to be a responder to events rather than a reactor, it requires you to slow down. You need to engage with each moment with an attitude of pause and reflection.

Without this practice and discipline, you won't have the time to ask the three questions. Let me remind you what they are... Is my position one of truth or am I trapped in my own point of view? Is what I'm about to do or say kind or am I simply being driven by the force of habit and the need to be right? Is there really any benefit in the position I'm adopting, or would it be wiser to maintain silence?

To have the presence of mind and sufficient poise to stop and consider these questions requires a lot of determination and attention and yet the more you embroider these considerations into your way of thinking and acting, the more you will feel that this is a perfectly natural way of being. You'll have the feeling that time slows down for you. This is because you are being more mindful and sensitive, truer to each moment, and so it is as if time gives you an extra window through which to view events - which is a primary characteristic of the lovingly detached position.

Taking every interaction and transaction through the three gates may at first appear time consuming and cumbersome but in fact it buys you time and gives you a better pair of eyes with which to view reality. The more you practise applying The Three Gatekeepers the more you'll come to the point where it's only the third gatekeeper that needs to be satisfied. The other two questions become more and more redundant.

This is because those who are sincere in their intentions and outlook increasingly seek out and tell the truth and kindness is woven into all of their dealings. And so, only one question remains... is there really any benefit in saying 'this'? Will it harm or liberate? Unless the person is convinced of the benefit then they simply retreat into silence.

By becoming a disciple of this great practice, you will find you will not be impulsive at critical moments. You will shy away from being reckless, because you'll remember those moments when your heart was damaged by insensitivity and unkindness and you'll have no desire to administer that to others.

Try to build this way of being into the three aspects of consciousness and your life will become one in which you are a joy-giver, a peacemaker, an enabler, creating the conditions for inspiration and empowerment wherever you go.

Theodore Rubin said: "Kindness is more important than wisdom and the recognition of this is wisdom".

The more you apply The Three Gatekeepers to your life, the more you'll become the single gatekeeper, so conduct yourself with poise, patience and grace and that will make the three gates into one.

The three 'A's – the key to perpetual growth

The importance of the three 'A's cannot be overstated. I would go as far as to say that every client I've ever had the honour to walk alongside has in some way been suffering with a deficiency, which relates to at least one of these: attention, affection and affirmation. In the vast majority of cases, they have had no idea that this is at the heart of the issue.

I spoke at some length in chapter 3 about the importance of the three 'A's. The formation of our personality and character is dependent on how much we are exposed to these key nurturing qualities. Where there are secure attachments, all three 'A's have been adequately met. With regards to the three insecure attachments there is always some deficiency.

Socialisation has a lot to do with how children are shaped. Although things are changing, we are still a long way from raising boys and girls in the best possible way. Girls are generally encouraged to have a broader range of emotions and feelings and as a consequence more readily display them. Boys on the other hand are encouraged far less to express the full range of emotions and as a result their emotional development can be stunted. They are much more likely to express anger, which perversely is much more tolerated and accepted. How often have you heard the term 'he's only being boisterous - that's what boys do'? How often have you seen what might be considered feminine traits discouraged in boys, directing them much more towards their 'natural' proclivities?

Is it true that girls have a greater emotional range than boys, and therefore we should continue to foster these biases? - or as the nature plus nurture dialogue is illuminating, is it more accurate to say that when we nurture and educate our children, we unconsciously steer them down gender-specific pathways?

There is so much conflicting research and debate on this topic. Take a look for yourself - I will leave you to make up your own minds, but my experience convinced me a long time ago that it is nurture that bends the brain and with it the mind in the direction of gender stereotypes.

In other words, the brain does not have a sex or a gender and even though we can find some evidence of what is described as hard wiring in the first thirty months of life, there are many social scientists who would argue that the messages of gender are being given to the child long before then, from its very first transactions with its caregivers. From the beginning we are treating boys and girls differently - even when they are in their cribs and cots, they are imbibing our non-verbal and verbal queues and the moulding process begins from there. This is why we can see changes in the brain as early as at thirty months.

Daphna Joel at Tel Aviv University, Israel, received the Alon Fellowship for young Israeli scientists and acquired her doctorate in psychology in 1998. She has subsequently gone on to be an accomplished psychologist and neuroscientist. Here's what she has to say about this topic: "Cranial differences between the two genders are a myth. The theory goes that once a foetus develops testicles, they secrete testosterone which masculinises the brain. If that were true, there would only be two types of brain."

However, her research calls this paradigm into question. Using brain scans to investigate sex differences between human brains (2015) – which is the first study of its kind – she and her team revealed that most people have a mix of male and female characteristics in their craniums.

Professor Joel and her colleagues analysed brain scans from one thousand four hundred people aged thirteen to eighty-five, searching for variations in the size of brain regions as well as patterns between them. The group identified twenty-nine brain regions which were repeatedly different in size and these were not able to be classified as either male or female. In other words, looking at the brains themselves without knowing the identity of the individual, one was not able to guess the gender – hence the conclusion there are not only two types of brain.

When the group looked a bit closer at each individual brain scan, however, they noted that very few people had all of their sex's brain features. In fact, those that might typically be classified as all male or all female brains made up less than 8% of all of the subjects.

Professor Joel and her team concluded that male and female brains are not wired differently at all. While sex differences in brain structure do exist when viewed in the aggregate, an individual brain will more than likely have its own unique set of features.

Doctor Joel states: "Most people are actually somewhere in the middle."

This research has been well received by others involved in the field. Psychologist Meg-John Barker of the Open University said that the research provides biological verification that supports the premise that gender simply isn't binary, and it is more accurate to think of brain function on a continuum.

Bruce McEwen at the Rockefeller University in New York is a scientist who believes this research will surprise many in the scientific community as it is clearly moving us away from the male and female brain hypothesis... and so there's a need for a new conversation.

Markus Hausmann of Durham University, UK, has been studying sex differences in cognition, with particular emphasis on spatial awareness. His view of the study is:

"Across all kinds of spatial skills, we find very, very few that are sensitive to sex. We have also identified spatial problems where women outperform men when the binary model suggests it should be the other way around – the black-and-white idea of a male or female brain is clearly too simple."

Professor Margaret McCarthy, who specialises in pharmacology and studies brain sex differences at the University of Maryland School of Medicine in Baltimore says, "This study fights against the idea that these outcomes are based on biological differences, as opposed to cultural expectations. We always need to look at culture, environment, education and a person's role in society".

I think Professor Joel's research significantly changes the paradigm of what constitutes male and female in terms of the brain, opening our minds to a more complex definition. In addition, it supports my experience of working with those suffering minor to unimaginable tragedy and trauma and finding time and again that the things that have most shaped their reality are their experiences, not their biology.

That isn't to say that biology isn't relevant because it unquestionably is, but there is something even more powerful and it is the environmental context in which we find ourselves. The three 'A's I believe are the most influential of the environmental factors in terms of brain development and the wider human experience. When they are present in sufficient quantity, the mind and spirit are made magnificent and when they are absent, or exist in insufficient amounts, the individual is emotionally and psychologically diminished.

Unfortunately, we have created a position whereby if we are to address some of the biases that are already instilled in our social fabric, then we need to understand how the three 'A's need to be applied. The way that many boys and girls are currently raised means that the three 'A's, do need to be administered slightly differently. All of us need the three 'A's, of that there is no doubt, but the current position is that most boys will find that they are in need of greater affirmation. Whereas most girls will have a greater need for affection. In both instances, attention is needed in fairly equal amounts.

I make this point based on my experience and research. It's the way our families, communities and society are currently structured that has created an imbalance which means the needs of one gender are slightly different from the other. And although the picture is somewhat more complicated as the research has indicated, if we start from this position of awareness, we can move towards individualising children's needs as we connect more deeply with them and come to understand where they are on the three 'A's continuum.

We do need to address the bigger picture but that is going to take time. We have to first deal with the current imbalances. If you are in a position where you are in any way helping to shape or influence young, impressionable minds, please bear in mind the idea that brains are being moulded all the time according to the environment and so we need to be more mindful about our interventions and their consequences.

If you're examining yourself and you have hitherto struggled to understand some of your own behaviour and responses, maybe you need to view your behaviour through the lens of the three 'A's. Maybe then you'll understand their impact on you and your behaviour. From there you can plot a different course.

I believe that when you take an honest audit of the situations and circumstances you find yourself in, you'll discover that the three 'A's are critical to the way you are - and by having a better understanding of them you can dramatically change your fortunes.

Perception, personality and performance

The three 'P's have become synonymous with our approach. In chapter 2, when explaining the four environments, I made reference to how dehydration affects perception, followed by personality and performance. These three 'P's are critical to understanding our relationship with time, space and events. We are always being affected by time and what's taking place within the spaces that we occupy. Added to this, the wider social context in which we live also influences our reality. Therefore, it's not only dehydration that affects perception, personality and performance. In fact, all stress, whatever form it takes, biological, emotional, psychological, financial, environmental and spiritual, impacts on perception, personality and performance.

Perception is nearly always the first one to be distorted. If you have a terrible headache or migraine, how you perceive things significantly changes. It's very hard to be positive and optimistic when you feel your head is being crushed in a vice.

Consequently, your mood dips and the way you interact with your environment changes. You're no longer able to give your best.

Equally, if you're challenged financially and can't see how you're going to meet the bills come the end of the month, the stress skews your view of your situation and circumstances and your personality is easily wrestled into submission. You struggle to be the best you can be because you're more depressed and down on yourself as you feel the fatigue of never quite having enough to make life comfortable.

Anxiety and panic provide a good illustration of the dynamic between these three 'P's. When someone is in the grip of a panic attack, hyperventilating, their heart racing and their bowels need emptying, they are trapped in the belief that the end is nigh, and that they will never be free of the crippling fear that they are feeling in that moment. Panic steals their clarity (perception) and even common sense evades them. Personality and performance are both equally crushed.

You will almost certainly have experienced the relationships between these three 'P's during the last week, without actually understanding you were under their spell. Such is their all-pervasive nature.

Although it's nearly always perception that is the first thing to be affected, personality and performance can at times be the first to show signs of fragility, causing the other two to stumble and fall.

The doom and gloom merchant who finds fault in everything and where they can't find it, they create it, is someone whose personality is always going to be leaning in the direction of low mood. The way that they see everything is condemned by this perspective. Even if they were trying their very best, they'd simply be unable to achieve the results they are capable of. Here we see personality responsible for the decline.

Performance can be equally undermining. You may have experienced carrying out a task, feeling really confident at the outset – then something unexpected derails your performance and your perception of yourself and what you're doing rapidly changes - and with that, your personality is deflated in the process.

It's important to state that although stress, fear and anxiety can send these three 'P's plummeting, it's equally true to say that by learning to recalibrate your consciousness you can maintain your perception in the face of adversity, which means you're able to maintain your attitudes and moods, so your personality doesn't impact negatively on your performance. In fact, the more you practise introspection and the many things covered in this book, the more you will find that your perception is something that you can steer in the direction you wish to go. Once your perception is strong and true, your personality is able to remain stable in the face of turbulent winds that would otherwise steer you off course.

There's no such thing as total immunity. We can all be affected in some way by life's challenges, but what we can achieve is the clarity and the strength required to become victors rather than victims.

The next time you're challenged by a situation at work, by a physical ailment, by a difficult relationship or circumstances you would rather not face, remember that your perception will shape your personality (how you feel and your way of being) and this will in turn affect how you respond and what energy you can bring to that situation. In other words, it will show up in your performance.

By creating a culture of self-care and self-nurture, your self-respect will grow, your love for yourself will deepen and your ability to stand firm in the storm will be assured. It's time to become captain of your ship.

It should be said for balance that the three 'P's also work in the opposite direction. I have explored the negative aspect because the more we understand the mechanics of this, the easier it is to turn it around and make the three 'P's work for us rather than against us.

The other three 'P's – a lifetime obsession

The three 'P's are well documented in many other pieces of work I've produced – they are practice, patience and perseverance. However, I want to go a little further and invite you to think of them as a lifetime obsession, as three allies you can never afford to be separated from. I promise you, if you can bind yourself to them, they will support and protect you at every turn.

Much of the modern-day personal development movement is focused on quick fixes and the promise that your very best self is waiting for you at the next workshop, retreat, the latest all singing, all dancing internet package, especially the gold and platinum offers - at discounted prices. In my experience these are rarely delivered and where there is some attainment, it is often short-lived.

What all these things have in common is immediacy and that with little effort the unimaginable can be achieved. For some, this may well be the case... but I have found that this is the exception rather than the rule.

If what you're looking for is a sustainable, lifelong solution, then you are going to need to make on-going and consistent effort. Some areas of your life might need minor modification, whist other areas will need a complete overhaul. Making out that you can create the change you want but not have to focus any effort on maintenance is like saying I've eaten for the first thirty years of my life, so I'm not going to worry about the next thirty years!

Let me take your mind back to chapter 1, Energy Contracts. There is nothing in the known universe that can be maintained without on-going sustenance of some kind. All energy needs energy and we literally do get out what we put in. If you or I want a future that sustains us, then we need to understand what the rules are. It could be argued that achieving positive change is the easy bit and that it's sustaining that change which is the greatest challenge. Again, this has not only been my own personal experience, but my professional experience too.

I've many times climbed to the top of the mountain, thinking I have arrived, and then spent my time celebrating my achievement, busily dancing away thinking how wonderful... I've done it... only to discover weeks or months later that I'm lying on my back looking up at the clouds, wondering how I got back here. The simple answer is complacency, ignorance and some arrogance, thinking that having reached my desired destination the job was done. Nothing could be further from the truth.

When you reach your desired destination, it's time for a new task, arguably the real one. That is, sustaining your achievement. It took me over ten years to get this and that's even after thinking I had understood all the mechanisms at play. This is the folly of knowledge, believing that understanding a theory or concept is wisdom. Wisdom knows that without consistent application one really knows very little.

I can't emphasise enough that if you want to meet your best you and keep her/him close, then these three 'P's must become a healthy obsession. Let me expand. Knowledge plus application equals personal power. This formula summarises what The Reach Approach is about, practice, practice, practice. You need to keep doing the right things to the best of your ability. This is the cornerstone to sustainability. Nothing will work without this.

Do not fall into the trap of thinking that the momentum that practice generates needs no further input from you. If you keep doing the right things, practice will keep its promise, that is to address any vulnerability, fragility or need that you might have. Practice promises to carry you over the line, to help you fulfil your potential. Practice gives you access to those untapped reserves. It promises to soothe and heal every wound. Don't think of practice as a chore, but rather think of it as your ally, your faithful companion that will never let you down. It will keep turning up when others disappoint.

Make the pledge to yourself that you're going to keep practising those things which are life-enhancing. Once you make this promise re-state your pledge to yourself each day. It will only really become bound to your heart and soul when you recite it each day. I would recommend you start with thirty consecutive days, and if you reach thirty days, why not go for sixty and then ninety. Make the promise, keep the promise and your practice will hold you up in any storm.

Next is patience. I have discovered for myself and from my work that patience eventually unlocks any door. She who can wait will find that all things eventually come to find her. I know how hard it is to be patient, so I make this request with no illusions about how difficult this is. However, if you can learn to wait you will discover you are more than you could ever have imagined.

I have had so much misfortune to deal with myself and at times the burden has felt unbearable. I've not always known whether I could or would make it. I remember when my brother was killed under vicious circumstances by a gang of youths. I wasn't sure that I could deal with such a loss. We were so close having been bound together by poverty and disadvantage growing up. We became each other's comfort blankets. And so, the hole he left in my life was enormous. That was a long road back.

My wife had a long battle with Motor Neuron Disease and caring for her over a nine-year period became the most important focus of my life. Doing this whilst raising our children and continuing to work was an enormous undertaking. Fortunately, I had a few allies who supported me in the management of these demands. However, caring for someone's every need, whilst juggling all the other things that need tending to - and also trying to meet the expectations of others, is arguably one of the most difficult things one could be asked to do.

The pull on my time and energy didn't end there. For seventeen years I played a pivotal role in caring for my mother and in the final five years when a third stroke had finally broken her body and resolve and vascular dementia took over, even more was needed and this was the most difficult and heart-breaking phase, as I watched her slip away too.

I share this not to illicit sympathy but to help you to see that I really do understand what it takes to walk this path and without practice and patience I would never have made it this far and without these two, you are unlikely to either.

Wherever you find the need for patience, tolerance is not very far away. We often have to tolerate the intolerable to discover what we are really made of.

So, when things seem as if they couldn't get any more difficult, or when you feel that you're literally on your knees, when you think you can't take any more, just pause and have faith in your practices. They will rescue you from any fate, but you must keep the faith. At that point you need to have faith in the process, faith in yourself and faith in all that you have learned.

Just as practice requires patience so that we learn to wait for the fruits of our efforts, so too patience needs perseverance to remind us it's not how many times we fall that matters, it's only how many times we rise. As Maya Angelou, in her beautiful poem, reminds us, 'and still I rise'. This is the essence of perseverance.

Perseverance is an unwillingness to give up. It's an unwavering tenacity, a 'never say die' attitude. It's a knowing, somewhere deep in one's soul that if I can just rise one more time then victory will be mine.

My request to you is no matter how many mistakes you have made, no matter how inadequate you feel, no matter how many times you have failed in your promises to yourself and others, make this moment the last time you choose that path. Your life is a contract between free will and fate but in order for you to fulfil your promise you need to refuse to lie down. You need to say to yourself, again and again, I refuse to stay down. I will not let yesterday decide today or tomorrow.

You will almost certainly as you make these pledges be hampered by self-doubt. You may well look back on a field of broken promises and disappointments but it's important to remember that those disappointments and regrets only have as much power as you invest in them. Use the word perseverance to remind you of what you need to do...

P is for practice, practice, practice.

E is for effort. Make it unwavering and consistent and there you will find power.

R is for routine. Build rituals because there is power in building a timetable that you honour.

S is for silence. The more you embrace silence, the more you'll discover your hidden treasures.

E is for experience. The more you practise the more the power of experience will lift you up.

V is for victory. See yourself breaking that tape, winning your own race. You're not competing with anyone but yourself.

E is for epicentre. You have to stand at the centre of your own life and become the master of your own destiny.

R is for rotation. Have a timetable but to keep things fresh, move it around. Don't allow it to become stale.

A is for attitude. Maintain an attitude of gratitude. Keep counting your blessings especially the small ones.

N is for natural. Be yourself. The more you connect with your nature the more natural you will be.

C is for courage. The more we take leaps of faith the more fearless we become.

E is for empowerment. Remember empowerment is our natural state and every positive thing we do is taking us back to ourselves.

The perfectionist, the procrastinator and the people pleaser

These three 'P's are like silent assassins. We don't tend to notice their work until they have long left the building, leaving a trail of devastation behind. We probably all recognise one of the traits in ourselves, maybe more, and we will certainly know others who possess them. They are quite pervasive, but do not make the mistake of treating them as inconsequential.

The perfectionist can appear full of virtue and can charm us into believing that this is a destination we should be pursuing. However, the perfectionist is generally one who is discontent, dissatisfied and unfulfilled. Rarely is their mind at peace, rarely do they find comfort in their chosen activities. In their pursuit of excellence, they often create ruination. They undermine and destroy relationships because nothing is ever good enough.

The perfectionist sits in a place of perpetual expectation, expecting to meet a standard they can rarely meet themselves whilst expecting that of others. And in both cases, they are devasted when that expectation is not fulfilled. Their philosophy on the face of it seems admirable. Why shouldn't we try to achieve perfection? Surely this is the way to best fulfil our potential. Unfortunately, this philosophy is inflexible and unflinching. It does not move from its obsessive focus, and it expects everything to align itself to its position.

If you are a perfectionist, you will know that moments of happiness are few and far between, because you are only ever truly happy when you think you've cracked it. If you know a perfectionist you will probably find them intense, overbearing and relentless in their demands. Despite your best efforts, nothing seems enough to nourish them, and you're left feeling inadequate.

Perfection is not the goal of life. It's better to choose progress, and if perfection comes as a result of that, well that's a beautiful side-effect. It is important for us all to strive for excellence in what we do, but that must not be at the expense of our humanity or at the expense of others. If we've achieved perfection in something, but have brutalised our own hearts and broken our most sacred relationships in the process, can one say this was worth it? I think not.

I believe a perfectionist is unlikely to reach their desired destination. I have not, to date, met a happy perfectionist. These are individuals who cannot live with their contradictions and shortcomings. They are unable to love those ugly, undeveloped parts of the self and as a consequence, they make things worse in their world, both internally and externally.

The antidote for being a perfectionist is simply not to pursue perfection. Become passionate about being your very best. Be so kind that the ugliest parts of you move out of the darkness and seek the light. Be so brave that no matter how inadequate and insufficient you feel, you keep looking for the solutions. Be so understanding that you look past your misdemeanours and mistakes and find the lessons in each one. Be so honest and courageous that you can look your demons in the eye and make them your friends.

Perfectionism often denies the truth as it is, because it wishes it were another way. But this is its great mistake. One has to be able to accept things as they are to have any chance of finding perfection and it's through that acceptance that one grows and fulfils their reason for being. Choose progress and you will 'perfect' yourself. You'll find your perfect self is more than enough.

The procrastinator is so persuasive, alluring and seductive. It can have the best of us doing tomorrow what really should be done today. It has a plethora of reasons why 'this' can wait and why 'that' can be done at another time. Its rationale is well constructed and seems to make total sense.

If you look closely, you will see the procrastinator is one of your cleverest defence mechanisms. It often emerges when you're afraid that you might not be able to meet a deadline or complete a task. So, your fear of failure gives you a 'legitimate' reason to back out or to leave it. But what it doesn't tell you at the time is the consequences are unlikely to be ones that you're happy with. That part of the contract is usually written in small print and it's when the consequences turn up that you're then racked with disappointment and guilt and the feeling of 'if only' consumes you.

Procrastination doesn't only turn up because of our fear of failure, it can equally turn up because of our fear of succeeding. Success is probably what most people are pursuing whether they are aware of it or not, but most people don't know what to do with it when it turns up because it's not quite what they expected it to be. I've worked with many successful people who have everything most people would give their right arm for, and now they have what they've worked their whole lives for, the size of the responsibility and expectation is more than many of them can bear.

And so, procrastination becomes their friend. They defer and put off for fear of more demand and responsibility. They try to find different ways of avoiding the thing they had so frantically pursued. They begin to hide from the life they've created and now are looking for a different kind of fulfilment, an inner peace and contentment.

Procrastination can turn up in many forms but if you are to discover how your procrastinator is sabotaging your best efforts and dreams, you will need to take a closer look. And I'm sure you will find either a fear of failure or success is lurking somewhere in the shadows.

It's easy to think of procrastination as being about laziness. Rarely is this the case. It might on first inspection look like laziness, but in truth that apathy, that lethargy is just a way of not facing the fear and the challenges that come with that.

Next time your procrastinator turns up, realise she is trying to protect you, because she's not been persuaded that the task or the goal ahead can be met with the current resources and so, putting your plans onto the list of deferrals is a clever and sophisticated way to avoid the pain of disappointment and failure.

The antidote for this is to be excruciatingly honest. Recognise what's really going on. Look at what you're really afraid of. Is that fear real or is it simply a habit, a pattern of familiarity that has been running your life because of some earlier experience that you've never made peace with. The closer you look at your procrastinator the more you will find it's running away from something and by deferring 'doing' it will hopefully never bump into that fear.

You must change your inner narrative. You must overturn this lie. And to do that you have been given a map throughout this book which shows you how to reach that destination. Build healthy obsessions, talk to yourself positively and kindly, treat others with compassion and empathy, pursue those activities that make your heart sing and honour your truth. The more you can be honest about what's going on in you, the less the procrastinator will turn up and eventually s/he'll have no reason to be there.

The people pleaser is busy trying to fit in, to be liked, to be loved and she will generally do anything to ingratiate herself. The problem with the people pleaser is that she easily loses her identity as she gives up her authenticity and adapts herself to the needs of her audience. She's like a chameleon.

The people pleasing character has an outward appearance that is likeable and attractive, as she gives the message 'I'm here to meet your needs' and who amongst us isn't happy when someone is willing to meet our needs? But it's important to realise this character often has underlying expectations and is not performing those acts of kindness unconditionally.

This is a very powerful subpersonality, because its philosophy is that one must do what's necessary to be part of the in-crowd and it doesn't care what the cost is. If you have people pleasing traits, you will recognise the ease with which you give up your convictions if they put you at odds with those around you. In fact, you'll notice there are times when your passionately held views and opinions, like a weathervane, change direction, according to the way the wind of public opinion is blowing.

People pleasers live uncomfortably within their own skins because rarely do they honour what's true for themselves. Many people pleasers have gone so far down this route that they no longer know when asked what their opinion is. They look around for some nudge or clue from somewhere else to point them in the right direction.

If you don't recognise yourself in this text, you probably recognise a people pleaser in your life, because he is busy trying to make everyone else happy, when he is clearly not happy himself. He's busy pretending all is right in his world but when you look more closely what you discover are feelings of uncertainty and anxiety driving many of his choices and decisions. This is why people pleasers tend to be hyperactive depressives. On the one hand they can be the life and soul of the party, but when you see them behind closed doors, they are often flat and empty – exhausted by the demands of their role.

In order to be free of this character, we need to first work out who we really are and where we are heading? If we have no clarity about either of these questions, we'll continue to take refuge in other people's ambitions, goals and dreams. We'll attach ourselves to that which helps us to best get our own needs met, whilst unwittingly sacrificing our true natures in the process.

Aspiring for authenticity is the easiest way to disassociate yourself from the people pleaser. By all means value, respect and even admire those who are examples of integrity, humanity and kindness. Those who use their creativity and ingenuity for the greater good. But don't make the mistake of losing yourself within that admiration. Be inspired, emulate those who provide us with positive templates, but most of all find out who you really are. Don't be afraid of that journey.

Then you will find the song of your own heart and when you do, sing it regularly. Organise your own choir and blast out wonderous tunes that uplift, encourage and move you. Align yourself to those things that are right and true for you and don't give away your power by being influenced by the last conversation or the next one, unless it resonates deeply with your heart and mind.

To fully free yourself of the people pleaser characteristic, you have to have the courage to be yourself - and you have to cultivate the faith that even if you can't see it yet, you are worthy of your vote. Vote for your own magnificence and it will turn up in your life.

The perfectionist, procrastinator and people pleaser are responsible for so much deception and damage. Listed above are some of the ways they can infiltrate our lives. This isn't a definitive list, so don't be afraid to see how they might be infiltrating your life and skewing your decisions and choices in the process. Become free of these three 'P's and your life will be richer and fuller.

Next is the final member of this community of threes...

The three realities

What is reality? It is a question that would be answered in many different ways, as the answer would be shaped by one's education, upbringing, faith, religious influences and culture. Given this, can we ever know what reality is?

I have no interest in challenging anyone's view or perspective on the subject because I recognise that we are all living within the world of our beliefs – unless of course we are willing to step outside of the messages we have unknowingly and knowingly imbibed, then we may be able to see things differently.

This section of all the threes is really about providing a framework for those of you who are interested in the synergistic perspective that we at Reach have constructed over the last four decades.

Some of our classic and unique subjects include: N.O.S.E, The Three Aspects of Consciousness, Persuading the Body, The Pyramid of Shame, The Four Aspects of the Mind, All You Need to Know, The Journey of Enough, The Journey of Becoming and of course the centrepiece, The Story of Health. Pulling all these subjects together has taken a great deal of time, research, patience and skilful navigation through all those things that make us human.

Creating a cohesive, fluid, integrated model that works from whichever angle you view it has not been an easy undertaking and yet I believe we have done just that. The Three Realities actually embraces all of the concepts listed above and much more. It provides a wider context in which we can understand our place in reality (however we see it) - our stated agenda at Reach has always been to provide people with the options and opportunities to grow and flourish. We are just as happy with the person who accepts everything versus the person who accepts very little. As long as they've taken what they need we believe our job has been done.

As you consider what The Three Realities might mean for you, as Buddha said, (paraphrased) 'Only adopt something in your own life if it stands up to the scrutiny of your experience'.

THE THREE REALITIES

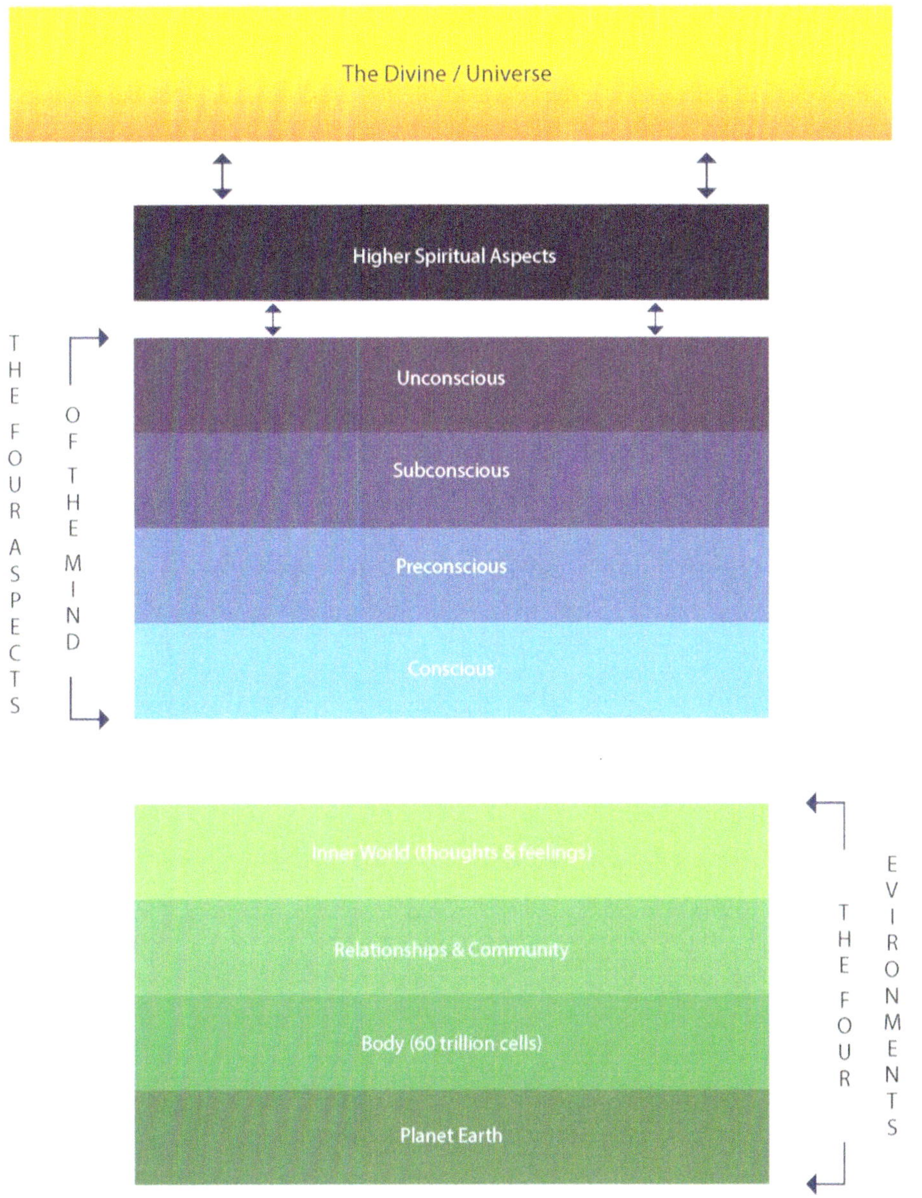

If you look at the diagram you will see the four environments are laid out in varying shades of green and the four aspects of the mind in varying shades of blue. Beyond the four aspects of the mind, higher spiritual aspects are depicted and beyond that in yellow you will see the divine/the universe. The primary reason for presenting the diagram in this way is that I wanted to convey the idea that these different expressions of energy occupy their own bandwidths.

The four environments are all played out in the world of matter, the material world in which we live and with which we are familiar. This is the world of the five senses, where sensory perception and logic tend to dominate the landscape... this is certainly the case in our modern world.

You will see in the four environments, that the planet is depicted at the bottom as it is the foundation and all life as we know it depends on Mother Earth's nurturing and sustenance and of course the intimate relationship she has with the solar system.

The body comes next - this extraordinary organism made up of sixty trillion cells. The complexity of tasks that it performs is simply mind-boggling. There are numerous systems performing their individual functions, but the real miracle is how this vast and intricate network operates synergistically, with unimaginable numbers of conversations taking place simultaneously. This is the true wonder.

The next bandwidth is that of the relationships that we form with our families, friends, colleagues and the wider community. It's the context in which most of us live and given that we are social beings, is vitally important to our mental health and well-being. Many of us identify ourselves by the relationships and the community we are either born into or grow into through our experiences.

The final bandwidth is the inner landscape, the world of our thoughts, emotions and feelings. This, albeit taking place in the material world, is where the world of the metaphysical meets the physical. Even though we have begun to measure, analyse and decode what is taking place in this dimension, through disciplines like: neuroscience, PNI, cognitive neuroscience, noetic sciences and neurotheology, we are still some distance from being able to classify all the wonders of inner space. It could be said that we understand much more about outer space than the inner cosmos.

As previously stated, these four environments have an intimate relationship with one another, which can be either harmonious or disruptive. This is the first reality - and our personal experiences influence our view of this reality.

The second reality is made up of the metaphysical, the invisible reality of the mind and spirit. This bandwidth is primarily experienced through an introspective habit. As you know, the four aspects of the mind are specific layers of consciousness each with its own role and functions (as explained in chapter 4). These four aspects are not only able to express themselves in the world of matter but also their unique attributes give all of us access to the spirit (our essence).

In this second layer of reality, what we see is the metaphysical meeting the material world of matter. Consciousness, or what can be called our identity is made up of mind and spirit. Spirit, as described in The Story of Health, is that feeling we all know and have... the feeling of 'who am I when no one is looking?' It's not the feeling of how we appear in the world it's the feeling of how we really are. If you stop performing your role, stop living up to the demands and expectations placed on you, you will discover either a feeling of dissatisfaction and unease, or a feeling of unassailable peace - a state of ambivalence and confusion, or a feeling of clarity and insight.

For most of us it is not a stable state, it is forever in flux - joy and contentment in one moment followed by doubt and fear in the next. This is why for so many there exists a state of inner torment with a perpetual pursuit of some soothing balm that will heal the mind and bring tranquillity to the spirit. Those who choose stillness and positive silence are able to create equilibrium.

The third reality refers to the Divine. For some this is God, or a Deity and for others, the Universe has become the best description for this aspect. This reality is experienced in many ways because as previously suggested it is dependent upon one's life experience and indoctrination. The most important thing about this reality is that it highlights a point where human consciousness extends beyond itself and connects to something in which it has faith.

Around the world, that 'thing', that force, energy, presence is talked about and related to in a multitude of ways. With regards to this third reality, I do not make suggestions about what one should pursue because I believe each one needs to find what works best for them. That might be following a particular religious tradition. It might be the humanism approach or a modern interpretation of an ancient ideal. The vehicles of expression are also likely to be different - for some that will be contemplation and prayer, for others meditation and mindfulness, or an appreciation for life in all of its majestic forms.

Regardless of a person's philosophy and the application of their beliefs, what is important to this reality is integrity – honouring one's conscience and acting in a way that does not cause harm. This is where our values and codes of conduct connect us to that which is greater than ourselves.

As depicted in the diagram, the higher spiritual aspects are supported by the mind's functions and enable us to connect with the Divine. What this means in practice is the more we live in alignment with our faith and beliefs the more we can build a fortress of peace. Those who live in these higher spiritual aspects keep their promises and pledges. They live a non-negotiable life. As a result, they are replenished by their disciplines and routines. These are also individuals who have a non-violent code. They value and respect difference. The more we respect others who may have differing beliefs but who equally seek to cause no harm, the more we can establish a reality that is harmonious and nurturing for all.

The Three Realities helps us to understand the world of matter and our position within it. It also gives us a simple map where we can clearly see the interface between consciousness and the physical world, whilst encouraging us to draw on the values of kindness, compassion, humility and integrity. It emphasises that we are spiritual beings having a human experience and what binds us is greater than that which divides us.

To experience all three realities, we need to have the courage to become those who live by the code of threes. Those that do are time travellers, as they remain in conscious contact with the past, present and future, making the best decisions and choices along the way. They commune regularly with the three different levels of consciousness, moving between the three positions, according to the situation, time and need. They nurture themselves with the three 'A's and share the qualities and virtues accrued with all that they meet. They sit confidently with the three 'P's waiting for the fruits of right action, knowing they will eventually turn up at their door. They walk hand in hand with the three gatekeepers, ensuring they cause no harm. Where they make mistakes and fall short, they do not chastise and condemn, they look for the jewel on the ground, claim it and rise again.

When we make the decision to live like this we are forever standing at the door of infinite possibility - and waiting on the other side are futures and fortunes yet to be claimed. Why not go and claim yours!

"The best and most beautiful things in the world cannot be seen or even touched – they must be felt with the heart".

Helen Keller (1880 – 1968)

Points to Remember

- The Memoried Self, the Experiencing Self and the Anticipating Self are useful descriptions for conceptualising our relationship with time. They summarise the confluence between the moment we're standing in, the moment that has just slipped away from us and the moment we are yet to step into. When we have a conscious arrangement with time we can relate better to the past, benefiting from the many lessons and experiences we have had. This enables us to be more present in the now... capable of handling whatever comes our way... and it provides us with the foundation to thrive. From there the future holds no fear for us, as we embrace life with courage and confidence.

- Time is the holder of so many secrets and if we can be still and focus our attention on her in the right way, then those secrets move towards us. They can emerge in so many ways – through conversation, a dream, a difficult experience, listening to a play, a piece of music or maybe an epiphany. Whatever form it takes, if you're open and accessible, time and the universe will speak to you.

- When you create a world that supports the position of 'healthy self', you will find moving to the position of 'other' becomes increasingly effortless. Be under no illusion, to cultivate this position does take practice and time, so do not think that this will just happen by itself.

- Advanced empathy requires us to step away from our viewpoint and look at the world from the other person's position. This means stepping into their skin and attempting to experience their reality as it is for them. Listening from 'over there' is a completely different way of interacting with another. It gives you a perspective and access to feelings that can't be gained from passive listening. Passive listening is almost always 'waiting to speak', waiting for the next gap, so it can express its point of view, because it believes its thoughts, opinions and ideas carry greater importance.

- The lovingly detached position is like being in a stadium, sitting in all the different positions simultaneously, enjoying every dimension of the game or event you're observing. You feel like you are watching each moment in slow motion, as if your respect for time has given you longer to process and evaluate things in real time. This allows one to see the context as clearly as the content - it's this ability to see both that enables us to the make the wisest decisions. Remember, the lovingly detached position is not concerned with being right, it's only concerned with what is right.

- The three gatekeepers ensure that you do not cause harm to others. They encourage foresight rather than hindsight. To ensure that you move through the world leaving a beautiful fragrance wherever you go, remember to walk with truth, kindness and benevolence.

- The three 'A's are the cornerstone of emotional and psychological development. A deficiency in any of these three (attention, affection and affirmation) will be reflected in how we see ourselves and the world. Find positive ways to meet these needs so that the patterns of the past do not continue to shape your choices and decisions.

- Male and female brains are not different. The brain is not bound by gender. It's our exposure to the environment and socialisation that has the biggest impact on brain development and the identities we form.

- Make the three 'P's a lifetime obsession. Practise doing the right things as often as you can, and that virtuous cycle will elevate you above all obstacles. He who practises patience will find it will eventually unlock any door. Those who make perseverance their ally always rise one more time than they fall.

- Understanding The Three Realities reminds us that we are spiritual beings having a human experience and so should not be limited by the physical world of matter. This understanding invites us to respect the relationship between the physical and the metaphysical and pursue a more principled life, one which is not merely self-indulgent, but is more expansive, generous and kind. Those who better understand the relationship between consciousness, matter and the divine become true disciples of all the threes.

A meditation to remind you of the primary themes of this chapter...

The number three has a deep significance... and it's worth remembering the many insights it offers me... firstly, it deepens my appreciation of time as it teaches me how to better relate to the past, present and future... it reminds me that the past will define me if I do not resolve those things that haunt me... it also reminds me that the future will equally rob me of peace of mind and joy, if I am tethered to its anxieties and fears... finally, it reminds me that the present is a gift I must keep unwrapping...

The number three reminds me of the subtleties of consciousness... and teaches me to move between self, other and lovingly detached... so I might better see myself and the social context in which I live... it also encourages me to pursue a better way of interacting with others... as it reminds me of the three gatekeepers... a higher code of conduct that I now seek to make part of the way I live within the world...

As a result of the number three I have come to understand the central importance of attention, affection and affirmation with regards to human development... and I now look for healthy ways to incorporate these three aspects into my life...

All the threes have helped me to understand my relationship with perception, personality and my performance within the world... they have helped me to develop a new respect for these three key characters... they determine so much of how I meet each day... and whether I am equipped for the ebb and flow of life...

Practice, patience and perseverance become an obsession for me... I know that without this special trio I am unlikely to make it to my dream destination... so I choose today and every day to embrace practice, patience and perseverance... they are my greatest allies on this journey of becoming...

The three realities open my eyes to the many illusions I have been bound by... they enable me to see the advantages and limitations of each reality... and how by having the awareness of these three dimensions I can become more than I could ever have imagined...

All the threes are wonderful reminders of the infinite possibilities that stand with me in every moment... and so I choose to live by the code of threes...

CHAPTER 9

FITTING IT ALL TOGETHER

"Vision without execution is just hallucination".

Thomas Edison (1847 – 1931)

In this penultimate chapter I want to try my best to pull everything together because I'm well aware of the diversity of topics covered and as my aim was to provide a guide for 21st century living, then it feels important to dot the 'i's and cross the 't's.

Discipline – becoming the disciple of...

It's hard to know where to place the blame because there have been so many contributors to the idea that discipline is somehow wedded to punishment. In every culture I've researched and studied, I can find evidence of this terrible disservice. I could spend time giving different interpretations around the history of all this, but I honestly do not believe it would be a good use of time.

What I think is far more valuable is to talk about the true meaning of discipline – to correct the misinformation so that we can all steer a better course.

Take a look at the word discipline and nestled at the heart of it, you can see the word disciple. A disciple is one who faithfully follows a particular doctrine. She is a student, an ally to the cause. She is one who has been persuaded by the merits of a certain ideology or philosophy. She follows those teachings with a passion and a willing heart. This is not someone who is beaten into submission and begrudgingly follows the path laid out. In fact, her adherence comes out of a deep understanding and respect for that which she has aligned herself to.

It's a terrible shame that when most of us hear the word discipline it conjures up images of having to do something we would rather not do. Rarely do we think of it as something that we want to embroider into the fabric of our own lives, something that would enhance and empower us.

If we worked to this idea that discipline is becoming the disciple of something, then we would be driven to inculcate doctrines that made sense to us. We would passionately pursue them, not because we think we ought to and merely to fit in, but because they make us feel completely alive.

My message is simple, become a disciple of what you believe in, become its student, inculcate its values and messages, because they make sense to you and because you wish to weave them into your own life and heart.

To become a disciple isn't doing something out of fear but to do something out of love and intoxication. And if you do passionately believe in something then where it is beneficial to others, share it with them, in non-evangelical ways.

Wisdom never seeks to indoctrinate. It simply offers its message, never seeking a return because it understands that giving is its own reward. It needs nothing more.

The more you become a disciple, the more you will find discipline and routine become your natural allies. You come to understand that putting the things you believe in into practice clarifies your reasons for being here and underlines your own value in the world. As a result, you fall in love with routine, because you experience its daily elevation of your mind and spirit. This is why I use the phrase again and again 'routine is power' and the disciple experiences perpetual empowerment. This is their bliss.

If you are persuaded by any of the values, principles and philosophical thought contained within this piece of work then rather than thinking of it as stuff you have to do, pursue it with love and you'll experience the freedom that comes out of that. Reject the idea that discipline has anything to do with punishment and become the disciple of what your heart holds dear.

The simplicity and complexity of The Reach Approach

The Reach Approach is a vast model, embracing so many disciplines, ones which naturally align and ones that are seemingly unrelated. One could easily be forgiven for thinking it is more confusing than clarifying or it's trying to be all things to all people. But the fact is that at the heart of what may appear complex is a very simple message... that everything is connected. Only when we look at those connections can we see the true nature of the problem(s) and with that identify the solution(s). We cannot heal that which is concealed, which is another primary theme of the model.

If we are only looking at the presenting issues, we are only ever at best performing first aid. This is not a psychological formula for therapists, this is a formula for life. All humans need to understand that we are multidimensional. There are numerous aspects that influence our experience of ourselves and the world and if we are to effectively address our fears, worries, inadequacies and self-loathing, then fixing what we can see and ignoring the rest will deny us sustainable solutions and happiness.

Although I have covered a broad range of topics in this work - the role of the oceans, the climate, what's happening in our bodies and our minds, how waste is contributing to our dereliction, how energy is at the heart of all transactions taking place in the world and how introspective practices such as LKM, meditation and mindfulness can save us from a toxic fate – what pulls all these things together is The Story of Health. In some way or another they are all included in this contract with life.

The Story of Health is the first lesson and it's the last one. It's where the self-examination needs to begin and it's where, if we want to live our optimal life, we will find the answers. Please, for those of you who don't feel sufficiently familiar with The Story of Health, take a look at what is written on the Reach website, or read the prequel to this book.

Try not to let the diversity of topics overwhelm you. Trust me, they really do all belong in the same conversation. The conversation that we all need to be having which is how do I best fit into the world? What is my primary responsibility as a human being living here on earth? Surely, it's to make a positive impact whilst causing the least amount of harm. Surely, it's to leave a legacy that I can be proud of

- to be remembered for all the right reasons and ensure I've left a positive trail for those generations that follow.

This is not a complex model. It's one that brings simplicity to complexity. It shows you how everything relates to everything else and invites you to connect with all aspects of life, becoming a metaphysical magician in the process.

When you have a better understanding of what's really going on you will find there is greater peace in giving than receiving and your desire is to be a true philanthropist. Then your account with life is always in the black.

Inside Out

We are living in a world where we're so busy trying to fix what's going on outside of ourselves that most of us barely recognise the crumbling of our own internal state. We passionately, in many cases, righteously, want to change 'out there' whilst missing what needs to change 'in here'.

I honestly believe that without an 'inside out' policy we are doomed. We have to get our own internal politics right. This means getting our own government in order. Mattering on the inside first does not mean ignoring the problems in your external environment, but it does mean always prioritising the inner one.

If your own internal government is in chaos, shouldn't you tend to that first before taking to the streets? Or at the very least address your own disorder/anarchy at the same time?

I talked earlier in the book about The Inventory of Incongruence, which is an invitation to look at your contradictions, those things that create an inner conflict. This I have found is the best starting point for getting your own government and society in order.

A question that I've often been asked by those undertaking this exercise is 'I find it difficult to identify my own opposing forces, so how do I do that?' This led me to write Professed Beliefs and Actual Beliefs and most people have found this combination very helpful.

If you are struggling to identify your incongruence, then I encourage you to compare what you say you believe in and how you actually live your life. When we explore this position many of us find that there is quite a chasm between what we say we believe in and what we actually do believe in.

Once you start stripping away and examining your professed beliefs a number of them become exposed as lies that you tell yourself. You discover that you don't always believe what you're saying to others. In fact, many of the things you profess, are what you think you ought to believe and where you find the greatest comfort. They paint a version of yourself that is most attractive and maintains your public persona.

At this point your professed belief, even to you, can seem like your actual belief. On many occasions I've engaged in this exercise with individuals who at the end of it are shocked to discover, usually through their tears and heartache, that they claim to believe in one thing but when push comes to shove, that belief crumbles under the weight of deep-seated doubts that have lain well camouflaged.

Looking at our contradictions and hypocrisies is extremely valuable because it illuminates the difference between our professed beliefs – statements we passionately declare to others (and ourselves) and our actual beliefs – as revealed by our actions, which are the true markers of what we really believe. We cannot find peace of mind and contentment whilst claiming to believe in something yet spend so much time living at odds with that claim.

One should not feel shame about these discoveries. The real shame comes from hiding, denying and justifying them. It should be said at this point that most people aren't even aware that they have professed beliefs and actual beliefs. What has become clear from my work, is that most believe their professed beliefs reflect the truth of their position. It's only when they are faced with some significant trauma or loss that this might be exposed or when they are invited to take a closer look at their inner world and actions that they see the glaringly obvious discrepancies between what they think and say and what they actually do.

You may not like all that you come to see, but as long as kindness is never far away you will be able to gently hold yourself in a place of growing awareness and increasing clarity. Please remember what I've said about living with ambivalence. Those who can do this are the most contented. With this attitude you can begin to generate positive change. Any growing pains you experience are just part of the paradox of progress.

Progress is peppered with many peaks and valleys, mirages, oases and climatic extremes. As long as you can treat all of these variables and conditions as opportunities for growth and learning, none of them is a real threat to your progress - so any pain or relapses you experience along the way are all part of making you more complete.

Living an inside out life means that most of your decisions and choices are influenced more by your internal governance than your external environment. What this means in practice is that you have the courage of your convictions. You're not easily swayed by the masses. You're only influenced by truth and integrity. Only those who develop a truly introspective habit can see the terrain clearly and plot their course accordingly.

Make your party-political slogan 'inside out' and you will win every election.

Making a Story of Health Plan

The Story of Health is the first thing we need to understand on the journey of becoming our best selves, and it is also the thing that we have to maintain for the rest of our lives if we are to achieve a sustainable position of health and contentment.

What is a Story of Health plan and how do you go about creating one? Throughout this book and also in this chapter you have been invited to look at how you're really living and how aligned you are to your beliefs and your faith. Exploring our contradictions and incongruences is an excellent place to begin from when working out your story of health plan.

THE STORY OF HEALTH

Spirit
• Sense of one's own value, worth
• The need to belong, to be loved
• The need for a purpose
• The need for meaningful, uplifting relationships
• Altruism, benevolence
• Honouring your heart
• Integrity, congruence
Environment (circle)
• Creating a physical sanctuary
• Managing pollution
• Work, vocation (Creating the right conditions)
• Healthy relationships
• Applying metaphysical laws and environmental principles
• The art of living at ease in your head
• A social conscience
Lowering of spirit can lead to
Neurosis and / or physical ill health can lead to
Psychosis and / or chronic ill health
Mind
• Meditation, still time, personal prayer
• Positive affirmations, 'I ams'
• The need for a set of non-negotiables
• Forgiveness and gratitude
• Clear vision statement
• Respect for time and resources and the need for a clear strategy
• Pleasure principle
Body
• 90 Nutrients per day for vitality (vitamins, minerals and EFA's)
• Stretching, exercise, and body strengthening
• Hydration, hydrotherapy, detoxification
• Diverse and balanced diet
• Bodywork (eg: bowen, acupuncture, osteopathy, massage etc…)
• Deep restorative sleep
• Pampering

If you look at The Story of Health diagram, you'll see listed the needs of the mind, body, spirit and environment. Looking at this list and seeing how you fare when you compare yourself against each of the four categories, will also be a good way to assess where you are and what needs to be addressed.

Try as you undertake this exercise not to be overwhelmed. It's not a question of having to tick every box and successfully complete every column, nor are you required to overturn your unhelpful habits and patterns all in one go. Lasting change is a process and hopefully by now you appreciate it's unlikely that any one thing is going to get you there.

Kindly compile your list and carefully plan the way forward. I like the acronym SMART. There are a number of variations around this acronym. The one I like best is Small, Manageable, Attainable, Realistic, Targets, because that is exactly the approach that is required here.

In chapter 4, I made reference to eight being the magic number - hopefully I made it clear that we need to build a set of non-negotiables around mind, body, spirit and environment. A good starting point for this is identifying two things in each of these four categories that you can focus on to deal with any imbalances in your life.

Even though establishing eight positive activities is the primary objective, let me underline that the best way forward is to find one thing that you can consistently do for the body, the mind and the spirit and identify one thing where the environment can support you in this endeavour. This would mean coming up with four things as part of your plan but if this feels overwhelming it may be more sensible to only try to do one or two things when you first set out. If that is the case, you need to identify where your initial efforts are best focused. Each person is in a different position when they begin on this journey and so they need to work out what their best starting point is.

If after consideration you're not sure where to start, then experience has revealed time and again, that where the body and environment are significantly compromised, choosing something to redress that imbalance in one or both is probably the best place to start, as these two can have a very destabilising impact on the mind and spirit.

Once you've chosen your starting point, I'd like you to think in blocks of six weeks. Some research suggests that doing anything for twenty-one consecutive days is sufficient to create a habit. I believe it's sufficient to create momentum, but a habit takes longer to be formed. I've found that anything done for less than six weeks is unlikely to find enough traction to get the individual to their desired destination.

Don't be intimidated by the idea of needing to do any of your chosen activities for that length of time. Try just to focus on doing it one day at a time because remember, this is not something you're planning to do for a while, you're seeking to change your lifestyle, your whole way of being. And if six weeks feels daunting, how will you maintain these lifestyle choices for the rest of your life?

Try to enter into this agreement with yourself in a light-hearted way. Treat this like a marathon and not a sprint, remember how important it will be to pace yourself. The race is not for the swift but the who can endure.

I mentioned this figure of twenty-one days not to undermine what is considered to be possible by some, because I do believe some individuals and conditions can respond in shorter time frames. However, I wanted to offer what I believe to be a more realistic time frame, one where I can honestly say I have seen individuals reach milestones they never thought were possible - and even six weeks is not always enough for that. It takes approximately ninety days to create a habit, to build the momentum that will start to turn events in your favour. It's at this point that most people report a feeling of power, a feeling of controlling the direction of their choices and decisions. But don't think of ninety days as an end point, see it as when the next chapter of self-empowerment and greater inner governance begins. At this point there is a feeling of quiet confidence and growing belief in the unlimited nature of your spirit.

Whether you began with one or two things or felt able to practise one thing from each of the four areas, it's at ninety days that you would consider adding another one or two things. For some reaching the six-week mark may have brought enough momentum and confidence to add to your list but if that weren't the case then that is absolutely fine, because you should choose stability and momentum over speed and haste.

Remember what I said about impatience. It is one of the primary enemies of growth. So, please don't force the process... work with it.

Hopefully by around nine months you will have established eight non-negotiables, they will probably be all at different points of evolution but no matter. What's important is to keep each of the plates spinning. Some of you may reach this point sooner whilst others may need longer. Find your own pace.

It's important if you need it to get support. This might be from a therapist of some persuasion, a support group, a friend, your family, whatever works for you. Please don't be afraid to seek out the support you need.

My experience tells me that those who can reach this magic number of eight continue to grow and evolve as they need to. These are the individuals who continue to flourish. Remember the real proof of growth is not about things necessarily looking better on the outside (of course we wish for this too), but the real evidence is finding serenity in the storm. Begin working on your plan today.

Silent revolution

The Reach Approach is part of a silent revolution. This has a dual meaning. On the one hand we're inviting people to take refuge in silence rather than sound. Our world is so busy and so hectic that we are literally being deafened by the noise and the pollution that surrounds us. We're also being deafened by the increasing din of materialism, that strange idea that acquiring objects is more important than decorating our spirits.

We are promoting the need to create silence, sacred moments in each day where we can transcend the noise, the pollution, the demands, the expectations of the modern world and find refuge in the glory of just being. Silence is where the real work is being done.

The other silent revolution that we're a part of, is the one where we spread the message of self-empowerment. Not through a single messenger or a figurehead. We believe that the message is the messenger, that the message itself is divine and only the message should be revered and not any one individual. This is why we conduct our activities under the slogan 'principle before profit'.

We are not prepared to trade away our principles and values in the name of personal recognition or the acquisition of wealth. We are certainly not 'anti' anyone who has acquired wealth or status, as long as that has been acquired in ethical ways. We're simply not promoting something where the pursuit of profit comes first. Our agenda is to enrich the soul, society and the planet. And to that end we are whispering rather than shouting – spreading this message around the globe via a number of platforms and various pathways.

We have numerous websites where most of the material we have researched, written and produced is freely available to everyone, in all the languages of the world. We have produced hundreds of audio-visual materials (which can also be found on our websites and on YouTube). Many of these are in a variety of languages too.

Our psycho-educational model does not end there. We have established a library of Explainer Videos (which can also be found on our websites and on YouTube), offering short summaries by way of an introduction to the depth and diversity of our approach. This is in response to the interest we've had from around the world. We keep finding ways to make our message more accessible to all.

We've produced an award-winning app Happy Hints, which is available both for the iOS platform and the android market. This is a simple application, which sends a positive message each day to the user's device encouraging them to change their self-talk and helping them to realise that happiness is a choice we can all make. The app is packed with a variety of additional resources all designed to help promote a positive mental attitude and has recently been upgraded with a host of new features and content.

In 2014, after fifteen years of running our successful training programme, we produced three original, accredited postgraduate courses, one for coaches and two for counsellors, psychotherapists and others who specialise in the talking therapies.

Our postgraduate courses have been designed for those who are already qualified therapists in one of the disciplines – and have either taken The Reach Approach journey themselves with one of our trained and qualified therapists or have been sufficiently motivated to undertake the journey through a combination of supervised and self-directed learning.

All those pursuing our courses are passionate about The Reach Approach and are keen to spread the holistic, integrative and person specific message that we are renowned for.

As a result of our postgraduate training programme, we have coaches and therapists around the world training with us seeking to develop their own learning and growth whilst making a difference to the part of the world that they inhabit.

And so, as you can see, we have numerous vehicles trying to mobilise the hearts and minds of many and we hope you too will join the silent revolution by finding a way that best suits you and fits into your life.

"Educating the mind without educating the heart is no education at all".

Aristotle (384 BC – 322 BC)

Points to remember

- A disciple is one who faithfully follows a doctrine, one who is persuaded by the merits of that ideology or philosophy. This is not someone who is beaten into submission and reluctantly follows a path laid out by others. Their adherence comes out of a deep understanding and respect for that path, and they pursue it with a willing heart. This is what true discipline looks like.

- The more you become a disciple, the more you will find that discipline and routine become your natural allies. You come to understand that putting the things you believe into practice clarifies your reasons for being here and underlines your own value in the world. As a result, you fall in love with routine, because you experience its daily elevation of your mind and spirit.

- At the heart of The Reach Approach is the simple message that everything is connected. At every point it is encouraging the mind to move away from a siloed way of thinking to a synergistic attitude and outlook. This is because we are multi-dimensional, and we can't possibly fix our problems if we refuse to see the depth and complexity of our natures. So, look for the connections, the points of convergence and there you'll find the truth and the antidote to your ailments.

- The Story of Health is the first lesson and the last one. It's where our self-examination needs to begin and if we want to live a rich and full life, it's only by addressing the deficiencies in all four areas (mind, body, spirit and environment) that we can ascend to the pinnacle of our potential. Begin with an honest audit, there you will find the problems, but do not be intimidated by them, actively pursue the solutions. The good news is, for a mind that is willing and open there is a plethora of strategies to choose from.

- We need an inside out approach to life. For far too long we have valued the external and neglected the internal. We have chosen image over substance and as a consequence we are drowning in our feelings of inadequacy, shame, fear and low self-worth. Valuing the inside does not mean neglecting the outside, that too should be treasured. What it means is prioritising the inside, which in practice involves closing the gap between our professed beliefs and actual beliefs. Pretending to the world or ourselves we are one thing when inside we feel something else simply diminishes us, our energy seeps away and we become mere shadows of ourselves. Although you may not like what you see at first, lovingly embrace your ambivalence and your spirit will rise.

- Make a Story of Health plan built around non-negotiables. Start with one activity that you truly commit to in each of the four areas, then when you can add another activity in each area. Don't go more quickly than you can manage. When you're up to eight things that you are consistently doing at least 80% of the time, you will find there is an energetic shift in your life. You are propelled forward in a completely different way. From this point any inclines you are confronted by feel much more manageable, as your internal resilience and stamina grow. Eight really is the magic number, it's the turning point. Don't stop there though, see it as that point where the positive 'spin rate' of your life choices has now taken you beyond the grasp of the negative forces.

- Find ways to become part of the silent revolution. Don't look out at the world and think "what difference could I possibly make?" It's easy to be daunted by the size of the task of personal transformation, especially if we've tried many times and accumulated a number of failures. See those failures and mistakes as stepping-stones, each one bringing you a little closer to the dawn. Realise that the main reason we have failed is that we have not had the right method and strategy. There's nothing fundamentally wrong with us - we've simply not known how to access our best selves.

Now you know that synergy is the answer you can, with kindness and love, reinvent yourself in the image of your choosing... Do that today.

A meditation to remind you of the primary themes of this chapter...

Discipline reminds me that it is my friend not my enemy... it's an invitation to become a disciple of right action... an ambassador for the truth... it helps me to understand and accept my ambivalences... and reminds me not to define myself by my limitations... discipline reminds me that I am unlimited... and if I embrace this feeling, everything becomes possible...

Having taken this incredible journey of self-examination and expanding my mind beyond myself... I realise that the way to make the best contribution to the world, is to matter from the inside out... this does not lead to neglecting the world... to the contrary, it ensures that I remember that the world I inhabit is sacred... and I can only truly respect it when I respect myself... from that position, I am able to make a greater contribution to the world... and I do...

In order to respect me, I need a set of non-negotiables... I need these heart-pledges to help me commit to a plan for positive change... intention is not enough on this journey... only consistent action will do...

I make my own story of health plan... which meets the needs of the four heroes, mind, body, spirit and environment... the whole drama of life depends on the needs of these four being sufficiently met... I now deal with any areas of neglect... I now make good on those promises that I have previously broken... I now remember the importance of forgiveness, gratitude, integrity and kindness... without these, my fortress of peace cannot be constructed...

My non-negotiables hold the fortress of peace together... they are the bricks and mortar... once in place they will weather any storm... starting from today, I commit to a plan that I will obsessively honour...

I can now see clearly the wonderful prism of synergy... where all the different coloured lights merge... and become the one stunningly bright light that illuminates my spirit... that light also illuminates my hopes and dreams... it unveils the path that I need to follow... I no longer walk blindly through my own life... my eyes of awareness are now completely open...

I can clearly see how it all fits together... and I can see my own magnificent part in this wonderful drama called life...

CHAPTER 10

THE REACH APPROACH IN ACTION

"I hear and I forget. I see and I remember. I do and I understand".

Confucius (551 BC – 479 BC)

Questions and answers on a variety of topics

Every day I receive approximately one hundred and fifty emails from around the world. About half of these are posing questions in relation to the person's mental and physical health, seeking answers for how they might better manage their circumstances and symptoms. I also receive at least forty calls a day, from individuals seeking help and support with their emotional, psychological and physical challenges.

I had considered, as with the previous book, including another batch of case-studies to further illustrate how effective a truly holistic therapeutic approach can be, across a wide spectrum of issues. However, I decided a more effective way of showcasing The Reach Approach would be to present a cross-section of questions that have been posed to me, along with my responses.

They cover a wide range of topics and issues to illustrate the fluidity and flexibility of the model. I hope to demonstrate to you how when you use The Story of Health as your lens you can always find something that supports the individual on their journey of self-improvement.

This question-and-answer chapter has been compiled in such a way that the individuals' identities have been concealed. The questions have been abridged due to the complexity and length of many of them, but the answers do reflect the context, to help the reader make best sense of my responses.

Before beginning this journey it's important to say that the answers offered are specific to the individual and cases presented. And so, the advice/suggestions made, should not be considered applicable in a generic way to other individuals and scenarios. The Reach Approach is a person specific model, which means it adapts itself to the needs of the client. The examples here are by way of illustration of the model in action; but should not be replicated without taking appropriate advice from a qualified and experienced practitioner.

Question:
I work with pain management and have found that the more I've studied and researched the subject, the more unsure I am about what the best strategies and techniques are, to help those who are suffering. I'm interested in your approach, and I wonder what you have to say about this subject?

Answer:
My experience has taught me that with all pain, whatever its origin, a multifactorial approach is needed. If we create a treatment plan that addresses all the elements of the patient's life, we are more likely to secure the best outcome for them.

An important part of the strategy is increasing their self-knowledge/awareness. The better they understand themselves the more likely they are to be able to manage the experience.

Helping the patient to understand the aetiology of pain can also give them a greater sense of control. This, alongside self-knowledge, offers a valuable foundation for any other intervention/strategy.

I'm passionate about The Story of Health (mind, body, spirit and environment), which has developed out of my clinical experience and research. What I've discovered over the years, is that the best strategic response to pain is found by doing an audit of these four elements.

The origins and exacerbators of pain are many. What I have consistently found is that where the mind is still entangled in unresolved issues, this can have a significant bearing on one's experience of pain. A lot of clients I've worked with who've suffered with a variety of complex and chronic conditions, where nothing else seems to have worked, have found that facing and resolving their emotional and psychological problems, has had a huge impact on their pain and pain thresholds.

Therefore, when the client/patient actually deals with what is troubling them, consciously or subconsciously, this changes their relationship to and experience of pain.

Also, when trying to meet the needs of the mind, it is clear that conscious and consistent introspective practices make a marked difference to one's experience of pain. There is a lot of scientific data relating to pain management to support this observation. See the work of Dr. Fadel Zeidan around mindfulness and pain.

With regards to the relevance and importance of the spirit, I have found that it is meaning and purpose that matter most. Those who lack this have a diminished sense of their own value and usefulness. This emotional debilitation can accentuate their pain. herefore, ensuring the person has meaning in their life and is being supported to fulfil their potential, however small, really matters. This offers one greater capacity and resilience - and given how important mind and spirit are in the healing process, then elevating mood is vital to one's experience of pain.

We now have masses of data, confirmed by Psychoneuroimmunology (PNI), that mood elevation influences how our psychobiological processes and immune system work (see the work of Dr. Lydia Temoshok and Dr. Ronald Glaser).

In fact, as a result of the advancements in this field, especially in oncology, we now know that the potency and efficacy of natural killer cells increase, the more positive we feel. So, our thoughts and even more critically our beliefs really matter.

In terms of the body, there are many factors we can influence in relation to pain - and of course diet/nutrition and sleep are significant amongst those. However, something I have found that is equally relevant, and is often overlooked, is the principle 'structure governs function'. None of the body's organs or systems can work properly if we are misaligned. Where there's any misalignment in the body there will be a propensity for pain. Therefore, getting the structure right is pivotal because of all the inflammatory responses and other biological dysfunctions that misalignment can produce.

Finally, the environment. Both the physical space one inhabits and the relationships one has (or doesn't have) really matter to the interpretation and experience of pain. For example, the latest research (see the work of: Professor Sharon Macdonald and Dr. Jennie Morgan) tells us that exposure to a disorganised and chaotic environment is unsettling and can create feelings of disorientation and insecurity. It's also difficult to focus and concentrate under these conditions. This is why creating order in our physical space(s) can make an enormous difference to how we feel (mind and spirit), how our bodies respond, and how we interpret and manage pain. This disorganised and chaotic tendency is also very disruptive to one's relationships.

This brief overview offers some insight as to why I believe pain management needs to be viewed through the lens of mind, body, spirit and environment. Plato put it beautifully when he said, 'No attempt should aim to cure the body without the soul... Let no one persuade you to cure the body until they have first given you their soul to be cured, for this is the great error of our day... that physicians first separate the soul from the body' (paraphrased). I believe we are still making this mistake, 2300 years later.

There is much more I could say on this topic, but I think that is sufficient for now. I hope some of it is useful to you and the important work you are doing.

Question:
I've been ill for so long with a variety of symptoms (aches, pains and burning sensations) which no one seems to have any answers for. I've had countless tests and I am always told my results are in the normal range, but I don't feel normal. At sixty-five I'm feeling very tired, and some days cannot see the point of continuing. Can you help?

Answer:
It was a real joy to finally meet you (this was a Skype conversation) and to have such a meaningful interaction. I promised I'd send you an email with my thoughts to underline what we discussed. Here goes...

Thank you for your honesty and sharing so much of yourself with me. I only shared as much of myself with you as I did because I wanted you to know there is a way back from your personal hell.

Cognitive neuroscientists have now established that we have approximately sixty thousand thoughts a day. 95% of those thoughts are the same thoughts we had yesterday, five years ago, twenty years ago and so on... which means three thousand thoughts a day are new and original ones - little sparks of energy and hope that can become anything we choose. If we don't choose a positive course for ourselves, then these three thousand new thoughts join the family of the familiar and simply repeat what has gone the day before.

Sadly, this is the story for most people. They don't make a conscious choice to think differently, to change their self-talk and as a consequence their tendencies, patterns and habits don't change. So, they keep facing the same reality again and again and wonder why.

I promise you this, if you decide you're going to have a better today and a better tomorrow, those three thousand new thoughts will galvanise around your resolve, creating the foundation for a much better future.

Given what you shared with me on Saturday, your body and your brain are starving. You're getting nowhere near enough of the right nutrients to give the body a fighting chance. There's no pharmacy in the world like the body and there's no physician like the mind. It's time to write the daily prescription of determined thoughts. In that way the a hundred billion neurons in your brain and the sixty trillion cells in your body will be mobilised to create the health that you seek... but you must put in those nutrients in abundance to fulfil the prescription.

The 4 'S's are a good place to begin for getting lots of macro and micronutrients into the body. These are: smoothies, soups, stews and salads. All four provide you with an opportunity to introduce colour and diversity in terms of your food choices. There's no shortage of healthy permutations when it comes to these options. That said, I don't want you to feel overwhelmed, so don't try to include all four 'S's straight away. Pick one and begin the journey.

For many starting with smoothies is a nice easy option. If this appeals to you then I'd suggest you get yourself a Nutribullet or equivalent and have at least one green smoothie (three quarters green veg, one quarter fruit) a day. The green veg I'd most recommend is spinach, or kale. You can have others such as cabbage, lettuce, broccoli etc. The fruit should be those you most like. Amongst the best for you given your symptoms are all of the berries, mangos, bananas and kiwis. Pears and apples are very good too.

The key to a very good smoothie is to find a mix you like so you'll keep wanting to have it. The beauty of a smoothie is how many nutrients can be packed into one serving and when the body is getting that massive injection of goodness, you'll find that it will crave more.

You can also add, if you don't find it sweet enough, a little bit of Manuka honey and from the other symptoms you described you would also benefit from adding some protein powder to help your body repair itself. There are some very good protein powders out there. I would recommend those with hemp, spirulina, chlorella, wheat grass... because the best sources of protein come in a vegetable form.

I would like you to contact me in four months' time for us to have a further chat because it will take three to four months to really reap the benefits of what I've suggested, but you must have at least one smoothie a day (on the days when you've not eaten much, try and have two) - this is because I don't believe you can create an upturn in your health until you're putting in the vitamins, minerals and essential fats that can begin the job of repairing your exhausted body.

I would suggest always having one for your breakfast and then replacing one of your other meals with a second one when you can or need to. This is not something you can afford to be casual about. In my view nothing else is going to work without this kind of adjustment to your diet.

Your body is pulling down your mind so you must reverse that trend, then the other suggestions I've made to change your thinking patterns will have a foundation on which to build.

Question:
I'm struggling with feelings of guilt, shame, grief and anger – especially since my father has died. What would you recommend... because I feel stuck?

Answer:
It's difficult to offer generic answers for emotional issues because the reason we feel what we feel is made up of so many factors. That said, the thing to understand about shame is that it's a largely unconscious emotion. It lives in the dark recesses of our minds, which makes it more difficult to excavate. The best way to address shame if at all possible is head on. You may need support to do this - from someone who has taken the journey themselves. A non-shaming person is one who is unlikely to make you feel small and inadequate when looking at your shame, because they can relate to the experience having faced their own demons.

If you don't have anyone you trust to walk alongside you then taking this journey is much more difficult but not impossible.

You can make a list of the things you feel shame or guilt about, things you would rather not remember. Then maybe over a number of days or even weeks work your way through the list. As you come to each item deeply reflect on what it is that you regret. Be honest with yourself about your part. Try not to make excuses for your actions, but equally don't seek to condemn yourself either. Facing your shame is not an assassination of oneself, it's a recognition that we have behaved inappropriately and could have acted in a better way.

If what you did hurt the heart of someone, whether they are still in your life or not, you can imagine yourself talking to them and saying what needs to be said, apologising for the action you regret. Remember this is not about letting yourself off the hook and you are in no way seeking to justify or excuse your behaviour. As you give your account, do it in an unconditional way. The more sincere and heartfelt your interaction with that person, that regret, that memory, the more it will positively impact on your spirit. Sincere regret and apology really do heal the soul.

This is an exercise you may have to do several times for each thing you are seeking to resolve. Some shames, after one or two sittings, dissipate into the ether of the past and no longer haunt you. Others may take half a dozen or more sittings to be reconciled.

You can also, if you prefer, write a letter of apology to the one you have hurt. This might be a letter that you write numerous times, each time you will find the intensity of what you feel lessens. These are letters you may never send because it doesn't feel appropriate, but equally there might come a time when you do feel it's right to send one of those letters, because it offers the chance for reconciliation and healing.

I can say more about shame another time because it's not possible to deal with something this huge in one email.

I think with regards to anger it is helpful to understand its anatomy if we are to work out how it applies to us. Here's a brief overview.

Anger is a complex emotion because it has a hot and cold temperament. Hot anger is obvious and indisputable, whereas cold anger is much more incognito and somewhat nebulous. A lot of sadness and melancholy is to do with anger turned in on oneself.

From what you've said, you may not be suffering with hot anger, but make sure you haven't got cold anger lurking because it is more insidious. It does most of its work by withdrawing from a situation/person or withdrawing love and affection. Much of its activity is conducted in a disturbed silence. In other words, the person is not at ease with himself.

Your feelings of grief are complicated by not just the loss of someone you have loved deeply, but by the feelings of injustice that you have been left with.

Grief is one of the most powerful emotions in disrupting our equilibrium – it is arguably the most complicated of the emotions because it has numerous stages (denial, pain and guilt, depression, bargaining, anger, reconstruction/acceptance).

There isn't a definitive list of emotions although people classically refer to the five stages of grief, but forty years of working with grief and loss tells me the list is much longer and is more specific to each person. What classically happens is that people get stuck in one phase or another and can be trapped there for weeks, months, even years, especially if they have not done any resolution work.

You have quite a bit of unfinished business and even though your father has passed I think you need to have a heartfelt conversation with him. There are those who believe that when someone has died there is now no chance of resolution. This simply isn't true. Most resolution actually is between oneself and one's memories. If the person we want to resolve the issue with is still around, then it may be possible assuming they are willing, to resolve the matter with them, but even when the other party has no desire to resolve the issue or as in this instance has died, you can still make peace.

We are generally taunted by the memories in our minds concerning that person or event. And whilst those memories are not questioned and remain unchallenged, then their capacity to keep us stuck in our grief is unending. Every time we think back our grief holds us in a place that is connected to the most powerful things recorded in our memory banks, whether they are still relevant or not.

Please try striking up a conversation with your father. To facilitate this, you can use a picture of him if you have one or if there's a particular item that you associate with him that stirs up memories and feelings, that could be a vehicle for such a conversation. It might be that you can simply do this through your imagination, with no external aid. However you choose to go about it, this is an opportunity to say all the things you feel that have not been said, a chance to address the injustices that you're now hampered by. This will not necessarily provide you with an answer, but it will help you to move out of your current position.

The value of an exercise like this is that you're not left wedded to a moment which has gone and which you can no longer influence. The worst thing about any negative emotion is to be stuck in it, as this drains away your power. When you face grief head on in this way you create movement, and the emotion can find its way to acceptance and peace, which is the ideal destination for all negative emotions.

I would encourage you to start here and let me know how you get on because there is much to consider. Whatever you do, don't force this. Move at your own pace and please reach out if you need any more help.

Question:
I'm struggling with a list of dualities and contradictions, which leave me sometimes feeling like a fraud. I also think these may be contributing to my illness.

Answer:
I'm very sorry to hear how you are feeling and applaud your honesty. It takes great courage to own our stuff but until we do, we are imprisoned. Please take a look at N.O.S.E. on our website to find out more. I think you would also benefit from looking at Living with Ambivalence.

Feelings of duality are more common than you think. Many people I have worked with have felt like frauds and the tug of war caused as a result of those feelings has done them psychological harm - and for some there has been physical harm too.

The list you sent me of all your internal conflicts was really helpful because wherever there are incongruences and contradictions, the soul struggles to find peace and authenticity. At this point what happens is that the acquired selves, those personality traits that we have accrued in order to help us fit in and belong, dominate the landscape. They are better known as the private and public selves.

The tension caused between these two positions does not simply have a psychological impact, it has a physiological impact too as the body creates a disproportionate amount of cortisol, adrenaline, adrenochrome and other neurochemicals. Their impact on tissues, cells and organs is very negative indeed. In fact, the impact on the body is almost incalculable because it depends how much time we are caught up with these conflicts and the level of their emotional intensity.

From the things you've told me about your life and story you may need more professional support to assist you with your health issues. I'm happy to offer generic advice but I think you need more precise intervention given the nature of your complaints.

What I would say given the physical symptoms you reported, is that you're clearly dehydrated, and nothing works properly in the body without sufficient quantities of water. Because I believe you need to be following a detoxification protocol then water for you is even more vital as the body can't adequately get rid of toxins without sufficient water in the system.

What is often described as endotoxicity (the re-absorption of waste) is down to the body not having enough water to get rid of the 30 billion cells of waste we're producing each day. So please take water seriously because without the removal of those toxins, your body will struggle to heal, and your mind will also be negatively intoxicated.

When looking for the right therapist or clinician, ask them if they can help you detox the primary systems of your body with particular attention to your colon, liver, kidneys, lymph and blood. If you struggle to get this kind of help, please let me know as I can advise you further on how to cleanse the body in a systematic way.

Also try not to give yourself such a hard time because positive change comes most easily through compassion, as it reduces the internal tensions - and remember that every negative emotion is seeking acceptance and peace so engage in activities that encourage this.

Question:
I've been doing a lot of reading and researching around cancer and I'm wondering if the reason I have the condition is because of how selfish and inward looking I've become? I'm also wondering if I've been hiding stuff that I've just never faced?

Answer:
It's interesting to hear your take on why this illness has come because disease is a multi-factorial event. It's almost always emotional, psychological, biological and historical.

Bearing in mind everything you've said in your email, added to our conversations, I believe that the combination of all your experiences is relevant here.

When a child moves home often in their formative years, they are less likely to establish healthy attachments. Just as they begin to develop good roots they are literally uprooted and the process of developing new connections and relationships begins all over again. Each time this happens the growth process is inhibited, and the child has to begin anew. There are feelings of loss, sadness, maybe even trauma which means the child is more likely to move into the protective pose. It should be said, this is not necessarily every child's experience, but I've certainly seen far more children impacted in this way than not.

This feels like an accurate assessment of your position, which is why you have struggled with so many of your relationships and you're clearly not very good when a relationship is coming to an end. I don't believe you have developed adequate mechanisms to help you deal with endings and change throws up more uncertainty than joy for you.

What you've described as selfishness and a preoccupation with your own needs I feel is a simplistic and unfair description of your position. As I've intimated, I believe you developed a protective coating from your more than a dozen moves in the first sixteen years of your life. That protective coating has encouraged you towards self-preservation.

Because you've not known what the next moment will bring, you've learned to protect yourself, which can look like selfishness, but I don't believe it is in this instance. I think if you'd not learned self-preservation, you wouldn't have made it as far as you have. This has also probably led you to applying a veneer on some if not most of your experiences in an attempt to make them feel less painful.

This is quite a common position, where the unconscious mind, which seeks to protect us as best it can, can keep us away from the most intense emotions associated with our more painful experiences. It can do this by saving us from seeing the worst of what's going on and we in turn find alternative and preferable interpretations for what we are witnessing and/or experiencing.

This may have led you to develop a denial of sorts and now as you look back the veneer is blistering, and the true nature of those past scenes are being more accurately calculated. This often leads to a flooding in of emotions. For some this can even feel like a tsunami where all they had previously thought is now laid to waste as a different story begins to unfold.

I think your calculation about the emotional impact of past events is one to be taken seriously but it's important to not let these realisations define you. Please try working with the conscious breathing exercises we discussed, the forgiveness work and the lovingly letting go mantra as these will bring much needed relief.

With regards to the physiological side, there is much written about emotional causation in relation to disease, but as I've already indicated I think the picture is more complicated and I don't want to draw a simple correlation between your personality and the disease because although I know this is indeed relevant, what you've shared with me makes this only part of the picture.

What I will say is where we have a habit of holding onto our stuff - pain, anger, sadness and hurt – we do inadvertently make a psychological contribution to the story of disease. As you know, I believe dis-ease in the mind will create disease in the body and so your cancer has probably emerged as a result in part of your internal dissatisfactions.

The revolution that is currently taking place around epigenetics and psycho-neuroimmunology is clearly showing us that our beliefs, thoughts, feelings, attitudes, perspective and outlook are all critical in switching on or indeed off our genetic predispositions. This means we can be the architects of our own healing and recovery or contributors to our own demise.

Diet and very importantly hydration are key players in this story too, because they can also switch genes on and off. For example, many physical illnesses are triggered exclusively by dehydration because without adequate hydration waste products are not decanted out of the body, which leads to a re-absorption of waste (endotoxicity) – so instead of it ending up in the bowl, it ends up back in the blood.

This then means even if we're eating well, nutrients are not being fully absorbed and if we're not eating well that adds to the toxic picture.

Added to this picture is chewing, which also has a lot to answer for. Most of us do not chew what we eat thoroughly. We are meant to eat our liquids and drink our food. In other words what we eat should be liquid by the time we swallow it. Only then are the enzymes able to fully extract all the nutrients. Food that isn't properly digested ends up putrefying in the gut causing a host of bowel disorders. An important factor in all this is ensuring we don't drink whilst eating because that too can dilute and wash away enzymes before they have completed their tasks, which again means the food is not properly broken down and fully absorbed. As a result, other health issues, including a range of mental health disorders, can ensue.

If you take a look at the Reach website, you will discover there's quite a bit about the gut microbiome and its relationship to the brain. These two ecosystems are connected via the vagus nerve, which is essentially a dual carriageway transporting masses of data between the two. What is now clear is that when the gut microbiome is out of balance due to poor diet, pollution, infection, stress etc. then an inflammatory response is often triggered, which can lead to depression and other mental health problems.

Hopefully, this overview provides you with the answer to your question and will help you to form the best plan for yourself.

Question:
I feel at times overwhelmed by my physical restrictions and pain. I feel I'm doing all I can physically. How can I use my mind to better help me?

Answer:
I'm sorry to hear about the wheelchair incident. It does seem like you have to battle on so many fronts. I know how tenacious and strong you can be, but of course there are moments when it can all feel too much. On those days, think of yourself as the calm, focused Samurai because she is peaceful in nature but becomes powerful when required to meet the challenges of life's ebbs and flows.

Remembering that victory is sometimes knowing how to embrace defeat can also be helpful at these times.

I think you are incredible how you keep rising to the many demands on your body and soul - I do understand though how you must feel weary at times. I'm pleased you've got something extra from the Strength vs Force meditation. I hope this will sustain you at times of doubt, weakness and fear.

Pain is such a difficult thing to help another relieve because it comes in so many different forms and it is a subjective phenomenon. What might be bearable to one is completely unbearable to another. For some, meditation, mindfulness or chanting a mantra can help, for others, visualisations are an invaluable tool. Breath work can also bring great relief. Experience has taught me that one needs to experiment with different things to find what works best for them.

That said, I would like to make a suggestion based on my prior knowledge of you and what I have found has worked for many individuals at this point in their challenge.

I know it's hard to maintain the faith when you feel overwhelmed by events, but at these moments try immersing yourself in the meditation The Magic Waterfall - but instead of water, make it light. Imagine the light cascading down your body, coating you on the inside as well as the outside. Think of it like the Beyond Limitations meditation you enjoy so much, see the light changing colour according to what you feel you need. Imagine the light is calming, cleansing and purifying and as it makes its way through you it's also strengthening you at your core, providing you with emotional, psychological and physical resilience. Engage in this activity as often as you can.

Please try this in those moments when you feel most challenged, even defeated... I'm sure it will bring some relief. Focus your attention on the left shoulder, the left eye, the right leg and the vertigo. Invite resolution and healing.

Something else you might want to try is the Dearest Past exercise. This is essentially a visualisation taking you down the corridors of your past with a view to asking for forgiveness for all your past actions. It's where you offer up an unconditional apology to all those individuals you have hurt or harmed in any way.

When you undertake this task, make a request for mercy and forgiveness from all those whose hearts you know you have in some way been guilty of hurting. These may be people you know as well as those you may no longer be in touch with or even remember, nevertheless you have negatively impacted on their lives and probably even altered the course of their destiny. Seeking their forgiveness offers resolution and healing.

When you engage in this visualisation you're not in any way seeking to justify your actions. To the contrary you're taking complete responsibility for your 'known' acts of unkindness and even your 'unknown' acts of unkindness. Invite all those you have hurt to attend. Ask sincerely for their understanding and forgiveness. The more you can do this with sincerity, the more powerful it is.

This is an exercise you may have to perform many times to experience that feeling of release and relief. It's an exercise I have undertaken over the years and it has brought great healing and with that hope and inspiration.

Question:
Could you take a look at my diet sheet because although I think I'm doing many of the right things I often feel tired and exhausted? I also have sent you a list of my daily activities to help provide a better picture.

Answer:
Something that is highly relevant in your case and worth underlining as I suspect it has a bearing on your current position, is from your diet and activity sheet you are actually training too hard, given all the other demands and stresses you are having to deal with.

From what I can see you train every evening and a lot of it seems to be at quite a high intensity. This will have a marked impact on your physiology and psychology. In an ideal world you would train one day and rest the next unless of course you are a professional athlete and even then, if periods of rest are not built into your exercise regime, you can do more harm than good, not necessarily in the short term but certainly in the medium to long term.

This is because the body when we exercise too hard, is producing too many acidic compounds, which puts a lot of pressure on the lymphatic system, liver and other excretory organs. At twenty-eight you'll get away with a lot of the negative consequences of this, because the body is sufficiently youthful to manage these extremes. But as you get older the consequences of acidity will make themselves felt.

I would recommend reducing your exercise to no more than four times a week. I think any more is too much given the rest of your schedule... and looking at your diet it's clear you're not getting enough of all the necessary nutrients to sustain that level of activity anyway. This will in turn lead to a different kind of stress in the form of fatigue (which I know you've been experiencing), which is the doorway to so many physical and mental health problems.

Below is an overview of my thoughts pertaining to your diet sheet. If you need or want to come back to me on anything, please feel free to do so.

I'm aware that you're taking a number of supplements but as you didn't list them, I couldn't sufficiently factor them in, but even with the supplements, the following feedback still stands because supplements still assume that all the primary nutrients are being imbibed through the diet.

Dietary Overview:

Overall. there is lots of good food in your diet. However, the following are points of concern.

1. Beware of sparkling water - the carbonate (CO3) in it attaches to minerals and carries them out of the system, creating deficiency (you stated that you sometimes drink 2-3 pints at a time which is a lot.) Given the importance of minerals to mental health there is no doubt this will have a bearing on your moods. This is a good illustration of how mood can be significantly impacted by nutrition.

   Your point about cravings is another example of the interconnectedness of everything. A lot of cravings for sweet things are to do with inadequate amounts of trace minerals, particularly vanadium and chromium. This may not be the sole reason you crave sweet things, but I'm quietly confident it will be a factor.

2. Be careful about having too much caffeine. Although you don't drink excessive amounts, espresso is strong stuff and two cups per day is enough to be destabilising to your energy levels. Some individuals have a greater hypersensitivity even with small amounts of coffee, which can lead to a 'crash' mentally or physically at some point during the day.

3. You need more cruciferous vegetables, especially in your smoothies and/or juices. I couldn't see much evidence of this food group. Although there are quite a lot of vegetables featured in your diet, cruciferous vegetables have the particular property of detoxifying as well as containing copious amounts of nutrients, so we need to consume plenty from this group each day (including: broccoli, spinach, cauliflower, kale, cabbage, sprouts) – unless of course you have some digestive issue that would preclude this food group.

4. You need more pulses – chickpeas, red kidney beans, aduki beans, black eyed beans, butterbeans etc. They are full of nutrients and a very good source of protein and as a food group are second only to green vegetables.

   If you have difficulty with digesting beans and pulses, this may be because of a lack of digestive enzymes as the bean/pulse family can for some be a challenge to digest. But before we conclude there may be a deficiency, the first question is, do you chew them thoroughly enough?

   Based on my experience, most people do not, and that's the primary reason for the digestive issues – the beans have not been masticated sufficiently and so adequate enzymes are not produced to break them down, which means they are sitting rotting in the gut long after they are useful. It's especially important when having beans not to drink liquid at the same time, as that might also flush away the enzymes before they have finished their task. That said, there are those who do have intolerances to this food group, and this may need to be checked but let's see how you get on with my suggestions first.

5. Shakes and juices should be around 80:20 vegetables to fruit. The ones you noted on your diet sheet are fruit dominant and will give you a spike in energy, but that is also likely to lead to a dip in mood because the sugar (fructose) content does not sustain us sufficiently when compared to the sugars in vegetables.

6. Beware of too much processed sugar – in puddings, chocolate etc. Although you don't have excessive amounts of this, there does appear to be quite a steady flow, which when coupled with the sparkling water, shakes and juices that are fruit heavy, added to the caffeine intake, it all adds up to something that is potentially disruptive to your energy and mood.

Talking of disruptions to your energy and mood, another reason for craving sweet things is when blood sugar level is low (which also affects our mood). Under these circumstances we are much more likely to crave sweet things. This is particularly true when we over-exercise, because we are spending more energy than our bodies can afford and so again there is a dip in the physiology, which in turn impacts on the psychology. As you can see there's not one thing going on here, there are many.

Hope this helps you to plot a better course. Please let me know how you get on, so we can make any necessary revisions.

Question:
I've been taking a look at your website and enjoying a variety of resources that you have. I'm wondering if you can help me as I have started a new job and am suffering with anxiety.

Answer:
Thank you for sharing your concerns about the anxiety you're experiencing and how it's affecting your life.

Anxiety is such a huge topic, and the antidotes are many and varied, subject to the primary cause.

I'm sorry to hear that your professional life has been so difficult since you graduated. I can understand why after losing the first two jobs you would be so anxious about losing this current position too. As you commented, the first two roles you had were in a highly pressured and stressful environment, as sales jobs often are. It may be the case that the sales environment is not ideal for you and the role you are now in may simply suit you better.

Based on what you've told me, I believe the resources below will help you to focus your attention on feeling okay, capable and competent rather than focusing on the fear of failing.

The four meditation videos below can be found on our YouTube channel and are very useful ways of training your mind to become calm and positive. If you watch/listen to these regularly, over time this practice will allow you to become the best version of yourself in your current job and gradually your anxiety will subside.

Being the Best You Can Be, Conscious Breathing, My Inner Sanctuary and The Focused Mind.

There is also an excellent article on anxiety well worth reading. It's called, Anxiety – addressing the causes not just the symptoms, which you can find on our website (www.thereachapproach.co.uk) – on the Healing Habits page. It will provide you with a good overview of the subject and give you further ideas about how you can help yourself.

It's very important to try to develop patience with yourself during this process because positive change is best facilitated by kindness and compassion.

In addition, something that I find helps about three quarters of the individuals I've worked with who are suffering with anxiety is a herbal remedy called Passiflora Complex, which comes from the passionflower. It is an excellent mood modulator and can help with calming the mind. It's not a panacea, but it is very effective.

It also contains an ingredient called avena sativa (derived from oats) that soothes and calms the central nervous system. The brand that I have found to be the best (I have no affiliation to this organisation) is A. Vogel (also known as Bioforce).

The Passiflora Complex comes in a tincture and I would recommend you follow the instructions. Most people need twenty drops in a little water either before or after breakfast and the same amount before going to bed. What I like about this product is that it has no known contraindications, and you can take it for as long as you need it. Please give it four to six weeks before assessing its efficacy. Most naturopathic remedies take time to build up in the system before reaching optimum potency.

It is also important to know that anxiety is exacerbated by dehydration - and stress makes dehydration worse. This is a vicious cycle that one needs to be aware of. If you don't already drink significant amounts of water, please try to imbibe at least two litres per day. It is best that this is not tap water, so invest in some form of filtration system.

If you find my suggestions are not sufficient for your current plight, it may be the case that your anxiety is being sustained by some underlying causes and you may want to consider talking to someone about this at some point – maybe a friend or someone you trust. If you need a professional, then please don't hesitate to get back to me and I will try and identify the best help for your needs.

Wishing you all you need on the road ahead.

Question:
I'm in a new relationship and the person I'm with is struggling with leftover feelings from her last relationship. I'm not sure whether I should continue investing in this as I feel invisible, and my feelings are constantly overlooked. Can you help?

Answer:
Relationships are bound together by so many strands, only you can decide whether the personal chemistry is right here or not. You need to work out if the investment you're currently making is worth it.

The ambivalence your current partner is experiencing suggests to me that she has not fully resolved whatever issues she has brought with her into this relationship. Based on what you've said about her last relationship and how she was jilted without a proper explanation, it's hardly surprising that she's blowing hot and cold. I'm sure she's feeling insecure.

When someone has been discarded in this way, they are often left feeling 'what is wrong with me?' They internalise the other person's decision and this introjection as it's called means they feed their own doubts and insecurities based on that person's actions. This is tragic because the other person's actions tell us more about the other person than they do about the one being left behind.

Try to think about it in this way... Imagine someone set adrift, having left one shore trying to make their way to the other shore. Their ship has capsized and now they are caught between two positions. She doesn't know whether to turn back or continue going towards the other shore. The question is, where is she most likely to find safety? This is almost certainly how she is feeling.

You've now come along in your boat and offered to take her to her preferred destination. She's come aboard but she's not sure. Does she trust you to take her to the shore? Because she doesn't fully trust herself, she doesn't know whether to trust you - as the voice of her past experience is whispering doubts in her ear.

Can you see that she is now in uncharted waters with you? On the one hand she questions whether you are the lifeguard who will save the day and get her to the shore. Whilst another part of her is wondering will you create an additional current, which will make it more difficult for her to get to land.

Your options are clear... if you're ready to invest in this relationship, then you need to be understanding of her plight and give her time to process her feelings of uncertainty as they are quite natural. If you are not willing to do this and take the risk that comes with being patient, then please do not hurt her heart by adding further turbulence. In which case, you should kindly walk away.

Work out your own position and act with caution, conscience and integrity.

Question:
Although I know I'm seeing you on Friday, I'm struggling. I've relapsed again and lost my bearings. Could really do with your guidance.

Answer:
You have done so wonderfully well in recent years to climb up to the position you now find yourself in. However, the journey of progress is not without its pitfalls. Remember the paradox of progress - it is inevitable that you will have lapses in motivation, mood and effort (everybody does).

The trick is when those moments do come, feel them, acknowledge them and then lovingly let them go. I know this practice is not unfamiliar to you, but at moments like this it requires you to go beyond the theory.

To be honest, the practice needs to be obsessive. Nothing ever belongs to us until we immerse ourselves in it. It's that immersion that brings realisation. Realisation is the point at which an action has become part of your nature. It's easy for us to say we understand but real understanding comes from obsessively focusing on what it is we need to do to engineer the change that we seek.

This is where 'the paradox of progress' meets the 'journey of enough'. Please go and re-read both, just to remind yourself of their messages. Really immerse yourself in the words, sit inside these powerful concepts so you can better understand their depth and meaning. It's easy to read the articles and handouts and think you've got it, but without reflecting and re-reading, reflecting and re-reading, the words remain on the page rather than finding their way to your heart.

Given that you're feeling a little under the weather and viruses have a powerful effect on mood, I would encourage you, rather than using the B12 patches once a week to increase that for now to twice a week and also increase your vitamin C intake by 50%.

Whenever we are feeling physically low or challenged, we are more vulnerable to these dips in mood and disturbances in our consciousness. Something else that will help at these times is the attitudinal shift into gratitude. You know the power of counting your blessings, great and small and it's when your knees feel like they're going to buckle, and the ground feels like it's going to give way beneath you that the power of thank you can really help. It's at these times when we doubt ourselves that we must go back to basics.

Remember you have the gift of being the author of your own destiny. Don't take it lightly or for granted. What turns up in our lives always provides us with the opportunity of becoming stronger. Seize that opportunity today.

Question:
My wife is battling cancer and she's been knocked around by the chemotherapy and is feeling scared. I am too. A friend of mine said you might be able to help by giving us some advice about the things we could be doing for ourselves, so we don't feel quite so helpless.

Answer:
Let me begin by saying I'm sad to hear of your news.

I understand that the chemotherapy has been knocking your wife around, which I have to say is pretty common. Because I don't have enough information about her background and the factors that may well have led her to this position, it is difficult to be precise in my recommendations, as I don't like advising blindly.

That said, I'm able to offer some generic advice, which I believe will be helpful.

1. When the body finds itself in the cancer state, it is generally because of toxic overload, which is brought about either through too much stress or a lack of detoxification - or both – over a period of time. The bottom line is that the body has to dump thirty billion cells of waste each day and if our lymphatic system and other waste management organs are not working properly, instead of this waste being dumped in its entirety, we can end up reabsorbing a percentage of it each day. What this means is that your wife's system in some way is not working optimally, which is why it's reached this point of overload. Therefore, what is needed is to lighten the load, both in terms of any stress to the mind as well as ensuring the body is not taxed further.

   The things that will help in this process are eating a more liquid based diet, which includes smoothies (which need to be vegetable based - at least 75% vegetable 25% fruit), soups of all kinds, but heavily vegetable based and stews with the same constituents.

   Eating colourful food is vitally important and so eating as much salad as she can, would be beneficial. The thing to bear in mind with salads though is that they do require thorough chewing. Chewing really matters in these circumstances because her body will be very challenged at this point and whatever she consumes should be easy to digest as the body uses a lot of energy in the digestion process – and this is all about conserving energy, so the body is in the best position to repair itself.

   If she is disinclined to eat salads, try introducing as much colour into the soups, stews and smoothies as possible. A rainbow diet will really help ensure she's getting a diversity of nutrients.

2. Nothing in our bodies works properly without water. Every transaction depends on it and given what I have said about the thirty billion cells of waste that our bodies need to discharge each day, there is simply no chance of that being done sufficiently without water.

   Dehydration is experienced as stress by the body, primarily because the body then has to make tough choices about where the water is to be used when there is not enough in the system. It's at this point that the organs of detoxification – skin, kidneys, liver, colon, lungs and the lymphatic system –

struggle to remove the biological debris that threatens our health. Therefore, it would be very helpful for your wife to drink as much water as she can manage each day, to help the body flush out the poison, which includes the consequences of the chemotherapy.

3. With regards to the mind, she needs to consider some regular introspective practice, whether that be mindfulness, meditation, prayer, deep relaxation or some other form of contemplation. As I said at the beginning, both stress in the mind and biological stress (where the body is not detoxifying properly) are contributors to the cancer profile. Many would argue that it's the mental side that makes the biggest contribution.

   My experience would support this hypothesis especially where individuals have pushed down their thoughts and feelings over a sustained period and so have not resolved many of their emotional and psychological issues from the past. Obviously, I don't know whether this applies to your wife or not. Nonetheless, introspective practices can help re-train the mind and dump unwanted baggage from the past.

Below are some meditations I have produced and am happy to recommend. Some of them are around eight to ten minutes whilst others are twenty to thirty-five minutes. If your wife were to choose this route, then she may want to start with the shorter ones to build up her practice. If this does not appeal, then as I said, she may want to consider mindfulness, which is easily accessible from numerous sources - and/or prayer (if that fits with her faith).

Either way, I believe she needs to do some work which is around letting stuff go – any guilt, shame, anger or regrets that may exist and have not been adequately faced. These are usually the main protagonists. Subject to the nature of her issues she may need more help to address what may be lurking beneath the surface.

Here are my meditation suggestions. These are all accessible via the Reach YouTube channel which you can access through our website.

Shorter meditations:

i) Conscious Breathing

ii) The Focused Mind

iii) Dearest Past

iv) Dearest Fear

v) Dearest Body

vi) My Inner Sanctuary

Longer meditations:

i) Positive Affirmations part 2

ii) The Magic Waterfall

iii) Beyond Limitations

iv) Heal Thyself

v) Lovingly Let Go

vi) FALL (Feel it, Acknowledge it and Lovingly Let Go)

It's worth pointing out that I'm not suggesting your wife watches all of these, although there would be no down side to that should she choose to... but I've sent such a comprehensive list to offer choice because there may be some that she's more drawn to than others, plus having a variety will help to wash and clean the mind in different ways.

The primary goals here are to help her to detoxify, to make her mind a fortress of peace and do what she can to remove any negative thoughts and feelings that produce unhelpful neurochemicals.

There are three books you may wish to consider that offer some helpful insights. A significant number of people I have worked with who are undergoing the challenge of cancer have found them useful.

These are: Radical Remission by Kelly Turner Ph.D., The Mind Can Heal the Body by Dr. David Hamilton and Eat to Live by Dr. Joel Fuhrman.

Everything I've suggested here can definitely help and support you too. However, if you have any specific needs, please do get back to me. I would be happy to help.

I will leave it there because there is already enough to take in here, plus I wouldn't want to offer any more information without more background detail.

I will be sending love and good energy to you both.

Question:
My son who is 17 years of age has been suffering with migraines for a while now. They do seem particularly triggered by intense physical activity and he recently fainted after a football match. I think I'm getting most things right in terms of his diet but I'm not sure if there's something I might be missing. Can you help?

Answer:
Headaches, cluster headaches and migraines can be caused by so many factors – diet, climatic changes, insufficient sleep, dehydration just to name a few.

When I'm working with these kinds of issues I like to have as much information as I can about the person's background and lifestyle. Given what you've shared in your email about your son, I think the following factors are relevant.

I definitely think hydration is an issue here because your son isn't even hitting the two- litre mark, which is the minimum recommended daily amount. Given this most recent episode took place immediately after a sporting activity, and he was probably already in a semi dehydrated state, then it's not a surprise that the body was tipped over the edge in this way.

Added to this, you said that there's a history of migraines in your family, which means he almost certainly has a genetic predisposition towards this condition. Going forward he needs to take water much more seriously. I should say genetic predisposition does not mean we will necessarily suffer with something that runs in our families, but it does mean we are more prone to those conditions, especially if we don't take the right precautions.

The other thing that's nearly always implicated in migraines are food sensitivities and intolerances. If this pattern continues you may want to go down the road of a food intolerance test. I have found The York Test to be amongst the best because their tests offer the most comprehensive analysis of food intolerances and based on my experience, I suspect that this is a factor in some way. It's certainly worth checking out if improved hydration on its own does not address the problem.

It's also worth pointing out that a lack of chewing, which is rarely cited in these cases, can also be a significant factor with regards to migraines. It is often said you are what you eat, but this is actually not precise enough. You are what you absorb from what you eat, and absorption begins in the mouth. So, it's very important to make sure that he is chewing his food. There is now a plethora of research around the consequences of gut health on mental health. I have found (although less reported on) that when you can clean up digestive issues many of which are down to poor mastication, that headaches and migraines markedly improve.

If he's a 'cut and swallow' person, he will not be properly digesting his food and therefore not getting all the nutrition from it. Poorly digested food creates toxic waste in the body, which is then reabsorbed via the blood back into the cells, creating a host of biological issues. This could well explain the vomiting that you described.

One final thing, which you mentioned and should also be taken very seriously, is the length of time he goes between meals. Those who are prone to migraines are better suited to grazing and not having long periods of time between their meals.

There are of course other factors such as worry and stress, anxiety, blood sugar issues which we have previously talked about, but I think what I've outlined here is the best starting point in this instance.

If you have any more questions or concerns, please let me know.

Question:
I'm having one to one therapy, couple counselling and am in a support group – all because I'm trying desperately to get well, save my marriage and support my family. I believe I'm doing everything I can to improve my mental and physical health and yet I can see very little evidence that I'm getting better, which is so disheartening. Can you suggest anything?

Answer:
You certainly do appear to be trying to address the concerns of your life on several fronts and for that you should be commended. It takes great courage to look our demons in the eyes.

That said, doing many things simultaneously does not always bring the best results. Often it can even bring about more confusion. I've discovered that less is nearly always more. Targeting one's efforts is more effective than trying to address things on several fronts. This can at times even camouflage the problem.

From what you've told me about your relationship there are many problems that I think need to be resolved. You seem to have very little physical energy and yet in an attempt to keep your relationship intact and meet your family's needs you are engaging in numerous activities, which leave you exhausted.

You cannot on the one hand be plying your body with all the necessary nutrients to restore your health and then almost simultaneously behave as if you are Wonder Woman doing all the cooking, cleaning, looking after elderly relatives and engaging in frequent sexual activity when you say you can barely keep your eyes open.

It seems to me that you need to be sitting down and having a heartfelt conversation with your husband. If he really loves you in the way you've suggested, then hopefully he will want to find better strategies for supporting you. Keeping quiet and saying nothing is not a strategy, it's denial.

It's obviously your choice how you manage your marriage, but if these things are not being talked about in your couple therapy, then I do think you're wasting your energy, money and time. Trying to fix things elsewhere whilst ignoring the elephant in the room doesn't work.

From what you've told me, your personal therapy is helping you unveil the issues, but you seem to lack courage when it comes to talking about it with your husband and family. Maybe in your support group, you could share your dilemma and concerns.

Groups can be good places to gird your loins and then summon up the courage to express yourself where that most needs to happen. If the group is willing you could try acting out the scenarios through role-play. Rehearsing how you might face and manage situations can be very helpful - even if it's only taking place in your mind, it can be very strengthening. If doing it within the group doesn't appeal to you then you could act it out in your one-to-one therapy. Either of these options would be better than your current approach.

I think until this primary issue is faced you are likely to keep going around the same loops.

Hope this helps.

Wishing you all that you need on the road ahead.

Question:
I live in Italy and I've been faithfully following The Reach Approach for some time. I love the simplicity and clarity of it all and I have made good progress. I've found my way back to work, my marriage is on the mend and generally I feel better about myself.

Taking the journey on my own has at times been difficult, and I now feel stuck. Could you give me some advice please?

Answer:
First of all, I want to highly commend your efforts. Taking the journey with someone is challenging enough. Doing it largely by yourself deserves special praise.

There are now many thousands of people around the world, who like you are trying to do the work themselves and where we can, we always offer support.

Below are some questions that I think are helpful to ask yourself when you feel stuck. Let me begin by saying that they won't all apply to you, but where they do you will find they are useful probes that will get you to look more closely at your life and they can highlight something that is staring you in the face that hitherto you have missed.

1. Is the balance of your life right? Use The Story of Health to help you assess this.

2. Are your primary relationships positive and healthy? Are you able to speak your truth in those relationships and do you feel valued and heard?

3. Do you listen to your body and act on its cues?

4. Have you really left the past where it belongs - behind you?

5. Do you understand that what's happening emotionally is mirrored in the body and vice versa?

   This is a particularly deep point because mood swings can be both psychological and biological in nature. What this means is inadequate nutrition can impact on blood sugar levels and on mood. Too much stress, worry and anxiety can bring the mind to its knees... and the body too.

6. Have you let go of victimhood or do you still find yourself caught up in cycles of 'poor me'?

7. Are you taking responsibility for your life? Do you really understand that personal responsibility holds the key to your transformation?

8. Are you paying enough attention to your self-talk? – because the endless chatter of the mind can keep you in a place of blame - condemning others and yourself.

9. Compassion is the quickest way to bring about change in yourself. Are you kind enough and sufficiently caring to yourself?

10. Is your life filled with sufficient meaning and purpose?

11. Order creates peace. Chaos creates peacelessness and confusion. Is your environment in alignment with your aims and objectives?

12. Do you have a sanctuary, a place where you can let go and just be?

The answers to these questions I have found help to highlight where the problem areas exist. And once you've identified them, you can decide what you want to do about those discrepancies, any omissions and shortcomings.

Once you've done your own soul searching, please do get back to me with any further questions or queries. I will be happy to help.

Question:
I find it difficult to control my outbursts of anger and no sooner are they over than I have terrible feelings of regret and self-loathing. No wonder all my relationships eventually fall apart. What can I do?

Answer:
The thing with anger is that it is more often than not masking pain and sadness. This does not legitimise your behaviour, but it can be helpful in identifying the real problem.

Anger has two common manifestations. There's hot anger, which can't be hidden because of its explosive nature and it tends to be out there in people's faces. The other common expression of anger is cold anger. This is less obvious but is no less destructive. It tends to express its hurt and pain by withdrawal of affection, silence and through negative emissions - vibrations that change the atmosphere in the room.

Generally, men are considered to exhibit hot anger and women cold anger and due to the way that social engineering has influenced how we raise boys and girls, this is largely true. The expression of our emotions has been shaped by our family history, the absence of the three 'A's and the cultural influences we've been exposed to.

That said, your description of your pattern suggests to me that when you don't feel valued and heard you lash out. The example you gave of your wife calling you a shit and mocking you for being less than a man speaks to those damaged bits in you that are still not healed. You did your best to tolerate this attack but when you reached your threshold you reacted in kind.

Although I understand why you felt so hurt, this is not a mature or helpful way to deal with such issues. I know it's easier said than done but at those points you need to reach across the divide and find a way to communicate your feelings with less hostility. If you feel unable to do this, it is better to walk away – rather than stay there until you reach boiling point and then lose your composure.

It seems from what you've said that these toxic episodes with your wife are never revisited until the next slanging match, which is another mistake. It is far better, at the earliest opportunity, once the dust has settled, to try and have a peace summit with your wife. Papering over the cracks - as you both appear to do - simply doesn't work.

By never resolving anything, when the next challenge turns up, you'll find that the unresolved elements of the last incident will bring their representatives to the event in order to try and win the argument.

You have both created and continue to contribute to a pattern, which guarantees more of the same. Rather than waiting for the next episode, why not find ways of reconciling your differences. Please take a look at The Four Stages of Couple

Therapy on the Reach website. This document offers a useful roadmap for how you can navigate your way through the tensions and problems you are both facing.

You may also need to consider joining an anger management group or working with a therapist on your unresolved hurts and pains. Maybe if your wife is willing it's something you could work on together. Whatever you decide, do not retreat into anger. It causes harm to your mind, and it poisons your body and can irreparably damage your relationships.

If you really listen to what your anger is trying to say, rather than leaving it to spill over, you will find that there are some important messages that will lead to your emancipation.

Remember, peace is only ever one thought away.

Question:
Why does my life just keep going around in the same loops? Every time I think I've resolved something I realise I haven't because I'm right back where I started... help?

Answer:
We live in a time of evidence-based practice. The science says that until we have the evidence, we can't really trust our experience because it's subjective. But I believe passionately in practice-based evidence. Practice-based evidence gives merit to the subjective experience because it knows it offers a rich source of data and insight, which can better help us to make sense of our reality.

This doesn't mean I discard the scientific evidence that supports good practice because I don't, I simply don't draw exclusively from that arena. This is because my clinical experience has taught me so much more about the human story and I have come to trust its guidance above all else.

My answer to your question comes from what I have repeatedly experienced to be true when working with individuals from all walks of life.

When we keep finding ourselves going around the same loop, having the same experience and nothing seems to really change, there is always something we still need to learn. There is something that has been missed and until you identify what that is and address it, the situation is unlikely to resolve itself.

To get to the bottom of this requires an honest audit. You have to try and stand outside of the scenario and look in, as best you can, objectively. It's important not to apply negative judgment as this will lead to your defence mechanisms emerging and at that point, nothing will be learned. When our defences kick in it means we have gone into a protective pose and as a result the opportunity for learning and growth is restricted. You need kind and honest eyes to evaluate what's going on.

Be truthful with yourself about what you're missing. What are you doing that's repeatedly contributing to the situation? Ask yourself if you are in denial. Are you justifying, pretending or trying to be something you're not? Are you speaking the truth, first and foremost to yourself, but also to those who are entangled in this behaviour and/or pattern with you?

Try not to be afraid of the answers because without answering these questions truthfully, you're unlikely to break free from this negative cycle.

It doesn't matter what the pattern is. If it keeps turning up in pretty much the same form, then it is trying to get you to see what has not yet been seen or understood. You can't graduate to the next place in your life until this lesson has been identified and learned.

Remember, you need kind, honest eyes to see what you're missing.

Question:
I've been reading The Four Aspects of the Mind and the Pyramid of Shame and I am fascinated by the concepts of drivers and minor drivers, the relationship between the unconscious mind and the conscious mind. And there are four main forces I believe that are driving my life. These are: fear, shame, lack of trust and lack of self-love. Given that I am now 60, isn't it too late for me to break free of their influence?

Answer:
Understanding how our drivers keep our beliefs, patterns and habits going is in my view one of the most powerful realisations we can have. It gives us the opportunity to move out of mental slavery into spiritual liberation.

Many of us believe we are driving our lives when in fact we are being driven. We are often being driven by things we no longer believe (if indeed we ever believed them). Patterns we've inherited continue to act out. Their power is maintained by never being adequately interrogated or challenged and so they occupy territory in our internal world, behaving as dictators, commanding us to behave in outdated ways, usually driven by fear, shame, regret and guilt. To establish healthy control and self-mastery we need to understand our slave masters' power. Otherwise plotting our escape will be little more than a pipe dream.

The list of your unconscious patterns and drivers is very interesting. Fear and shame are opposite sides of the same coin. The one who carries shame is always living in the fear of being found out - the fear of not being good enough. This fear generates a low-grade all-pervading anxiety, which of course is disabling.

The one who lacks self-love either trusts the wrong people or invests in the wrong things, or has no trust at all, therefore living in a place of perpetual uncertainty. A lack of self-love and trust are intimately bound together.

Given this mix and the relationship that these patterns have to one another, it's little surprise that they are still sloshing around in the depths of your being, simply sustaining each other.

However, the personal work that you are undertaking with me will convert these old energies into new forces, but it does take time, kindness and patience. Remember, change is a process, not an event. The fact that you are 60 is not a barrier to sustainable change. The only barriers to that are complacency, ignorance and arrogance – the three common faces of the ego. If you keep your mind and heart open, positive change is assured.

The experiential work we are doing, all of which is using trance as a vehicle for reaching the unconscious realms, will give you access to the hidden powers that lie dormant within. Trance, used correctly, leads to 'trance-formation' and positive change.

Your fear and shame will become courage and self-belief, leading to a more fearless way of living. Your lack of trust and lack of self-love will become the very foundations on which your inner confidence and certainty in your own value will be built.

See you soon for the next chapter of this epic journey.

Question:
Having done so well over these recent months adhering to your dietary advice, I have had another flare-up of my psoriasis and I'm wondering what this means, as I've continued to follow your advice?

Answer:
First of all, I'm very sorry to hear that you've had a relapse, but I cannot pretend to be surprised. The journey of healing and recovery is a paradox and there are almost always relapses along the way. This is because when you create any change in the body there is a 'die off' process.

This means that the toxic cells that have occupied space in your blood, tissues and muscles, as you improve, have to be broken down and got rid of, and expelled by the cells, lungs, kidneys, liver, skin and colon.

This process is known as the Herxheimer's Effect, better known as a healing crisis. At this point of die off, it's not uncommon for people to have headaches, flu like symptoms, other aches and pains, sweating and nausea.

A healthy body produces about 30 billion cells of waste each day. This is just the consequence of being alive. When the body has been challenged over a significant period of time like yours, you're probably producing anything up to 50% more waste. Coupled with that it's highly likely that the waste is not being properly expelled from the body, due to blockages. Remember, I did also point out that when you're making the kind of changes to your diet that I've asked you to make, this will also create some challenge to your system. Even when making positive adjustments, the body has to work hard to accommodate the changes. This recalibration can feel like you're not making progress, when you are.

All this means that your body is under great stress as those organs responsible for detoxification (which I listed above) are working up to capacity and at times beyond that. It's because of this that periodically these healing crises occur, which to the person going through it can feel as though they're getting worse. This is a relapse that is to be expected when making such changes. Please don't lose faith, it's nowhere near as bad as you may think.

Relapses can also occur because of change in circumstances or environment. I don't know if anything has changed recently, however, keep doing what you have been doing... this is very important because lasting change takes about nine to twelve months to achieve.

When working with any biological changes, you need to think in blocks of three months. The first three months are about creating the new habits and removing blockages and creating healthier pathways. The next three months are about consolidating those changes, re-educating the body in the process.

From six months to nine months most individuals find that the body is now entirely cooperative. The remedial detoxification phase is usually over by then and your new health paradigm has been installed. In truth by this point, most conditions have been arrested and unless the person reverts back to old patterns, they are unlikely to experience any further major relapses - but up to this point relapses can occur. Hopefully this makes things clearer for you and you can embrace this episode with understanding, knowing that it is only a phase in your journey of recovery.

When the twelve-month mark is reached, it is very difficult to go the other way. One would actively have to undo their efforts by recreating blocks and poisoning the body with the wrong food and dietary choices.

Having said all this, please remember, this is not a journey just of the body. The mind is an important factor in these things because stress produces too much adrenaline, adrenochrome, cortisol and other inflammatory chemicals, all of which change the pH in the body, creating a more acidic environment, which can cause all the symptoms you've described.

Therefore, you really do need to be - in addition to putting the right things in the body - feeding your mind with the right thoughts. Because when the body is moving in a positive direction the serotonin, dopamine and oxytocin that is produced along with other healing hormones help to maintain balance in the blood and other systems. As a consequence, flare-ups are less likely.

Please reflect on my response and I will expand and develop these concepts further when we next meet.

Keep the faith and the faith will keep you strong.

Question:
I'm really scared that my sister might be contemplating suicide and I really don't know how to approach this, if indeed I should?

Answer:
Suicidal ideation is such a difficult issue to address. The stark truth is that if someone is determined to take their own life, there is very little we can do. This doesn't mean we shouldn't try to do something, but the truth is we cannot be with someone every minute of every day.

That said, having worked with a lot of self-harm, which includes attempted suicides, I would say that the vast majority of these cases are actually a cry for help. The person isn't really wanting to end their life. They've simply reached a point where they don't know how else to express how they're feeling. This can be a way in.

If we can find a way to hear what they're really trying to say, then there is often a way back. Nearly all those my colleagues and I have worked with have found when you can find the hook (that thing that has brought them to this point) and listen to what the person is feeling, if you can help them to find a healthier way of expressing it, then you can talk them off that ledge.

Suicidal thoughts and feelings are actually not uncommon, and the research is showing an increase across all sectors of society. The reasons for this hike in the numbers are many, as individuals battle with their self-image, over-trading, meeting the expectations and demands of others, battling with their regrets, shame and guilt and all this taking place in an ever-shrinking world, where social media perpetually makes us feel like we're under constant scrutiny.

In this case you have to tread more carefully because having found your sister's diary and read these entries, if you are to intervene without being sensitive to her position, then what is likely to be perceived as your betrayal may damage your relationship beyond repair. If she feels she's been betrayed (especially as you've talked to other members of your family too) this could make the whole situation more precarious as you all now have information, she didn't want you to have. I at this point would encourage you all not to approach her... I think you could do more harm than good.

It's unfortunate we don't know the dates of these entries because if they are a while ago, then we could say she has moved on and is going in the right direction but if, as you suspect, they are more recent, then I am troubled by that and yet I would still say it's important not to overreact. Overreacting will not help her. Whatever you do has to be sensitive and measured.

It's important to reiterate that suicidal ideation rarely leads to suicide, it is often a phase - a time when the individual feels overwhelmed by the thoughts, feelings and images that occupy their mind.

These entries in her diary may represent the fantasy of how ending her life might look and what could follow - and are therefore an opportunity to process her feelings in a safe way. Therefore, they may not be a desire to end her life.

This is why you have to tread carefully because if writing in her journal provides her with a safe way of expressing these feelings and you confront her, then the very thing you're afraid may happen could be facilitated by your actions.

It could be argued that she feels free to have these thoughts because she has the safe harbour of her family, that place she can always come back to. So, fantasising about the ending of her life is more a form of emotional release never to be acted on. I've seen many such diary entries and heard many end-of-life declarations, and rarely do they end in the loss of life. They are either a cry for help or as I suspect in this case a way of safely processing her emotional turmoil.

This doesn't mean we shouldn't take this seriously because we should, but the situation is complicated by the fact that your sister doesn't want any help, otherwise she would have asked for it. The first step in helping her to get past what she's feeling is to continue to shower her with love and affection and to support her in the things that are important to her. By all means watch her and respond to any concerning behaviour, but please remember it's important you respond rather than react.

If at some point she does reach out, then seeing if she's willing to go and speak with someone who's appropriately qualified to help with these matters would be a good next step.

Of course, if there is anything else I can do, then don't hesitate to ask. I hope this helps in giving some clarity and maybe a little comfort.

Question:
Although my son is now in his thirties and I am approaching retirement I am ashamed to say that I am still very much entangled in his life in a way that I believe is spoiling our relationship and yet I don't know how to break free.

Answer:
Given the backstory I'm not surprised that you are so enmeshed in your son's life. You didn't only flee a violent marriage, but you have emigrated twice and all of this to save your son from the terrible uncertainty, fear and threat that shrouded your life.

It was right that you removed yourself and your son from these violent situations but in the process, you have become overly attached to him and he to you. This over-identification is classically referred to as enmeshment, which usually happens between a parent and a child and it's where their identities become so entangled that eventually they can think and feel as if they were one brain and one mind. It may at first be a good and positive thing but as the child grows older different tensions begin to impact on this dynamic.

When your son was small and you were doing all the things you were to save him, your own identity was distilled down into his needs and requirements. You considered yourself and what was important to you less and less. All your major decisions around where you lived, his schooling, extracurricular activities, put him first.

On his side, he has grown to expect this and at times demand it. This has increasingly felt normal to him and to you. The problem with this dynamic is the boundaries become blurred. He has unrealistic expectations of you, which you fulfil even when they go against your instincts and if you don't, he feels angry because you've not met his needs, and you feel guilty, and the vicious cycle continues.

Now he has a serious relationship, and they are talking about starting a new life, you feel excluded and are frightened about being left alone. So, although you want the best for your son, your over-identification with him for all these years is now highlighting what's missing in your own life and some part of you is expecting him to meet your primary needs. After all, look how much you've sacrificed for him.

Your feelings are hurt because at this point it's clear he doesn't see it that way – and why would he? You've inadvertently taught him to look to you to fulfil his needs and now someone else appears to be doing that you feel relegated, which is why you feel disappointed and hurt. Your years of sacrifice seem to have meant little.

The truth is that you've unintentionally created this problem, but the good news is you can fix it. It's in your hands to do so. You are going to need to be courageous because you now need a new life plan. You need to create a different destiny for yourself, one which is built primarily around your needs. You have not really cultivated your friendships or your interests. You've been successful in two things, your career and in rearing your son, and both are now on the brink of change. This is an opportunity that you need to meet head on.

As hard as it may be, encourage your son to move in this new direction, if it's right for him. Also, if it feels appropriate, sharing these insights about yours and his relationship could be helpful to him too, so he might better understand himself.

You will probably need help working out a new life plan because it's been so long since you put yourself first that you've probably lost contact with your own desires and what's really important to you.

You may be able to do this by yourself, but if not, I can help you with this or direct you to someone else who can.

Good luck!

Question:
What do you mean by aspiring for authenticity?

Answer:
Aspiring for authenticity is a term I first coined thirty years ago because it summarised my own efforts. I knew I was flawed, and I knew my preoccupation with my mistakes, shortcomings and weaknesses was perpetually undermining me, making everything more difficult.

I decided I could either endlessly torture myself (which I'd become very good at) or I could find acceptance and peace in the truth that I knew I was trying to be my best in each moment, even when I fell short. In accepting this I found a better way to live. As long as we are aspiring to be authentic - being the best we can be in any given moment - then peace and contentment will never be far away. Aspiring for authenticity, to me, is the highest destination.

The journey might be long and slow, but when there's no hurry, it's exactly as long as it needs to be. It's the hurried mind that tortures us because the mind that is truly present doesn't care about the time. It's too busy making the most of and enjoying the journey. There is no greater gift than the present. The present is a gift that needs to be perpetually unwrapped and there you will find your bliss.

Question:
Can you remind me of those eight points of success you shared with me? I feel my spiritual leg is the weakest on my Story of Health table and believe these points would particularly help me through this phase in which I'm questioning everything.

Answer:
Here is a summary of what we discussed. Apply the ones that feel most appropriate to you and your situation.

1. I came alone, and I will go alone - it's important not to be defined by the opinion of your tribe. Too many decisions are made based on how you will be seen by others and yet you came into this world by yourself and will exit it by yourself. So have the courage of your convictions.

2. The art of revealing and concealing - there's a right person, right time and right place to say something, so don't give away your heart and your secrets to those who've not earned your trust. The biggest mistake we can make is speaking about our hopes and dreams prematurely; silence is indeed golden.

3. The only destination is right action - those who worry too much about the outcome rather than doing the right thing lose their moral compass. Those who remain true to their code of ethics will claim the prize.

4. Speak slowly, softly and sweetly - those who are measured in their delivery do not become anger's puppet because to do anger's bidding is to already have failed. Anger steals both clarity and virtue. Remember, the truth is rarely heard when the presentation of our message is unkind.

5. Routine is power - success depends on practising doing the right things again and again. It is not enough to have good intention... we also have to build a portfolio of healthy obsessions. Then the destination takes care of itself. Routine is a magnet for success.

6. The secret to health is the removal of waste - if we do not seek out and remove the waste in our minds, bodies, hearts and lives, we will continue to be undermined. Remember, waste weakens us.

7. Single pointed awareness – first of all we have to be clear about where we're going, then obsessively focus on what needs to be done. This is a state of being where you think about it, dream about it, live and breathe it. This level of focus has to be balanced with doing the right thing in the present.

8. Virtues only ever travel in pairs. It's not enough to be right. Context is everything. If I am right but I make my point in the wrong way, I am wrong. If I am kind but my kindness promotes the demise of another, then this is not kindness. Wisdom is to do the right thing in the right way. Whenever you're about to do something, consider if your virtues are appropriately paired.

If these 8 jewels become part of your way of being in the world, you won't have to look for your destination because your destination will come and find you. Real success seeks out those who are virtuous. It's about always having all that you need, it's about peace of mind and contentment that carry you through the demands of life.

I hope you will see where these apply to you and proceed to inculcate them in the best way you can. I'll leave you with the equation that I believe most guarantees success... Knowledge takes you to the door of understanding, but it's only courage and application that take you through that door. Experience and wisdom then await you on the other side.

Question:
I'm battling with gout and nothing seems to be helping. My diet is shrinking and so is my motivation... can you help?

Answer:
Gout is such an excruciatingly painful condition and usually takes many years to develop. It exists because of an overproduction of uric acid, which finds its way into the blood stream and can affect one's joints. Its most common manifestation is in the joint of the big toe, but it can affect other joints too such as those in the hands.

You already know that there are many foods that those suffering with gout are encouraged to avoid such as: spinach, cauliflower, kale, beetroot, mushrooms, oranges, papaya and lentils and as you're a vegetarian this complicates the story for you even more. For now, focusing on removing or limiting these foods in your diet might be in your best interests as this would help lower the acidic burden in your body - but I do not believe this is the sole solution for you because gout is not simply about diet. What I believe is more important is to detoxify your body in order to improve the pH of your blood.

There are a number of ways to do this but in your case the first thing that needs to be addressed is chewing. Because of all the problems you've had with your teeth, you have had a long tradition of not chewing food thoroughly. This cannot continue because I'm quietly confident that this is the number one reason for your flare-ups. When food is not properly digested a more acidic state in the body is created, placing a greater challenge on all your organs, tissues and cells. This is why I initially recommended digestive enzymes to you whilst you got your teeth sorted out, because they would at least help with the breakdown of your food.

Secondly, your intake of water is intermittent at best and water is critical in maintaining the fluid balance in the body. There is a daily exchange taking place within the cells which depends on water. Water carries the nutrients from the extracellular fluids into the cells and the intracellular fluids are responsible for the removal of the waste products. Without adequate water in the system, both functions along with other activities are compromised leading to a build-up of waste products in the blood, which can then become trapped in numerous pathways.

A body that is not adequately hydrated cannot efficiently deal with uric acid, which then puts the liver and kidneys under a lot of stress. This causes blockages in the system which when coupled with poor mastication leaves the body reeling. One of the things you said you were doing when we last spoke, and I would encourage you to continue doing twice a day, is drinking water with freshly squeezed lemon in it. This can be helpful.

Amongst the foods you should eat more of, are those with high amounts of essential fatty acids (omegas 3 and 6) as they help to decrease the inflammation and pain. So, your olive oil and tarragon meal, with your bowl full of lettuce and extra virgin olive oil is a very good choice, as extra virgin olive oil is high in those essential fatty acids and makes a great dressing for salads.

Seeds and nuts all properly chewed are also fantastic (do you still take the omega oil that I recommended in the liquid form? - because of course this is a wonderful antidote to gout too). I'm not sure if you're a fan of peanut butter but that's very good if you have the unprocessed version.

As for carbohydrates, they are generally good for gout sufferers because they are lower in purines, which reduces uric acid levels in the body. Of course, when considering increasing carbs, there is the problem of negatively impacting on blood sugar levels, with all the consequences that this can bring. And given your type 2 diabetes, you will need to keep an eye on this. The carbs you don't need to worry about are sweet potatoes, beans, oats, wheat crackers and rye products... with all these foods you want to have them in an unprocessed state where possible, but again remember chewing is the key.

We were also talking about the value of vitamin C the other day and this is critically important. I know that you are having organic cherry juice, which is great given its long heritage in reducing gout symptoms and cherries are also good for your blood sugar levels, so there's a double benefit for you.

It should be said to avoid purine is impossible and the research is mixed around whether all foods containing purines cause gout attacks at all. This is why the avoidance of all the foods listed is not always helpful because some people are not affected, for example, by the green vegetables that you listed. We need to be more person specific than this. Therefore, some experimentation on your part is needed to work out what foods actually cause your attacks.

Gout attacks can also be brought on by stress. Stress comes in many forms. I've laboured the point about chewing only because it's critical. When food is not properly chewed, the digestive system, the immune system and the cardiovascular system are particularly impacted. Dehydration is also a terrible stressor. Insufficient sleep has substantial consequences too, because it's during sleep that reparation and renewal take place. As you can see, stress is not just about what's happening within our minds. That said, keep practising your conscious breathing and meditation. They will help with the toxic fallout of waste thoughts and produce healing hormones – this is an important part of your strategy.

Finally, I wonder if you're still taking the digestive enzymes I recommended, which contained bromelain amongst other things? If you are, please continue because the bromelain is very good for helping reduce uric acid levels. There are some other products that I could recommend such as urtica and urticalcin – both of which are great at dealing with uric acid. However, at this point I don't want you to do more than I've currently recommended.

Let us review the position in 4-6 weeks.

Question:
I've recently been diagnosed with bipolar disorder, but I'm confused. For the last fifteen years I've been operating under the diagnosis that I was given in my teens that I am schizophrenic. I was told you might be able to help which is why I'm making contact. Can you?

Answer:
I'm not willing to offer diagnoses in the absence of a more detailed profile. The problem with the mental health continuum, even with the help of the DSM-5 (diagnostic statistical manual) is that you could see ten practitioners and end up with four or five different diagnoses. Even though it is considered the gold standard for assessing a patient's mental health status it nonetheless leads to varying conclusions. In other words, this is not a precise science.

At Reach we don't work within the rigidity of labels. They can be a very useful starting point, but experience has taught me they can also be very misleading. Your position is not as uncommon as it might seem. I've come across many such cases and although mental health is probably getting more attention than ever, misdiagnoses are still quite prevalent and obviously where there is misdiagnosis the wrong treatment will inevitably follow.

In order to help you further, I need a full case history. I would also need to know when you were first diagnosed with schizophrenia, what have been your symptoms and what medication you have been on during that time. Also, when did the diagnosis change and what are your current symptoms – how do they differ from the past if indeed they do? Only then could I draw up a personal plan specific to your needs.

It's important that I underline that if you're looking for a purely allopathic approach then I would encourage you to stick with the conventional route. Our approach is naturopathic and complementary, which means working as far as possible within the parameters of a natural approach and, if beneficial, incorporating other modalities which includes allopathy.

Allopathy is a system of medicine, which tends to rely on synthetic chemicals and compounds to address our biological and psychological needs. Sometimes this is achieved to great effect and at other times the allopathic remedies either don't work or they cause secondary issues/side effects.

We at Reach are not against allopathic medicine but it would be disingenuous to say that we think allopathy is the answer for our modern ailments because there are many occasions where this is not the case, which is why we are passionate about a holistic and integrative approach that adapts to meet the needs of the individual. We have to be careful when working with labels that we don't keep trying to get the person to fit into our description or diagnosis.

Therefore, the help I would be offering you would not work purely within the confines of your current diagnosis. This is because I would work with 'you' rather than your symptoms.

It's staggering to see that many people with mental health issues, when eating the right food, drinking enough water, taking appropriate supplementation and addressing their environmental issues, start to change with no other intervention. I've also seen many times, that just by dealing with intolerances and/or allergies a shift in consciousness and well-being can miraculously emerge, leading to a whole new strategy and approach.

I'm not promising that this would be the case here but if you ignore the fact that the environment impacts on the body and the mind, you're in danger of chasing symptoms and never addressing the causes.

If this approach appeals to you, then please do get back in touch.

Question:

I remember you saying that creating order in my environment could impact positively on the whole of my life. Can simply tidying up my office and making some improvements in the garage and the hall change the way that I feel about myself? It seems too much to hope for.

Answer:

It does seem overly simplistic to suggest that these relatively small changes could have such a marked impact, but I do stand by what I said.

Researchers at the Princeton University Neuroscience Institute published the results of a study they conducted in the January (2011) issue of *The Journal of Neuroscience* that relates directly to uncluttered and organised living. The report was entitled: Interactions of Top-Down and Bottom-Up Mechanisms in Human Visual Cortex. Below is the primary conclusion of their research.

"Multiple stimuli present in the visual field at the same time compete for neural representation by mutually suppressing their evoked activity throughout visual cortex, providing a neural correlate for the limited processing capacity of the visual system".

Put in more accessible terms, the conclusion of this research was that clutter and disorganisation creates a state of information overload where the brain is trying to process too much via the visual cortex simultaneously. As a result, different parts of the brain shut down to accommodate for this state of overload, which means we struggle to be clear and focused. In other words, we are unable to process information in the same way when compared with an ordered, uncluttered environment.

The researchers gathered the data by using functional magnetic resonance imaging (fMRI) and other physiological measurement tools to map the brain's responses to organised and disorganised stimuli.

This research showed that we would all be distracted less often, able to process information better, therefore be more productive and less irritable with an uncluttered and organised home and office.

Dr. Christine Carter, a sociologist with a particular interest in health, goes on to support the findings that came out of Princeton University. Her research indicates that an environment that is cluttered takes away some of our ability to manage other things in our lives well. This can lead to the avoidance of emotional challenges and issues because we don't feel we have the energy to meet them head on.

Hopefully this helps to answer the question. The research around decluttering is happening around the world, as social scientists, psychologists and specialists in environmental matters are increasingly taking this subject seriously.

We are also exposed to far too much information and data and our mental health is suffering as a result.

Let me conclude by saying that although I think decluttering would make a marked difference to your situation, this alone is not going to transform your fortunes, but it's a very good place to start.

Question:
Can you offer me anything quick, straightforward and simple that can help me improve my life more quickly?

Answer:
Everyone I've met on this journey (including myself) has been looking for a quick fix. I'm often criticised for appearing to speak against the current trend and the prevailing wisdom, which would have us believe that there are swift antidotes to our ailments. For some this is true but for a far greater number and especially those with more complex issues, the quick fix in my experience rarely offers a sustainable outcome.

I believe change is a process, not an event and so I don't promise quick fixes. I promise sustainable solutions, ones that are designed for that person, as mine is not a 'one size fits all' approach.

Therefore, what I'm offering may not meet your needs as I want those who take this journey to understand what it takes to reach a point in their lives where they really are in control of themselves and their destiny... and that this often takes time.

Having given this context, these are the four things that I have seen bring rapid change for many. They are not a quick fix per se, but they can lead the person to move through the transformational process at a greater rate of knots.

1. Forgiveness is the foundation of a clean mind, a mind where the streams of consciousness flow clearly. If we are unable to forgive ourselves for our mistakes and those who have trespassed against us, our minds and hearts remain muddy and muddled. Then our best efforts never seem sufficient to turn the tide.

2. Gratitude - the grateful mind has no room for complaint. When this first dawned on me it enabled me to dig myself out of many holes. The more we stay stuck in complaints, criticism and blame, the more we dirty the soul. We stay stuck in our patterns, our beliefs and opinions and are unable to reach our destination. Develop an attitude of gratitude and watch your fortunes change.

3. The reason our struggles are accentuated is because we walk alone. What is it that you believe? Whatever you believe in, anchor your faith to this. You'll discover the more you honour what you believe, which is the essence of integrity, the more you are able to access the reservoirs of strength which reside inside of you.

4. Kindness. Every day, perform at least one act of kindness for no reason at all, simply because it's the right way to be. The one who lives in the place of kindness finds that time, destiny and fortune are kinder to them.

I hope this goes some way to answering your question.

Question:
You said to me that there is a difference between information, knowledge and wisdom and I am still struggling to understand the distinction. Would you mind summarising it again please?

Answer:
We are all indoctrinated with an ideology, usually the one we are born into, and it takes time and special effort to de-robe ourselves of that conditioning.

Thich Nhat Hanh puts it beautifully when he says, 'you can only truly know and understand, when you renounce what you 'think' you know'.

Let me provide you with a brief overview of what I said. I hope this will help you better understand the difference and assist you to navigate your way through the torrent of data and information, which is assaulting our senses.

Information is a form of data collection. It's where individuals collect 'stuff' from numerous sources and have not always adequately cross-referenced that data. This information begins to form the basis of their thought processes and beliefs around a particular topic. This in turn is reported by the consumer of this data as fact - when factoid would be a better description (information repeated often enough that people believe it's true). Now the virus of the mind is born – contaminating our thoughts, ideas and feelings with things that do not necessarily carry any credibility.

The internet is both a beneficial source of data and information but it's also a terrible source too - current estimates suggest that at least 58% (and this is a conservative figure) of what is posted online could be categorised as either inaccurate, misinformation or misleading. This is because there is no regulation on the internet, and anybody can post anything. If we are not sure of our sources, how do we know what we can trust when surfing the internet?

A poll conducted by The Centre for International Governance Innovation (CIGI) in 2018, found that 86% of us were duped by fake news stories, further underlining the danger of information. We need a better lens through which to examine our reality.

Knowledge is more sophisticated than information. It's where we've taken on data, researched it up to a certain point and started building concepts and structures around it, which then begin to shape our own ideology and ways of perceiving and being. There are many people in the world who could be described as knowledgeable and we seem to revere these individuals, sometimes with good reason, but we should be aware that being knowledgeable can also make us blind and dogmatic. It's easy to be misled by someone who's knowledgeable especially if they are charismatic and have the ability to express and convey their ideas well, but this should not be mistaken for wisdom.

Wisdom is unique. It is where knowledge and application meet. It takes the mind and the spirit beyond logic and the senses. It's a realm rich with experience, where the questions asked are answered, not just in words, but in the beautiful amphitheatres of silence. There is no guessing, no theory, no hypothesis at this point. This is because one is elevated to that special point of awareness and can see with the eyes of experience. From this giddy height, all things can be understood.

Very few people experience this state of being because they become trapped in either the information gathering phase which can confuse as much as clarify, or they are seduced by the trappings of knowledge which can lead them to believe that because their intellects have understood something and can explain it, this must be the answer. But as I said earlier, we can only truly know when we surrender what we think we know. Very few undertake this journey because they are so wedded to their culture, tradition and ideology.

Experience is where true knowing lives.

I hope this answers your question sufficiently. I'm happy to talk more about it when we next meet. The most important thing is striving to become wise and to do that we need great humility.

Question:
I'm trying to understand how breathing can help me deal with PTSD. There are some sexual memories that I have that periodically overwhelm and incapacitate me. I'm tired of this and I was told breathing can help. What do you recommend?

Answer:
There is no panacea for trauma. There are some things that work well for some people and for others they make little or no difference. You may need to experiment before you find the right fit for you.

Amongst the things that I can say I consistently see working are EFT (emotional freedom technique), EMDR (Eye movement desensitization and reprocessing), clinical hypnotherapy, counselling/psychotherapy and breath therapy. There are also some bodily interventions that can bring about emotional release such as: TRE (Trauma Releasing Exercises), deep tissue/remedial massage, Five Rhythms dancing and acupuncture – but this is not a definitive list.

However, as your question is focused on breathing, I would encourage you to make sure when engaging in this exercise that you're breathing correctly. There are a number of great templates to help you with this. Please take a look on our website or a source you trust. You might also want to consider learning some breathing techniques from a yoga teacher or someone with equivalent expertise.

Breathing is such a powerful way to affect the relationship between the amygdala and the hippocampus. Putting it simply, the amygdala stores all of our emotional memories and experiences and is particularly bound up with the fear response. Its primary job is to protect us from harm.

The hippocampus provides context to those memories and experiences as it has a relationship with the wider brain via the neocortex. What often happens in trauma is that there is a disconnect between these two organelles. This leads to our fears taking an irrational path as the amygdala hijacks the brain, disabling the contextual information of the hippocampus.

Breathing correctly introduces, via relaxation, a bridge of communication between the two (this is achieved as the hypothalamus, the mood centre, is engaged). If then, whilst breathing deeply, you repeatedly introduce the thought 'I relax and let go' the reduction in anxiety re-engages the hippocampus, bringing much needed context to your thoughts and feelings by regulating the amygdala's dominance.

The other things that help to arrest the amygdala hijack are mantras and positive affirmations. Coming up with a batch of these that you have readily available to you could also be part of your survival kit. Phrases like 'every day in every way I'm getting better and better', or 'I am safe and secure in the world', or 'I'm cool, calm and confident in every situation', can all be very powerful antidotes to negative emotions - especially when you repeatedly recite them. Neuroscience has explained for us the process of synaptogenesis, which put simply is 'neurons that fire together wire together'. This means, the more we string together positive thoughts, the more we build new neuronal pathways, which generate feelings of hope and positivity.

Visualisation is another wonderful activity that you can use alongside breathing. The mind loves mental rehearsal because the more we 'see' something in the mind the more we become comfortable with it in reality. This activity makes us feel safe and secure, especially when walking into undesirable situations. If whilst breathing you can see yourself in your mind's eye feeling safe and secure, confident and calm, the combination of these two activities can bring great results.

Revisiting in your mind the traumatic events you have described is something you might be able to do by yourself through the practice of conscious breathing. However, I would only recommend this if you feel confident, because you don't want to expose yourself to further trauma by reintroducing memories and feelings that you find overwhelming. This is a judgment call you will need to make. It might be wiser to take this part of the journey with someone who's skilled in these matters.

I hope this is useful. If you want to discuss any aspect of this further, please get in touch.

Question:
What is anxiety? I'm so confused by the differing descriptions. Can you offer a simple overview to help me get a better handle on it please?

Answer:
This is a huge topic. Probably half of all the people I've worked with are suffering with some kind of anxiety. I don't think there's an easy way to answer your question, but I think this overview could be helpful.

Basically, there are two types of anxiety – endogenous anxiety and exogenous anxiety. Endogenous anxiety is an anxiety which rises up from within the individual, but they are unable to name its source. This form of anxiety tends to be more difficult to treat because there are no obvious triggers which can leave the sufferer confused, frustrated and even terrified.

Exogenous anxiety is where there is an external stimulus (trigger), something the sufferer can point to as a reason they're feeling anxious, which doesn't mean they'll feel any less terrorised but it does offer a starting point for a resolution and/or treatment.

Whatever the reason the person is suffering from anxiety, what I have found all anxiety sufferers have in common is they are somehow disconnected from their sense of self. Something has either fractured their self-concept or alienated them from it in some way. Being able to identify what that is, is critical to a successful outcome.

I have also found that the other thing all anxiety has in common is that it is trying to protect the sufferer.

Although I said exogenous anxiety has some starting point, I should point out it doesn't follow that that's the reason for the anxiety. That may merely be the presenting issue or symptom and under further examination it becomes clear that this is not the primary cause at all.

With endogenous anxiety, although it can be more confusing as it has no obvious trigger, the same questions need to be asked; why does it exist and what is the anxiety trying to protect you from?

In both instances there is something so overwhelming (real or perceived) that it threatens your equilibrium, and the anxiety state (the mind and body's alarm system) has been triggered.

Whatever course of action you take, try and understand what your anxiety is protecting you from because when we find the problem, we also find the solution.

Question:
I hate the feeling of being vulnerable. It makes me feel weak and although I hate to admit it, I despise it in others too. Can you help me to overcome this?

Answer:
First of all, what a great question. I love the honesty and courage of it.

So many of us hate the feeling of being vulnerable and when it's staring back at us in the form of our connections and relationships it can leave us feeling uncomfortable because it exacerbates our own feeling of ambivalence and self-loathing.

What's sad about this is that often the answers we seek are to be found within our vulnerability and so if we despise it either in ourselves or others, we remain trapped. Seeing vulnerability as weakness is our first mistake. Vulnerability tells us that some part of us is in need of tenderness, love and care.

It's a call for greater awareness, sensitivity, care and compassion. Any other response is not only harmful, but it denies us access to untapped reservoirs of strength.

My recommendation is the next time you witness vulnerability, whether that be in yourself or in someone else, ask yourself 'why has it emerged?' 'What is the vulnerability trying to express?' 'What can you learn from this moment?'

Whenever vulnerability turns up it's an opportunity to grow into the other parts of yourself. It's an opportunity to meet your true nature.

I hope you can find the kindness you need to silence the despising aspect, because that is where the real weakness resides.

Question:
I'm drowning in my need to be in control and yet I feel unable to act any differently. You know my story and how my losses have impacted upon me... and all I seem to do is hold on tighter, which leaves me feeling trapped. Help...

Answer:
Your need to be in control is understandable. As we've discussed many times your lack of a secure attachment at the time when you were most vulnerable as a young child in need of the 3'A's (attention, affection and affirmation), means you have a powerful propensity to try and shape and mould your environment in order to create some safety.

When a child has little or no structure and finds themselves in an environment where feelings of safety and security are lacking, then they will use all their wit and resources to find a way to influence what is happening in their personal space. There is often the illusion that if they can control people and events, then this will lead to the best possible outcome. Often this is not the case because the more you try to control your external environment, whilst your internal environment is not being properly managed, the more likely you are to do harm – both to yourself and others.

This is why you feel like you are drowning. You may remember I said to you that unhealthy control is like trying to get the wind to change direction, whereas healthy control is understanding you can't change the wind, but you can manipulate your sails and work with it.

This needs to be your approach now. Start by controlling your inner world. Remember your Story of Health plan and go back to your non-negotiables. Create healthy control through proper self-care. The more you manage your own environment, the more likely you are to positively influence your external one.

When others are not feeling that you are trying to control them, interestingly they are more likely to be paying attention to your input. The energy of control, forces and pushes, it's impatient and rushes things along. As a result, this energy damages and distorts, and alienates others. If you want to be respected, heard and valued, then let go, rather than hold on. Wait rather than push. Listen rather than speak. Step back and give space, rather than move in and try to make things happen.

Even though it is your past losses that are sustaining these patterns, those same losses can become the catalysts for a whole new approach. Take a good look around you and you will see that unhealthy control simply doesn't work. What have you achieved by it? Where has it got you?

Remember, going around the same loop is always a reminder that there is still something that you are not seeing... and I believe the message here is that it's by letting go that you're most likely to positively influence events in your time and space.

Question:
Everywhere I go I'm told I can be better if only I do 'this' or if only I do 'that' and yet I continue to struggle. Is it me?... and what should I do when I'm not feeling I'm good enough?

Answer:
It is difficult to keep finding self-belief when you fall and hit the ground, especially if you've hit the ground hard. It's very easy in the current climate, with advice coming from so many quarters, to conclude that you're the one getting it wrong because you've not been able to make that magic formula work. You've attended the special workshop, watched the life-changing film, bought the only book you'll ever need and still you struggle. Under these circumstances most people would conclude that something must be wrong with them.

I don't believe something is wrong with you. I believe that many of the methods offered do not make it clear that change is a process, not an event. And so, individuals are understandably looking for quick fixes and when they don't work, the obvious conclusion is 'I must be the problem'.

This is not what I believe... I believe that you have more potential than you imagine. I believe an understanding of the four aspects of the mind shows that most of us have access to less than 10% of our capacity and unless we learn the language of all four minds, we are merely shadows of our souls – unable to access the vast reservoirs of consciousness.

Relapses are an opportunity to see what is still missing. Relapses give us a chance whilst on the ground to take time to find the jewel. Next time you find yourself on the ground wondering why you find yourself here once more... change the question. Rather than wondering why is this your fate? Spend time in that place, observing, feeling and listening. Try breathing in what you need in that moment and breathe out what you want to let go of... Breathe in courage, strength and hope and breathe out anxiety, doubt and fear.

If you can be the contemplator, the listener, the one prepared to wait and not allow yourself to be shaped by the experience, then you can become the responder rather than the reactor. At this point you stand at the crossroads of positive choice, able to write the destiny of your choosing.

Try not to get too entangled in the modern message of immediacy. Trust in your heart and mind and use silence to access the reservoirs of the soul. Relapses are not negative events unless you perceive them to be, so change your mindset and see them as opportunities to flourish and grow.

Question:
What really is stress? There are so many explanations I've actually found it confusing to decide where I fit into those descriptions. Most of what I've read focuses on the psychological but having looked quite extensively at your site you seem to talk about the topic in a much wider sense. Are you able to offer me a better definition?

Answer:
Let me see if I can help.

As a holistic and integrative psychotherapist, I would define stress as the point at which the mind-body-spirit system is either under-resourced or over-trading. In many instances it is both. This tripartite system is perpetually interfacing with its environment and any deficiencies that exist in the environment also cause stress to that system.

This definition as you can see takes us away from the idea that stress is primarily a psychological event. It is of course a condition that affects how we feel emotionally and psychologically and that is well documented elsewhere. What is not spoken about with the same veracity and passion are the many other stress inducers, which are no less potent in their impact.

For example, dehydration is arguably one of the greatest stressors and certainly here in the first world where we have sufficient water available to us, many of us actually do not drink the minimum requirement - even in the face of the growing evidence that any trace of dehydration throws the body into an anxious state and has a marked impact on cognitive function. So, this is not merely a biological stressor - emotional and psychological aspects are also significantly affected.

A life of meaning and purpose is vital to our well-being and it is increasingly acknowledged that where there is a lack of purpose and direction then there is an increase in stress and mental ill health. The Japanese philosophy of Ikigai offers a wonderful template to the modern world of the importance we need to place on our reason for being. There is some excellent research that indicates that people in this part of the world tend to live longer and are healthier because the attitude and culture is focused on never retiring from the idea of usefulness.

In other words, regardless of our age, we all need to feel that we have something to offer and however small, find ways in which to do that.

In the field of PNI (Psychoneuroimmunology) where social scientists are looking at the consequences of poverty, redundancy, limited opportunity, alienation and familial breakdown, we see that stress is rife in the dynamics and politics of modern life. Our relationships with individuals, geography, class and other social factors can all cause immeasurable amounts of stress and the evidence clearly shows that our self-talk (inner narrative) changes and with that the neurobiochemical context of the brain also changes, creating untold damage to its organelles, the rest of the body and also our relationships.

The carbon cycle is another good example of a stressor. If we just look at one aspect, the combination of deforestation and airborne pollution continues at an alarming rate and the quality of oxygen in the atmosphere as a result continues to decline. We of course depend on that oxygen for optimal function because there is no organ or system in our bodies that can survive without the virtues of oxygen. When these systems and organs are underfed, they move from a state of growth and flourishing into survival and protection, which leaves us living in a sub-optimal state, which is a stressful condition.

Hopefully, with this brief overview you can see that stress comes in many guises and for each aspect of what makes us human (mind, body and spirit) there is a long list of stressors. The environment which interfaces with all three adds a fourth dimension which has a long procession of its own and we are directly affected by those environmental factors too.

This is why it is fair to say that stress is the number one enemy of health because it is responsible for so many physical and mental diseases, which is why a 'whole person' approach is needed that does not merely focus on symptoms but goes in pursuit of the cause.

Try and identify where the stressors are in your life and then create a plan for how you are going to address each of them. I think you will find it helpful to create a plan using The Story of Health as a template, so I'd suggest immersing yourself more in the depth of its message.

Question:
I'm confused! It seems to me that those around me (especially those I'm closest to) are resistant to my positive changes and in some instances actively oppose them as if somehow my transformation is offensive to them. Am I paranoid?

Answer:
Sadly, this is quite a common position and I've seen numerous reasons for this behaviour over the years. The most common reasons however do seem to centre around the fear that if you change, what does that mean for the other person.

Most of us are comfortable with not changing the status quo and/or pushing the boundaries to our limits - because change tends to mean something needs to happen and the question then arises, will that require sacrifice and maybe even courage? The thought that one has to possibly give something up, surrender one's position in some way, can be frightening.

Courage means doing something scary, which we don't necessarily want to do. So, when someone is changing, those around him start to wonder if they have to be different? Will our relationship have to change? This can create feelings of discomfort and insecurity.

In addition to individuals fearing what your change will mean to them, equally frightening, maybe even worse, is that you are holding up a mirror, which highlights what they need to change themselves. You are inadvertently exposing their incongruence and shortcomings.

My advice to you is to tread carefully and whatever you do, don't become evangelical about your newfound insights and ambitions. By all means be passionate about your discoveries and growth but only share this where it is appropriate. Becoming a better version of yourself is not meant to handicap anyone else and although there's nothing to be ashamed of, being mindful of how others may feel about your changes is actually very good for your awareness and learning.

Often an overzealous approach exacerbates these feelings in others. You can't change how others are likely to feel and it's not your job to do that, but you can influence that position with humility and understanding.

Keep growing with quiet passion, sensitivity and empathy, and remember to meet people where they are, not where you think they should be.

Question:
I feel insecure in myself and that translates to feeling insecure in my relationship. I find myself projecting all kinds of things onto my partner and although these are largely irrational, I don't seem to be able to switch them off. Can you give me any advice?

Answer:
Given your upbringing and the instability you were exposed to, where there was no modelling of a healthy relationship between your parents, it's hardly surprising that you lack the knowledge and resources that are needed for a healthy relationship. What you witnessed was conflictual communication and a lack of intimacy. Even at times of affection there was a feeling of unease, as if at any point the environment could erupt.

Therefore, your internal model is one of uncertainty and skepticism, which you are projecting onto your partner, and based on all that you have shared with me, without justification. This of course threatens your relationship because your partner may well feel negatively judged and 'accused' even when you're not actually making accusations. This of course will threaten the bond of trust between you. I think that's already happening anyway and so something needs to change.

My recommendation is, sit and talk with her in a non-confrontational way. Share your vulnerability and fears. Speak from a place of love and kindness to the part of her that clearly loves you. If you don't feel you can do this by yourself, if your partner is willing, find a person you trust who can facilitate such a conversation, or a neutral third party.

Conversation conducted in the right way is almost always the antidote for this issue. You yourself may in addition need some personal help to process and resolve what's left over from your past. You may be able to do this through self-help techniques, such as mindfulness, tapping (EFT), meditation, body work and other introspective practices. If they don't feel sufficient, again maybe a trusted and skilled friend or colleague could help - or identifying a therapist with the necessary skills might be more appropriate.

Whatever you decide, don't sit in this position and do nothing as it will poison you and the well of your relationship. Remember, it's the things that we hide from ourselves and those whom we love that are most likely to harm us and them.

Find the courage and the honesty to take the next step.

Question:
You have explained numerous times about the detoxification pathways and how when blockages exist in different areas, we become more prone to particular ailments and conditions. I'm trying to get my head around this, and I'd be grateful if you could say a bit more.

Answer:
Given your particular complaints and how congested you are, I think it is important for a while that you limit/avoid mucus forming foods (dairy, too much meat and processed foods). In addition, chewing thoroughly is crucial because a lack of chewing can lead to an over-production of mucus.

With regards to what kinds of problems are produced when there are blockages in the detoxification pathways, this is a vast list which I couldn't possibly cover here in its entirety but here are some examples.

When there is a blockage in the colon, this can cause literally every disease that we know of, but the common ones are: IBS, ulcerative colitis, Crohn's, a variety of other bowel issues and cancer. In addition, there is an over-proliferation of bacteria and fungi (candida being the most well-known). These pathogens have a long list of consequences all of their own.

When there's a blockage in the liver, amongst the negative consequences are fatty liver issues, an inability to digest fats, cluster headaches and severe migraines and a myriad of skin disorders - eczema and psoriasis amongst the most common. The liver is involved in more than 300 primary processes and so any/all of these can be affected. When there is toxic build up in the liver there is also a whole range of bacterial and pathogenic infections that can run rampant in the body.

If the kidneys are blocked the most common ailments are urinary tract infections, hydronephrosis (swelling of the kidneys due to a build-up of urine) which can cause headaches, abdominal pain, nausea and vomiting. Infections here can lead to brain fog at one end of the continuum and dementia at the other end. There is also a greater propensity to experience fear, stress and anxiety. It should be stated for clarity that blockages anywhere along the pathways have the ability to generate emotional and psychological disturbances.

With the blood, blockages or toxic build up here can also cause headaches, moodiness and at the other end of the spectrum more systemic problems such as overall body pain like with fibromyalgia, lupus, rheumatoid arthritis and other autoimmune diseases. A range of cancers, like leukaemia, are also bound up with blood issues.

When the lymph is blocked, waste moves through the body slowly trying to find exits via the various drainage points. The body will do its best to excrete waste through all the pathways it can find but when there is back-flushing (waste not finding appropriate exits) that reabsorption of waste can cause nondescript aches and pains, lethargy, lack of motivation, noxious body odour, too much sweating, halitosis and headaches, to name a few.

A build-up of waste or a blockage anywhere along the detoxification pathways threatens homeostasis and our health - at its most extreme it is life-threatening. This is because waste products produced by the cell are not being fully excreted and therefore nutrition is not getting in and toxic waste is not being sufficiently removed.

Blockages in the cells can cause atherosclerosis, cardiovascular events, transient ischemic attacks (TIA), strokes, oedema, bloating and sharp pains which seem to have no explanation. Cellular dysfunction is heavily linked to a variety of cancers - as cells start to proliferate at an unhealthy rate.

I hope this provides you with a useful overview and underlines why a systemic approach to detoxification bears good fruit.

I'm happy to discuss the specifics with you further and how a systemic detoxification programme works.

Question:
I've been trying the 'listening in' exercise you recommended, and nothing has happened. I've been intensely practising now for the last month. Am I doing something wrong?

Answer:
From all that you've told me, you are not doing anything wrong, but it's really important to recognise that one cannot simply manufacture spiritual insights and life-changing experiences. This is a much more subtle process and requires time and patience.

It really helps to understand that the nature of all things is to grow. What is needed is for us to provide the right conditions for that to happen. When listening in, try doing this with no expectations. The non-expectant mind is able to hear and connect with the unspoken messages that float around in the ether of the inner world. As those unspoken messages are acknowledged, a deeper set of insights is revealed. What realisations emerge on the horizon tend to fall into one of these three categories:

1) The things you already know come more sharply into focus and probably for the first time you can see how the different aspects of your life could come together.

2) The things you have been feeling, have suspected and maybe even have forgotten, become crystallised, offering a whole new spectrum of understanding.

3) The things you didn't know at all, offering a new bandwidth of awareness and incredible insights, come to the fore. These insights are often breathtaking and are the precursors for positive change.

To have such experiences requires an inner stillness, which comes from the patient, accepting mind.

It's amazing how, when we stop frantically searching for the answer or the solution, it can as if by magic rise to the surface. It's a bit like the person who's drowning and is frenetically waving their arms and gyrating their whole body in an attempt to stay afloat. Their panicked movements increase the chance of drowning. If only in that moment they could find the presence of mind to be still and relax, their body would find its natural buoyancy.

Listening in is not only about noticing what's going on when we are sitting; it is also about noticing the nuances of life, whilst we are on the move. It's about learning to 'feel' our way through what is happening. Our emotional aspect is 50% of who we are, so to simply logic our way through things, ensures we will miss so much of what's really going on.

When you are feeling overwhelmed by life events, unable to cope, the current of doubt, fear and confusion can drag you into its vortex. In that moment of despair, it's so easy to give away the last vestiges of power and surrender to your demise.

But here's what experience tells us... at that very moment of white flag surrender, if you could find the composure to stop panicking and feel your way through the experience (which is a deeper kind of listening) you would then hear what you need to do. At that point the answer comes and finds you.

It can be hard to find the composure and courage needed in those moments because we are overwhelmed, but this is where the art of slowing down can really help.

The frenetic pace of the mind can deceive us. It leaves no room for pause or poise and when these two are absent, clarity and discernment fall away – we then become a bundle of reactions. And so, we are much more likely to panic and try desperately hard to stay afloat, which really is the wrong strategy.

If on the other hand, through regular practice, you learn to slow the mind down, what starts to happen is time gives you another perspective on what is occurring. It's as if you are watching the same events as those around you but seeing it all in slow motion. You feel like you always have a few moments more in which to respond and as a result better decisions and choices are made.

Try developing the non-expectant mind and listen with patience and acceptance. You will find magical things begin to occur.

Question:

My eight-year-old daughter, who was born premature, (she was under two pounds at birth), and needed to spend the first three and half months of her life in hospital, now has a number of social deficits. At times, she doesn't appear to connect with her reality. She is a very bright child and is doing well with most things at school, but she is having problems relating to her environment and other children. Lately she is being loud and disruptive and has begun lashing out. I'm afraid she will hurt another child or herself. I'm struggling to get any help or direction as everyone I reach out to refers me to someone else. Can you help?

Answer:

I'm sorry to hear of your struggles. You really are up against it and my heart goes out to you.

Given the complexity of this case, and its many different strands, what I am going to offer is an overview position. If you want any further help, I will need more precise information.

Here's a summary of my position.

1. It is often the case that premature children have emotional, psychological and behavioural issues that need some attention, and specific intervention, as they mature. This is because having come out of the womb early, their brains have not always fully developed because they have left the nutritious sanctuary of the womb too soon. This can lead to feelings of insecurity and uncertainty. Having left the womb prematurely, it's as if they are set adrift, their senses saturated by the new and unexpected sound and

light show of life. Emotions beyond their underdeveloped form, create disorientation and confusion.

2. As I said, the womb is a safe, nurturing space (other than when the mother is abusing herself or being abused) and when a child is prematurely removed from that space, or comes early through the force of nature, then attachment/developmental issues nearly always follow. This will have been compounded in this instance, because of how long your daughter spent in HDU. That lengthy period of incubation can be compared to a period of solitary confinement. During this time, she would not have been exposed to the love, nurturing and intimacy that a child needs from her primary caregivers. This will have been emotionally devastating, which is why relating to others can create feelings of challenge and threat. When we don't have those healthy attachment templates, the world can be a scary and confusing place, and we struggle with the boundaries that we're presented with.

3. Thank you for sending a summary of your daughter's diet. Although you say it is much improved since weening, it is nonetheless greatly lacking in vegetables, particularly the cruciferous family. That which is green is the most important food group on earth, given the breadth and depth of nutrients available.

   The second most important food group is also inadequately represented, which is the legume family, i.e., beans, pulses and lentils... so finding ways to increase their representation will almost certainly make a difference. Unless there are any intolerances or allergies you've not declared, incorporating these two food groups into a rainbow diet is the way to go. The more colour on our plates the more likely we are to be getting all of the essential nutrients. This is critical to brain health.

   The trauma of coming into the world before the physiological development is complete can be addressed by taking nutrition seriously. This is why premature children tend to improve with greater nutritional support, which helps to compensate for the early life deficiencies. The physiological deficits (psychological ones too) can be helped/rectified by precise food planning and targeted supplementation - ensuring there is a good representation of all the macro and micronutrients. You might need professional help with this.

What is also valuable to help with the disconnection and disruptive behaviour you report, is some form of psychological intervention, which can help with your daughter's sense of belonging, improve her understanding of the world, and help her with communication.

In my experience, both nutritional input and psychological support are needed - but the nutritional strategies should start first, otherwise trying to build the emotional and psychological bridges will prove more difficult.

4. Finally, when it comes to brain health, it's very important to emphasise the importance of water and essential fatty acids. There is good evidence in the research literature, highlighting the essentiality of water and EFAs and their positive impact on cognition, mood and behaviour. Nothing works properly in the body where there is dehydration. Dehydration causes stress - physically and emotionally.

I hope this overview is helpful because there is a lot you can do for your child with the right interventions and support. Please remember, whilst fighting for what's best for your child, to look after your own needs in the process.

If I can be of further help, please do get back in touch.

"Failure is unimportant. It takes courage to make a fool of yourself".

Charlie Chaplin (1889 – 1977)

FINAL MESSAGE

I hope after this journey that you've been persuaded that becoming a synergist is indeed the answer for living in the 21st century. It's not merely about our survival, it's about finding ways to thrive and supporting one another in that process.

I've taken you on a long journey from the cell to the ocean. I've tried to show you what is required to transform our darkness into light. I've explored the internal machinations of the body and invited you to gaze into the mystical manifestations of the soul. I've tried at each point to show that everything is connected.

There is a relationship between all energy and as we ourselves are energy, there's no buy-out clause for us. We're part of everything that's taking place... and even more than that, ours is the energy that can most bring about transformation, but we have to create new energy contracts by becoming positive signatories in all areas of life.

This will enable us to become co-creators, working with the physical and metaphysical, thereby establishing a new world order. We can no longer allow apathy and disinterest to sap away our energy and contribution. We need to focus on the changes required in the inner cosmos as well as the outer cosmos.

Becoming part of the solution means understanding our relationship to ourselves, our bodies, our families, our communities, society and the planet. If we really understand these relationships, we will begin to take responsibility in a completely different way. We won't be able to stand idly by and watch the fabric of our world falling apart. We will be compelled to find ways to make a positive difference.

Make a promise to yourself now that you will obsessively commit to positive change. Start with yourself and your home. Improve the nature and quality of your relationships, build a 'we' consciousness. Then take that kindness and benevolence from your own personal space into the world, into your place of work, your schools, hospitals, offices. Infect all those spaces with loving-kindness. Help to create a social conscience which protects the weakest and most vulnerable members of society and find peaceful ways to overturn injustice.

Although we have to save ourselves and each other, without also saving the planet, the environment in which everything else grows, then our very best efforts will be in vain.

Hopefully, I have been able to persuade you to write your own personal energy contract and you will use that as your template going forward. It's also time for us to make an energy contract with each other. It's time to say 'we, not just me'.

The world is on life support and needs us...

THE LAW OF CONSISTENT EFFORT

The primary equation that underpins our work is: **knowledge plus application equals personal power.** In fact, knowledge plus application will enable you to reach any goal where there is patience, perseverance, and heartfelt and sincere focus.

Below is a simple mathematical formula illustrating what happens when one makes small, consistent efforts over the course of a year.

As you can see, someone doing nothing over a year can expect nothing. Interestingly, the person who does as little as 1%, can achieve over 37 times more than the person who's done nothing.

DOING NOTHING AT ALL

VS

MAKING SMALL CONSISTENT EFFORTS

$$(1.00)^{365} = 1.00$$

$$(1.01)^{365} = 37.7$$

This equation underlines another one of our fundamental tenets, which is: **change is a process not an event.**

Put another way, it's by stringing together lots of little positive activities, over time, that we are most likely to create the change we ache for and desire... then even that which seems beyond our grasp becomes attainable.

This formula was brought to my attention by Zak Sagoo, who was a nineteen-year-old student at the time of sharing it with me. What's amazing about this young person is that he realised it represented everything we had been doing together. In fact, for the last year, he has conscientiously put into practice all I've asked him to do, and as a result, he is doing phenomenally well. He is a wonderful example of how small, consistent efforts create miracles.

ABOUT THE AUTHOR

Easton Hamilton is the founder and director of Reach and the model that he has created has come to be known around the world as The Reach Approach.

For more than forty years he has investigated and researched the relevant topics that speak to our humanity. He has not been convinced by philosophies that have claimed that only their modality provides the way to recovery, healing and salvation. For this reason, he extensively examined both the sciences and the arts, the physical and the metaphysical. He's explored and studied the different strands of eastern and western philosophy and how philosophy gave birth to psychology, with all its subsequent subdivisions. He has studied the history of the human race, the countless migrations that have led the world to its current state and the development of politics, culture and language as part of that evolutionary process. He's seen how geography and history have helped to create false divisions, prejudices and hatred and how the collective ignorance about who we really are continues to fund those divisions.

The more he's examined the individual paths we've taken, generally defined by where we were born and how those social, political and environmental factors have shaped us, the more he has concluded that what binds us is much more than what divides us. If only we could look beyond the limitations of geography, gender, race, religion and culture, we would find something more substantial... something more beautiful.

Is there really such a great difference between what humans want, wherever they are placed in the world? Hamilton's experience and research have shown that the primary differences are negligible. We all want health, peace and happiness. We all want to be safe and to belong to something caring and nurturing. We're all looking for meaning and purpose. However, whilst we stay true to the limitations of our own world view, unwilling to embrace the wider context, we will be denied the peace and harmony we all ache for.

Hamilton passionately believes that the 'siloed' approach to life is the enemy to synergy because it is divisive and has created a system of 'part-ology'. This keeps us in conflict with one another, as we are busy championing, often in dogmatic ways, that which we believe to be true, when we haven't thoroughly examined the other options.

In this, his fourth and final book, Become Part of the Solution, he tries to persuade us that another strategy needs to be found and it needs to be found quickly. He encourages us to stop wasting time in conflict, creating new theories, which are often old theories re-hashed, then standing blindly behind them, unable to see that the truth is not in short supply, only our willingness to see it.

The Reach Approach is taking a pioneering view of personal development and psychotherapy out into the world and is creating a new generation of therapists who understand a multi-factorial approach is needed to deal with the multitude of problems and afflictions in the world. It also offers every individual with an open mind access to the knowledge and resources required to create a habit of self-care and enrichment that will support the positive change we are all seeking.

We hope you will join the silent revolution!

"Science is really about seeing what everyone else has seen... but thinking what no one else has thought".

Albert Szent-Györgyi (1893 – 1986)

Printed in Great Britain
by Amazon

63159446R00224